Rehabilitation Counselling in
Physical and Mental Health

Rehabilitation Counselling in Physical and Mental Health

Edited by Kim Etherington

Jessica Kingsley Publishers
London and Philadelphia

First published in the United Kingdom in 2002
by Jessica Kingsley Publishers Ltd
116 Pentonville Road
London N1 9JB, England
and
325 Chestnut Street
Philadelphia, PA 19106, USA

www.jkp.com

Copyright © Jessica Kingsley Publishers 2002

Library of Congress Cataloging in Publication Data
Rehabilitation counselling in physical and mental health/edited by Kim Etherington.
p. ; cm
Includes bibliographical references and index.
ISBN 1 85302 968 8 (alk. Paper)
1. Mentally ill--Rehabilitation. 2. Rehabilitation. 3. Counseling. I. Etherington, Kim.
[DNLM: 1. Rehabilitation--psychology. 2. Counseling--methods. WB 320
R344162002]
RC439.5 .R4235 2002
617'.03'019--dc21

2001054517

British Library Cataloguing in Publication Data
A CIP catalogue record for this book is available from the British Library

ISBN 1 85302 968 8

Printed and Bound in Great Britain by
Arhenaeum Press, Gateshead, Tyne and Wear

Contents

Acknowledgements

As editor of this book I have been on a very steep learning curve which at times felt like being on a giant roller coaster at the funfair: exciting, scary and never knowing what I'll discover around the next bend! It has given me an opportunity to meet many people who have enriched me and extended my understanding through their stories.

I would like to acknowledge the hard work of each of the chapter authors and thank them for their patience with my endless requests. All of them are extremely busy people and I have appreciated their willingness to respond so readily and quickly. I would like to thank particularly the contributors who have written from the client's perspective; without their chapters we would only have half the story. This is the first time I have been able to include stories written by my husband and my son that link with my own story. I would like to acknowledge my delight in the way those stories enhance the final chapter.

Particular thanks are due to colleagues who have generously given their time to reading and giving me feedback on drafts of my own contributions to this book, notably Tim Bond, Michael Carroll, Pamela Griffiths, Alison Leftwich and Jane Speedy.

Once again it has been a pleasure to work with the team at Jessica Kingsley Publishers and especially Amy Lankester-Owen who has gone above and beyond the call of duty this time in offering herself as a 'pilot' for the interactive part of the last chapter. Her enthusiasm and encouragement bounce regularly off my computer screen when I open up my email!

As usual I have been sustained by my husband Dave, who keeps me well fed and watered and my computer running smoothly, and by my ever-increasing family (a new granddaughter and daughter-in-law have been added whilst editing this book) whose energy and love reinvigorates me and keeps my feet on the ground.

Preface

This book formed its roots within another which was published in August 2001, *Counsellors in Health Settings*. As the co-ordinator of the Postgraduate Diploma in Counselling in Primary Care/Health Settings at the University of Bristol (a post which I relinquished in December 2000), I had discovered that there was very little literature for and about counsellors working in secondary and tertiary health settings, although there was an expanding literature for and about counsellors working in primary care. Originally the course focused on training primary care counsellors, in line with several other courses that were supported by the Counselling in Primary Care Trust. It was a one-year course offered to counsellors who had already achieved a diploma level qualification. However, after two cohorts in this model we developed the course into a two-year postgraduate professional counsellor training and widened its scope to include counselling in a wider range of health settings.

This change was partly inspired by my personal belief that there is insufficient recognition of the need for counselling as part of the process of rehabilitation. There has been a vast increase in the numbers of counsellors working in general practice over the last ten years and counsellors working in other health arenas have a much lower profile. So I decided to attempt to address this imbalance by producing some literature that would be of use to people who had an interest in counselling in secondary and tertiary health care: literature that might also help to raise the awareness of these roles.

In my current role as co-ordinator and tutor for the MSc in Counselling (Research Unit) I have been impressed by the research undertaken by some of our students which highlights the work in which they have been involved in health settings. These students, having gained their diplomas, go on to achieve the MSc by becoming researchers and producing a dissertation. So I decided to ask some of them for their assistance in producing a book that would help disseminate this knowledge to a much wider audience.

During the early phase of planning for what was eventually to become two books, I became curious to know about other counsellors out there in the wider counselling community who were also developing services in health settings that were little known about and I wondered if they too might want their work to be included in the book. So I advertised in *Counselling* (Journal of the British Association of Counselling and Psychotherapy) asking if there were counsellors in this field who enjoyed writing and would be interested in this project. I was pleased and surprised to receive so many responses that allowed me to broaden my perspectives and include a much wider range of interesting chapters. The problem then was that I had too many proposed chapters for one book and I was reluctant to exclude any. There was a process of natural elimination as people withdrew once they realized how much work was involved and I eliminated some because of duplication. There were clearly some that did not fit into the remit for the book, but even so I ended up with more chapter offers than one book could contain. As I ruminated on this problem a pattern emerged and I began to see clearly how these chapters could usefully become two books, each with a separate focus.

The first book, *Counsellors in Health Settings*, focuses on the counsellors themselves and the issues that impinge upon their work: how they came to be counsellors; how they have created their services; what it means to work in a multidisciplinary team; the impact of their work on their lives and their lives on their work; the impact of their work context upon them and the counselling process; their training, supervision and support and the complex issues that clients bring in different contexts, such as adolescent sexual health, HIV/AIDS, infertility, cancer care, palliative care, mental health. That book also includes the clients' voices: a woman with cancer and another who describes her experience of infertility treatment.

This second book has a different focus. As I thought about the chapters on offer I could see the word 'rehabilitation' form before my eyes. My early training as an occupational therapist (OT) gave me a professional interest in rehabilitation in both mental and physical health. I had worked in a child guidance clinic, a psychiatric day hospital, a general hospital, a community for people with autism, and as a community OT with a social services department. I was still employed in the latter role when I began to train as a counsellor in 1987. So my role as counsellor was closely connected to and informed by my role as a rehabilitation team member. I had undertaken research and produced a dissertation in 1988 as a requirement for obtaining my Diploma in Counselling: the focus was 'The Disabled Person's Act 1986: the Need for Counselling'.

This title reflected my concern at that time about the lack of consideration for the emotional welfare of disabled people. The act highlighted a variety of practical needs: aids for daily living, holidays, etc., but nowhere did it say anything which indicated an awareness that some people may need emotional or psychological support to assist with the changes in their lives created by disability. Whilst I was working as an OT, making assessments for aids and adaptations, I had frequently listened to people expressing how they felt about their changed lives. Yet counselling was not identified as a need in the act, nor had it been offered to the clients I was meeting in my role as OT.

I began to notice that aids, wheelchairs, crutches and artificial limbs were sometimes left unused because nobody was listening to what the experience of disability and chronic illness meant to the individuals concerned. By ignoring a person's emotional needs we were in danger of ignoring a significant block to the person's process of rehabilitation and their future well-being. So the research for my dissertation focused on finding out from people who were registered as disabled with social services whether they had ever felt counselling would have been appropriate and, if so, how they thought that need could be met. The findings showed that some people did express a need for counselling and at that time there was no provision. Although my local authority employers acknowledged my findings as credible, they did not respond by providing counselling for disabled people.

I became increasingly frustrated about the inadequate service I delivered and in 1992, eight years after I became a community OT, I gave up that role and became a counsellor, counselling trainer and supervisor, having in the meantime gained an MSc in counselling training and supervision. So for two years I was out of touch with the world of health care and rehabilitation. My interests took me in other directions until 1994 when I became involved in training counsellors to work in primary care.

This book completes my circle back into the world of health and rehabilitation, but this time with counselling as my main focus: and things have moved on. The contributors to *Rehabilitation Counselling in Physical and Mental Health* have all been actively involved in rehabilitation, either as workers within the field or as clients. Several authors have first-hand experience of impairment disability and/or chronic illness. Others, like myself, have lived with a disabled family member at some stage of life. All bring a wealth of experience and knowledge to this book from their particular areas of interest.

Introduction

Kim Etherington

Rehabilitation

As I began to talk to people about the creation of this book, many of them asked 'What does rehabilitation counselling mean?' It became obvious through these conversations that the word 'rehabilitation' meant different things to different people. Some people in the counselling world understood it in reference to drug and alcohol rehabilitation while others understood it as physical rehabilitation. There were also those who understood the word in terms of mental health. More recently people have used this word in relation to refugees and ex-offenders. In the USA and Australia rehabilitation counselling has been a profession in its own right for decades and has an emphasis on vocational retraining for people who have become disabled and can no longer perform the work role they previously held.

This book focuses on rehabilitation counselling in physical and mental health and in recovery from drug and alcohol misuse. It attempts to approach the issue of rehabilitation counselling from a biopsychosocial viewpoint, recognizing that a person's physical, mental, emotional, social and spiritual needs impinge upon each other and that, as individuals, we are the experts on ourselves.

Counselling in a rehabilitation setting is offered on the assumption that the experience of mental or physical impairment, disability and recovery from drug or alcohol misuse can be supported by a relationship in which individuals are helped to explore and express their thoughts and feelings about what is happening in their lives. Although this view has been challenged (Lenny 1993), these assumptions have been borne out by disabled and chronically sick people themselves (Etherington 1988; Woolley 1993) who have spoken about their sense of fear and loss,

> My whole body shook and I seemed to be going down deep inside me trying to get rid of every ounce of pain in great sobs and tears. I must emphasise that this happened in a counselling session where I was quite free to express such emotion without being thought mad or without upsetting anyone else or without anyone leaping forth to stop me crying. After some time I stopped, blew my nose, calmed down, giggled for a bit and then felt very happy. The world seemed a great place to be in and I was glad to be powerfully alive. I was finally dealing with feelings of loss in the most natural way known to human beings. I was physically expressing grief, fear, anger and a whole range of emotion that had been locked inside me for 12 years. I was dealing with loss in a totally safe environment. (Woolley 1993, p.79)

The above quote seems to indicate the need for a safe space in which it becomes possible to release powerful and natural feelings, even a long time after the events that caused them, and how that can free the individual to feel more at home in his or her world. Stewart (1985) suggested that the feelings people experience strongly influence the way they co-operate with the process of rehabilitation. Counselling, however, focuses not only on feelings, but also sees their acknowledgement, expression and validation as part of a process in which people can gain control of their lives, tell their stories and honour their experiences. In my previous role as a community occupational therapist I frequently noticed how expensive equipment lay unused, artificial legs unworn, wheelchairs cluttering up hallways, because the person had been left alone to deal with painful feelings that needed to be addressed before they could intellectually and emotionally commit themselves to the process of rehabilitation. If we ignore these feelings it is like saying they are of no significance.

Chambers *English Dictionary* defines rehabilitation as: 'to make fit [after disablement, illness or imprisonment] for earning a living or playing a part in the world'. However, rehabilitation seems to have become an increasingly contentious word over the past fifteen years or so, particularly when linked with the role of professional rehabilitation 'experts' who have been described by Davis (1993, p.199) as 'professional disability parasites':

> Part of the process of gaining control over our lives involves us in resisting their attempts to box us into the pigeonhole of 'client' – and to

expose their self-styled, self-seeking efforts to elevate their second-hand knowledge about disability into a 'profession'. (Davis 1993, p.200)

I believe the above statement reflects the anger that some disabled people feel as they struggle against the oppressive and disabling forces in our society. However, being one such 'professional' and not being disabled myself, I would like to attempt to balance this view by acknowledging that I am by no means an expert in the field although my interest in rehabilitation has personal and professional roots. This book uses the word 'client' when referring to individuals who use counselling as an intervention as part of their rehabilitation, not because I wish to pigeon-hole anybody, but because I prefer that word to 'patient' which implies a very different kind of relationship.

The debate about definitions of disability, impairment, handicap and illness continues and the terms are contested by disabled people themselves. Words such 'spastic' or 'mongol' have become terms of abuse. Phrases such as 'the disabled' or the 'mentally ill' are seen as ways of depersonalizing and objectifying people (Barnes, Mercer and Shakespeare 1999). Although the word 'impairment' can have profoundly negative meaning, I have used it in recognition of the idea that a medical condition in itself is not necessarily the cause of a 'disability'. An individual with a spinal injury who uses a wheelchair is disabled when faced with a building that bars access, lacking ramps, lifts, thereby denying people opportunities for leisure, educational or social contact.

Clients whose stories are told in this book have either given permission for their material to be used and/or have been anonymized so that their identity is fully disguised. Some chapters have been written by authors who are themselves disabled and/or chronically sick; some write from the perspective of being a client; others write from the perspective of being an experienced counsellor in the field who has no personal contact with disability; some are writing from the perspective of being rehabilitation professionals who have experienced the impact on themselves of an impairment or disability of a significant person in their lives.

All of these perspectives are valid. In postmodern times we value the richness and diversity of 'intimate knowledge' which Miller Mair (1989, p.2) believes 'is likely to teach us more than distant knowledge'. Individual stories make a difference to our lives. These stories provoke other stories and may add something to our own stories, new perspectives that may help us re-author our own lives. Maggie Woolley sums this up as she reflects upon the value of telling her story of hearing loss: 'Our experience is always unique and yet when we begin to talk about it openly, we find that others begin to rejoice in those parts of our experience which have also been their own. My experience is no more invalid than any deafened person' (1993, p.83).

Counselling

Traditionally counselling grew from roots laid down by the early psychoanalysts who were scientifically trained in positivist thinking within the framework of the medical model. Behaviourists and cognitive behaviourists came later and were also within the positivist tradition. The humanistic movement taught that the individual was, at 'core', full of potential for growth and self-actualization. However, all of these approaches placed the individual at the centre of his or her problems, and each proposed that individuals, whether by gaining insight, learning new ways of thinking and behaving, or by actualizing the core self with its tendency towards positive growth, could improve their lives at least somewhat.

In more recent times people have begun to question the limiting views of the 'person', 'identity' and 'self' proposed by all of the psychological theorists, emphasizing rather the view that all these concepts are social constructions that depend on social, cultural and historical forces which inform the stories that people tell about themselves and their lives (Gergen 1991). Seeing these psychological constructs as only one of the many available stories rather than 'the truth' frees us to recognize alternative stories that position the individual 'amid a constantly changing web of connections and stories' (Speedy 2000, p.365). Deconstructing the 'dominant stories' of therapy and the 'taken-for-granted assumptions' of professionalism (Derrida 1981; Freedman and Combs 1996; Parker 1999) creates a shift in the power relationships between client and counsellor who become more equal partners in a process of exploration from a position of 'not knowing' and 'curiosity'. Counselling can then be understood in terms of a 'social process' (McLeod 1999) whilst recognizing the counsellor's part in the co-construction of the dialogue (Foucault 1980; Parker 1999; White and Epston 1991).

It is clear from what has gone before that a social constructionist view of an individual's sense of self fits readily with the process of counselling in rehabilitation, particularly in recognizing that people's experience of themselves and their illness and/or disability is powerfully influenced by attitudes held by affected individuals themselves and society as a whole.

An individual's experience of a particular impairment needs to be understood within its social context and processes of socialization.

Attitudes

A postmodern view is that the stories people tell themselves and others about their lives create personal meanings which influence their ways of being in the world and that these stories may also limit the person within a constricted set of possibilities (Bruner 1990; Geertz 1973). These limits may be as a result of attitudes towards self and the world that have been learned through a process of socialization. Thomas (1982) defined an attitude as:

> a set of ideas, feelings and beliefs about life, oneself and others. It is an acquired orientation towards or away from some object, group, person, event or idea. It is a disposition more enduring than mood yet capable under certain conditions of being modified or even reversed. Attitudes seem to have certain features, such as cognitive components (how a person explains, justifies or rationalises his views), a behavioural component (how a person behaves when confronted by the object, event or person which evokes the attitude) and an affective component (the emotions aroused by the object, person or event associated with the attitude. (Thomas 1982, p.56)

Attitudes cannot be understood only at the level of the individual; to some extent the attitudes a person mobilizes are a response to other attitudes elsewhere in a given network or system of relationships, for example, societal norms, stereotypes and generalizations. One of the purposes of an attitude is to guide the person's relationship to an 'other' in order to reconcile the feelings he has towards the 'other' with the norms of the social system that prescribes what beliefs and behaviours are appropriate (Katz 1960).

Society's response to people with disabilities was highlighted back in 1981 by one of the posters advertising the International Year for Disabled People which asked: 'Do disabled people make you feel uncomfortable? If so, their greatest handicap could be you and your attitude.' Our attitudes may create invisible barriers between ourselves and people who are physically or mentally impaired or chronically ill, thus increasing the social, emotional and practical difficulties which can accompany the experience of impairment (Swain *et al.* 1993; Van Dongen-Garrad 1983).

Societal attitudes towards people with mental and physical illness and/or impairments have been documented as far back as Aristotle, Hippocrates and Galen, but it was not until the Middle Ages that impairment became a source of fear, ridicule, persecution and mockery. At the time of Martin Luther, it was believed that the birth of a deformed child was proof of the parent's involvement with witchcraft or the result of the mother's intercourse with the devil. These beliefs survived until the nineteenth century and there is a muted remnant of them even today.

During the nineteenth century attitudes became more sentimental and philanthropic. In the early part of the twentieth century the belief developed that people with disabilities were unfortunate, different, oppressed and sick, followed by a more positive view that all things were possible. People with disabilities were encouraged to 'go public' and become active in shaping opinions about themselves and the nature of disability. In more recent times attitudes seem to have gone through several phases: a phase where disabled people were seen as helpless was followed by a phase of skilled professional involvement, leading to a third phase in which new determination by disabled people questions their role as passive recipients of help and aims to prove otherwise.

Mental illness often evokes fear — fear of our own madness and chaos that may cause us to react from a need to control. Some of my own early OT training took place in one of the five large Victorian 'mental hospitals' (asylums) that encircled London like a net to catch the fallout from life. There were locked doors, patients who looked like zombies from massive doses of drugs or lobotomies, conveyor belts upon which men and women were given electro-convulsive therapy which left them dazed in the short term and frequently without prior memory in the long term. Because our attitudes have changed so dramatically, the reader might find it hard to believe that I am referring to 1960 and 1961. But although attitudes have undoubtedly changed, there still remains in some quarters a need to eliminate any signs of psychological distress. One example of this is that in spite of it being well known that benzodiazepines are harmful when prescribed for more than the short term, these drugs are still being over-prescribed (Hammersley 2001) with serious long-term effects for clients.

Attitudes towards those who become addicted to drugs and/or alcohol are frequently punitive and rejecting. The antisocial behaviour that is often displayed by addicts (such as stealing to support their habit) and alcoholics (aggressive, noisy behaviour) makes them easier to reject than, for example, someone with a spinal injury or hearing loss, because their addiction is judged as self-inflicted and an aggressive act towards others. It is all too easy to lose sight of the person behind the behaviour and condemn both. We often make assumptions and judgements rather than offer a supportive framework in which such behaviour can be usefully challenged and new coping strategies developed.

An overview of the book

The impacts of many of the attitudes to impairment and disability in today's society will be found among the pages of this book as we hear individual stories of disability, marginalization and denial. Alongside this we also hear stories that challenge attitudes, stories that reject limiting beliefs and stories about changed behaviours. These attitudes can be demonstrated and influenced by the language that we use. I have been very aware of my need for 'political correctness' in my use of language throughout this book (although there will be inevitable lapses).

In Chapter 1 Pamela Griffiths tells us the story of the development of rehabilitation and rehabilitation counselling in the UK. She traces the history of rehabilitation from its earliest roots to the present day, highlighting the changing ethos in recent years, bringing in issues about training, research and locating her own developing story within the text. Pamela's travels in other countries show a global and colourful aspect against which to compare the UK story.

Pamela Griffiths has established a unique training in rehabilitation counselling for professionals with experience of working in the field, thus creating a pool of well-trained professional workers who value the emotional, social and spiritual well-being of their clients, alongside their mental and physical health. These professional counsellors (and those from the Bristol University course) will, we hope, be in a position to influence practice and policy in the field of rehabilitation as they develop their individual roles in a variety of settings. Perhaps we can look forward to a future when the 'ripple effect' of having such people within the workforce will be felt as they disseminate their learning through their modelling of good practice.

In Chapter 2 Julia Segal shares some of her vast experience of working as a counsellor with people who have multiple sclerosis (MS). Julia reminds us that people with multiple sclerosis are unique individuals and we should not lose sight of this by focusing solely on their disability. Disabled people have many of the same problems as able-bodied people, problems with relationships, parenting, work, abuse and a range of other life problems. However, many of these problems are exacerbated by chronic illness and disability, especially when additional difficulties are experienced as a result of the environment and societal attitudes.

Julia Segal addresses how our assumptions and attitudes as workers may also add to our clients' problems: if we respond fearfully to our help-lessness and inability to 'cure' or 'heal' our clients, we may withdraw from them or attempt to reassure them, thereby avoiding an opportunity to help them explore the existential anxiety that is part of our human condition and which may be brought into sharper focus for people with a condition that has an uncertain outcome. She points out that if we are to accompany our clients on this journey, we need first to undo our own denial and face our own existential fears.

Rehabilitation counsellors are quite a rare breed, so Diane Aronson's story in Chapter 3 gives us a fascinating glimpse into what it was like for her to develop this new role within a head injury unit in Bath. She gives us the background of how the role was established and funded prior to her arrival in the unit and takes us through some of the issues she had to deal with along the way. In her chapter Diane covers a wide range of complex tasks that were required of her: practical issues such as finding space in which to work that created a safe enough 'frame', making decisions about contracting and referrals and defining the role. Becoming a member of an already established multidisciplinary team can be no easy task: it requires tact and patience as colleagues readjust to the different boundaries around the role, such as confidentiality.

Diane Aronson then presents some of the powerful and complex stories about the nature of her work with children, families and adults, some of whom have cognitive difficulties following head injury which require particularly creative approaches to the work. She paints a vivid picture of the wide range of issues she and her clients deal with at many levels. Finally she reminds us of the potential strain on counsellors (or any workers in such a field) and the need for good support and supervision.

The quality of an experience is difficult to capture in words but in Chapter 4 Sally Lockwood manages to encapsulate the experience of stroke for younger people. She writes about the research she undertook to gain an insider's perspective of three different stages in the process of reha-bilitation after having a stroke: being admitted to hospital; the return home from hospital and the person's current situation. Sally's personal and narrative approach and the use of clients' own words create for the reader a real sense of those experiences. Poignant representation of clients' stories in poetic form distils their experiences with a powerful immediacy and clarity.

The experience of transition from health to illness or disability is impacted by many factors: whether the onset is gradual or sudden; whether the eventual outcome is known or uncertain; whether the illness could have been anticipated and therefore prepared for; whether the event occurred within the normal expectations of an individual's life stage. Stroke is rarely anticipated, occurs dramatically and suddenly and leaves sufferers with uncertainty about outcome: these factors all add to the sense of shock. Because stroke is normally associated with old age, when it happens to someone in the younger age group the shock is even greater.

In Chapter 5 Diana Sheppard tells the story of her personal experience of stroke as a younger person and how counselling helped her rehabilitation. This is a powerful story of hope and healing. Diana refers to the onset of her stroke as 'the day I died' and she leads us through the process of her recovery and self-discovery in a way that allows us to feel part of that journey. When we are supported through times of crisis we can find a way to use them as an opportunity for personal growth. Diana shows clearly how this can happen. Her story also highlights the importance of other significant people in her recovery: family, friends and those who have suffered similar experiences. Illness and disability can isolate and separate us from those we need to help us on our way. Sometimes people walk away, unable to be with sufferers in their pain. Diana understands this because she too would have liked to walk away from herself. Her determination and strength of character, along with the support from others, carried her through to a sense of renewal and rebirth as a different 'me'. Her relationship with her counsellor is woven into her story, showing us what she needed, what she didn't need and how counselling can be used alongside self-help and support groups. There is a clear search for meaning in her progression through her illness and a sense of finally reaching a stage of acceptance which she can use to offer hope and healing to others.

In Chapter 6 Ruth Morgan-Jones focuses on her work as a counsellor and researcher with people who acquire hearing loss, either suddenly or gradually. Ruth is in a unique position to inform us about this subject from the perspective of a counsellor whose own relatively mild hearing loss became profound later in life. She uses the words of her research participants eloquently to portray some of the issues that individuals struggle with as they adjust to the changes brought about by acquired hearing loss.

She shows us through her research the impact of hearing loss on intimate relationships, on how an individual experiences being a member of a group, as well as the impact on people's attitudes to themselves. Ruth also raises some important issues about the inadequate training currently available to people who support those affected by hearing loss and the need for these services to be improved. Once again we are reminded of the importance of viewing the disability as only one aspect of the person and maybe as only one of many factors contributing to the problems that people experience in their lives.

Modernist society has developed medical and surgical interventions that may greatly extend and/or improve the quality of life for some people. These same interventions may create new and different anxieties and problems as people grapple with their choices about how to live in the future. Transplant surgery, IVF, chemotherapy and other interventions raise ethical and life issues that were previously unconsidered. In Chapter 7 Gillian Thomas tells us about counselling people who are attempting to make a choice about one of the surgical interventions now possible for some sufferers of inflammatory bowel disease: the creation of an internal pouch from part of the intestine. She takes us through the process from making the choice, to undertaking the necessary operations and adjusting to life afterwards. This narrative evokes powerful images of the way people experience their bodies physically, emotionally and spiritually. Gillian's sensitive handling of these issues is doubly poignant in that she wrote this chapter whilst experiencing a flare-up of her own inflammatory bowel disease – thereby writing from a perspective that enriches our understanding and allows us to come closer to the experiences she is portraying. Although this chapter takes a very specific focus, the issues it raises can be understood in terms of a greater variety of medical and surgical interventions.

Chapter 8 moves us into the arena of rehabilitation in mental health. Kevin Brenton shows us how counselling training and personal therapy have enabled him to position himself differently from his previous role as a nurse in the field of mental health. Having initially been trained in the medical model, Kevin reflects on the shift of power when counsellors approach clients without the need to 'cure' and with the ability to stay alongside people whilst they find ways to recover from painful experiences in their lives. Emotional pain is difficult to face and sometimes bears a stigma of 'weakness' which is judged as wrong, especially in men – sometimes it is easier to say 'my head/leg/back is aching' than 'my heart is breaking'. Many of us have been socialized to keep our emotional distress hidden, almost as if it is shameful (stiff upper lip). Emotional pain may therefore become displaced onto our bodies and create physical symptoms which allow us to take time out, give expression to our pain and evoke sympathy from others, none of which might seem possible to achieve through an emotional route. Kevin shows us these delicate links between mind, body and spirit with the example he gives of his work with a client.

Richard Bryant-Jefferies writes in Chapter 9 about his work as a counsellor supporting people in the community as they recover from alcohol addiction. He informs us how alcohol impacts on the chemistry of the body and how this chemical dependency contributes to the psychological, emotional and social difficulties people face when attempting to stop excessive drinking. Richard demonstrates through his writing how a person-centred approach positions the counsellor alongside the person in an effort to help them through the rehabilitation process. He introduces the reader to a model of change that views relapse not as failure but as part of the process of recovery when it is consciously processed and understood. Richard also shows us the importance of enabling clients to reach out to others for support and how, in many instances, this requires retraining in social skills, especially when excessive use of alcohol has caused clients to withdraw from normal social contacts, or caused others to withdraw from them. As counsellors we can sometimes lose sight of the client's life outside the counselling room. This chapter reminds us of the necessity to keep the client's context in the world constantly in mind whilst, at the same time, providing a safe environment in which he can explore his internal world.

In Chapter 10 Cindi Bedor has created the story of a client who is an amalgam of several clients and is therefore easily recognizable to all of us who have worked in the field of drug rehabilitation. Cindi's style brings alive the complexity of this work and the important role that assessment plays in the recovery and rehabilitation process. She leads us gently through many important issues such as collaboration with other professionals and the issues this raises about confidentiality; attitudes towards and about people who are drug addicts and the impact of these attitudes on workers and on clients; the despair that counsellors may feel in the face of the client's chaos that seems to mirror their chaotic feelings in relationship with the client; the need to pace the work to match the client's readiness rather than the counsellor's need to work with underlying issues; and our need as counsellors to hold an awareness of our responsibilities towards clients and those for whom they are responsible alongside our duty of care towards the client. Cindi's writing takes us with a delicate touch into areas of darkness and despair, leading us out again into the light of knowing that our counselling relationship can sometimes make an important difference whilst acknowledging the reality that it is sometimes not enough.

In Chapter 11 we hear the other perspective on Cindi's story: the client's story. Frances Taylor gives us a personal and powerful account of her journey through drug addiction and recovery. She shows us how the addiction was created by her early life circumstances, the relentlessness of the battle against the force of addiction and the strength required for her to free herself. We hear how the judgemental and punitive attitudes of society added to the difficulties she faced and how the medical model reinforced negative self-esteem by pathologizing and marginalizing her as an addict. Frances tells her story without a trace of self-pity, marvelling at the patience and love of the counsellor who believed in her and stayed long enough to help her climb out of the pit of despair she had created for herself and her family. Person-centred counsellors know about the value and power of the therapeutic relationship, but rarely do we hear so clearly from the other person in that relationship – the client. The core conditions of respect, empathic understanding and congruence were fully experienced by Frances, who conveys that experience to the reader through her story of the important part counselling played in the co-construction of her identity.

This book is full of stories and I have encouraged authors to write in a way that allows the reader to create pictures in the mind's eye of the world of rehabilitation. Stories inform us in a way that academic theories and scientific research may not. If we can sustain an interest through a 'good story' we can stay open to learning and 'narrative knowing' (Bruner 1986, 1990) which we can place alongside paradigmatic knowing, and thereby learn to value both. So in Chapter 12 I have explored some of these ideas and invited the reader to become an active audience to my own stories about disability and those of some of my family. We all have stories about the ways in which disability, illness and other problems have touched our lives, because they are part of being human. As counsellors we need to be aware of how our own stories inform our ways of listening to and interpreting our clients' stories. We fill in the gaps in other people's stories from our own limited stock of experiences and knowledge so it is our responsibility to expand that range of experiences and knowledge by becoming familiar with our own stories and other people's stories through reading books, watching films and plays. Thereby we increase our empathic listening, our understanding and our ability consciously to resonate with the stories told by people who seek our help.

When we write stories we normally have to make do with an imagined audience. In my final chapter I invite the reader to become an interactive audience through the medium of technology by responding to my stories by email and letting me know your answers to some of my questions about your responses. And as I bring this Introduction to a close I would also like to invite you to respond to the stories that other authors have written in this book and to the book as a whole. Let me know whether and how this book contributes to your learning; whether or not it demonstrates a human-world understanding of rehabilitation in the arenas we have explored; whether or not it has opened you up to creative and new ways of thinking; whether it resonates with your experience and has affected you emotionally and intellectually; whether it raises new questions in your mind and/or has moved you to write or take any other action; whether it challenges your assumptions; and, finally, whether or not it has sustained your interest. My email address and further information about how your responses might be used can be found at the end of the last chapter.

And if all that seems far too much to ask, then do nothing but read on and enjoy.

References

Barnes, C., Mercer, G. and Shakespeare, T. (1999) *Exploring Disability: A Sociological Introduction.* Cambridge: Polity Press.

Bruner, J. (1986) *Actual Minds, Possible Worlds.* Cambridge, MA: Harvard University Press.

Bruner, J. (1990) *Acts of Meaning.* Cambridge, MA: Harvard University Press.

Davis, K. (1993) 'The crafting of good clients.' In J. Swain, V. Finkelstein, S. French and M. Oliver (eds) *Disabling Barriers – Enabling Environments.* London: Sage.

Derrida, J. (1981) *Positions.* Chicago: Chicago University Press.

Etherington, K. (1988) 'The Disabled Person's Act 1986: The need for counselling.' Unpublished dissertation for postgraduate Diploma in Counselling. Bristol: University of Bristol.

Foucault, M. (1980) *Power/Knowledge: Selected Interviews and Other Writings.* New York: Pantheon.

Freedman, J. and Combs, G. (1996) *Narrative Therapy: The Social Construction of Preferred Realities.* New York: Norton.

Geertz, C. (1973) *The Interpretation of Cultures.* New York: Basic Books.

Gergen, K. (1991) *The Saturated Self.* New York: Basic Books.

Hammersley, D.E. (2001) 'An exploration of how therapists view therapeutic process in relation to clients who are taking benzodiazepines', unpublished PhD thesis, Regent's College and City University, London.

Katz, D. (1960) 'The functional approach to the study of attitude change.' *Public Opinion Quarterly 24*, 163–204.

Lenny, J. (1993) 'Do disabled people need counselling?' In J. Swain, V. Finkelstein, S. French and M. Oliver (eds) *Disabling Barriers – Enabling Environments*. London: Sage.

McLeod, J. (1999) 'Counselling as a social process.' *Counselling 10*, pp.217–227.

Mair, M. (1989) *Between Psychology and Psychotherapy: A Poetics of Experience*. London: Routledge.

Parker, I. (1999) *Deconstructing Psychotherapy*. London: Sage.

Speedy, J. (2000) 'The storied helper: narrative ideas and practices in counselling and psychotherapy.' *European Journal of Psychotherapy, Counselling and Health 3*, 3, 361–374.

Stewart, W. (1985) *Counselling in Rehabilitation*. London: Croom Helm.

Swain, J., Finkelstein, V., French, S. and Oliver, M. (eds) (1993) *Disabling Barriers – Enabling Environments*. London: Sage.

Thomas, D. (1982) *The Experience of Handicap*. London: Methuen.

Van Dongen-Garrad, J. (1983) *Invisible Barriers: Pastoral Care with Disabled People*. London: SPCK.

White, M. and Epston, D. (1991) *Narrative Means to Therapeutic Ends*. New York: Norton.

Woolley, M. (1993) 'Acquired hearing loss: acquired oppression.' In J. Swain, V. Finkelstein, S. French and M. Oliver (eds) *Disabling Barriers – Enabling Environments*. London: Sage.

Further reading

Cooper, N., Stevenson, C. and Hale, G. (eds) (1996) *Integrating Perspectives on Health*. Buckingham: Open University Press.

Etherington, K. (2000) *Narrative Approaches to Working with Adult Male Survivors of Child Sexual Abuse: The Clients', the Counsellor's and the Researcher's Story*. London: Jessica Kingsley Publishers.

Finkelstein, V. (1980) *Attitudes and Disabled People: Issues for Discussion*. New York: World Rehabilitation Fund.

Finkelstein, V. (1993) 'Disability: A social challenge or an administrative responsibility?' In J. Swain, V. Finkelstein, S. French and M. Oliver (eds) *Disabling Barriers – Enabling Environments*. London: Sage.

Frank, A. (1995) *The Wounded Storyteller: Body, Illness and Ethics*. Chicago: University of Chicago Press.

French, S. (1993) 'Disability, impairment or something in-between.' In J. Swain, V. Finkelstein, S. French and M. Oliver (eds) *Disabling Barriers – Enabling Environments*. London: Sage.

Oliver, M. (1990) *The Politics of Disablement*. Basingstoke: Macmillan.

Oliver, M. (1996) *Understanding Disability: From Theory to Practice*. London: Macmillan.

Chapter 1

Counselling in Rehabilitation
The UK Story
Pamela Griffiths

Introduction

Over the last twenty years interest in narrative and storytelling has increased in the social sciences. In her pioneering book, Hollway (1989) hails the reclamation of subjectivity for 'valid and legitimate knowledge'. Her reappraisal of the concept of subjectivity, drawn from her research, has contributed to exciting developments in qualitative research with an emphasis on subjective reality for each person and a wider participation in the research process. This shift towards valuing the subjective experience has led to profound changes in how we understand and develop our health-care provision in the UK. Training programmes for health-care professionals have increased their core components of social sciences, recognizing the need for improved communication skills in all staff and knowledge of psychological and emotional process. The literature has seen an increase in published qualitative research and autobiographical or biographical accounts, demonstrating the lived experience of people with chronic illness and disability. Accountability to the health-care consumer has more recently become a theme in health-care planning, requiring consultation and discussion of project development.

These developments grew out of earlier initiatives which became influential in the 1960s and 1970s. Humanistic psychology challenged experimental psychology in the 1960s for not seeing the individual as a whole person. At this time, in medicine, Balint was leading pioneering groups for doctors and GPs where he urged them to listen to their patients, to reflect upon their responses to the patient and to move from 'illness-centred medicine' to 'patient-centred medicine'. He also attacked the power base of the doctor ('the doctor installed in the role of untouchable priest of a deified science' Bernachon 1972, p.297) and as one doctor put it 'revealed to us what we had been carefully taught not to see' (Bernachon 1972, p.297). However, increased recognition of the wider needs of patients raised new questions of a need for counselling which remained unanswered by participants in Balint's groups: 'Is it up to doctors to be better trained and to be able to assume this role of counselling? Is it for doctors to share their function with counsellors?' It was thought that many of the doctors attending the Balint groups had begun to ask these questions but 'no answers to these questions' were found at the time (Sapir 1972, p.17).

This is the beginning of the UK story of counselling in rehabilitation at the end of the twentieth century. I will now explore some of its historical and sociological context and contribute my own story in terms of my experience of the development of this field and my motivations for working in this area. An outline of the development of the rehabilitation counselling course at Brunel University, which commenced in 1990, will be given together with other relevant initiatives, and implications for future directions will be considered.

Recognition of rehabilitation in the UK

The industrial revolution, founded on capitalist principles of competition, maximization of profit and the free market, profoundly changed the social and economic organization of Britain in the nineteenth century. Cottage-based work, local markets and horses and carts were replaced by large factories in built environments designed to serve able-bodied interests. Ryan and Thomas highlight the change in working patterns created by this development:

> The speed of factory work, the enforced discipline, the time-keeping and production norms – all these were a highly unfavourable change from the slower, more self-determined methods of work into which many handicapped people had been integrated. (Ryan and Thomas 1987, p.101)

Finkelstein (1981) and Oliver (1993) have shown how people with physical impairments or learning difficulties were marginalized by these developments and many ended up in workhouses or asylums.

At the same time large numbers of people suffered physical impairment during the extensive building of the new industrial base. An example of this phenomenon is the building of the Manchester Ship Canal where figures of

1100 fatal accidents, 1700 permanent injuries and 2500 partial injuries were thought to be an underestimate (Whitworth 1892). Unusually, in this instance the contractor did endeavour to find more appropriate work for those who had been injured. By the end of the nineteenth century a few charities were beginning to recognize and give voice to the neglect of people with sensory impairment; for example, the British Deaf Association formed in 1890 and the National League of the Blind formed as a registered Trade Union in 1899. Thus at the turn of the century there was some indication of the emergence of a new sensibility towards people with physical or sensory impairment.

Previously casualties in foreign wars had been treated or left to die in the field. However, in the late nineteenth century it became possible to bring many casualties back to the UK by ship and a large naval hospital was built on the River Hamble in Hampshire to treat the wounded men. This venture was one of the earliest forms of mass 'rehabilitation' in the UK. War continued to be the impetus to develop and restructure the rehabilitation services in the twentieth century.

World War I led to high numbers of casualties and injuries on the battlefield, but many of those who were able to return to the UK were less visibly scarred; they were shell-shocked – a condition we might understand today as traumatic shock or PTSD. At Craiglockhart War Hospital in Scotland shell-shocked men in active service were sent for treatment. Some of the treatment meted out was crude, but one pioneer, Dr W. H. R. Rivers, began sensitively to explore the psychological impact of trauma. His work has since been recognized in the writings of Pat Barker (1992, 1994, 1996) and the film of her novel *Regeneration*. The poets Siegfried Sassoon and Wilfred Owen were both patients at Craiglockhart during World War I. Their use of poetry is perhaps an example of using a reflexive and symbolic medium (as in creative arts) to deal with their emotions and the memory of the trauma.

After the war, in 1920, the Tavistock Clinic was founded in London. There was an urgency to improve the understanding of the impact of trauma on individuals and societies and much of the early work of the clinic was associated with the understanding and treatment of 'war neuroses'. The clinic has continued to develop a clinical service and a national training role for mental health professionals.

Following World War II large numbers of injured servicemen returned to the UK and major initiatives were carried out to provide a welfare state. The National Health Service (NHS) was introduced in 1948 and many of the staff of this large employer were ex-servicemen and women. Several acts were passed designed to meet the needs of those with a chronic illness or physical impairment. These acts included the National Assistance Act 1948 and the Disabled Persons (Employment) Act 1944, which recognized that disabled people had a right to work. An impetus to create a more inclusive and caring society appears to be evident after the devastation of the world war. However, Oliver (1993, p.53) believes that the legislation was influenced by the shortage of labour at the time and 'the collective guilt of seeing ex-servicemen who had been disabled while fighting for their country'.

With large numbers of ex-service staff entering the newly formed NHS it was inevitable that models of health care and rehabilitation were strongly influenced by a service ethos. My own experience of training as a physiotherapist in clinical placements at a large London teaching hospital in the 1970s demonstrates this point. Staff groups were strongly hierarchical with uniform indicating levels in the hierarchy (e.g. different coloured epaulettes, belts or hats). Groups of staff often walked along the corridors in hierarchical formations. Staff were expected to change into uniform as soon as they arrived at the hospital and some sections had morning inspections. Standardized routines designed for efficiency, especially when dealing with large numbers of people, could also lead to a depersonalization of patients and a lack of opportunity for staff to acknowledge their own feelings and responses to stressful and challenging work.

More recently the Chronically Sick and Disabled Persons Act 1970 and the Disabled Persons Act 1986 have continued the post-war impetus to develop welfare provision. Although the acts made some improvement in available service, they have been criticized for reinforcing the notion that people with disabilities are 'helpless' (Shearer 1981) and for making unfulfilled promises (Oliver 1993).

Perhaps because of the Hampshire tradition of rehabilitating wounded naval veterans, the first Chair of Rehabilitation in the UK was established at the University of Southampton in 1977. This was soon followed by a second chair at Edinburgh University. Professor H. J. Glanville in his inaugural lecture at Southampton (1977) explored the theme of 'What is Rehabilitation?' It is clear from his address that the understanding of rehabilitation was in transition. Glanville defined rehabilitation as 'making able again' (from its Latin roots) and identified aims of promoting research in rehabilitation and training of rehabilitation therapists at undergraduate and postgraduate levels, as well as encouraging more doctors to specialize in rehabilitation. He called for more emphasis on home treatment and noted that remedial therapists were beginning to 'see themselves in new roles such as counsellors and teachers' where the role would comprise teaching and advice 'for people disabled whose families are prepared to care for them' (pp.21, 23). He envisaged staff working in 'parallel' at a time when interprofessional teamwork was still undeveloped. His characterization of rehabilitation as a 'new discipline' underlines the increased recognition this area was now receiving. The development of new technologies, the influence of social science studies and the beginning of a move away from institutional settings towards community-based care were all influential in this initiative.

Sociological perspective

As recently as 1996 sociologists have been criticized for not taking disability seriously by relegating this area to the margins of sociological theory (Oliver 1996). Key theories have been influential in studies in the area of chronic illness and disability and have been incorporated into curricula for medical and health-care professional training programmes. These include Parsons' (1951) analysis of the sick role which associated it with social deviance and introduced the idea of health as adaptation. Later Goffman's (1963) concept of stigma, a term traditionally used to mark those seen as morally inferior and therefore shunned by the rest of society, was influential in beginning to highlight the position of people with disabilities in society. He suggested that the 'stigmatized' such as 'the dwarf, the blind man, the disfigured ... and the ex-mental patient' are generally viewed as less than human. His theories drew attention to areas of segregation in society and found a resonance with Wolfensberger's introduction of social role valorization in the early 1970s.

Wolfensberger was particularly looking at service provision for those with learning disabilities and mental illness. He found:

> Once a society has made a decision (explicated or not) to come down hard on a devalued minority group, it will transact this decision through whatever technical measures it may take towards this group, even those measures that are interpreted as being to the latter's benefit. (Wolfensberger 1987, p.141)

Wolfensberger's work demonstrated the practical ways in which people with disabilities are segregated from society. Examples include communal buildings which are not close to public transport and isolated family situations where there is no place with access to meet other people. Furthermore these conditions cause people with disabilities to be invisible to society and their concerns, suffering, hopes and aspirations remain unheard.

During the late 1970s and early 1980s the concept of normalization became influential in the UK, apparent particularly in the area of learning difficulties. However, as government policy regarding the transfer of long-term hospital care to the community developed in the early 1980s, the principle was applied to other groups. Service providers and professionals adopted normalization more readily than disability activists who criticized the concept for implying that there will always be devalued victims, otherwise there would be no concept of normalization (Whitehead 1992). Normalization contributed to rehabilitation services in the UK moving from a treatment model to an advocacy model. However advocacy remains in the form of professionals speaking up for those with disabilities, resulting in no real shift in the balance of power.

These perspectives represent a challenge to the medical model of chronic illness and disability which regards these states to be a result of physical or cognitive impairment. The medical model seeks to return chronically ill and disabled people back to the '"normal" condition of being able-bodied' by curing or rehabilitating them (Drake 1996, p.149) and has been central to the organization and provision of rehabilitation services in the UK. However, the challenges put in place by the emergence of social constructionism in the social sciences are gradually leading to profound changes in our construction of chronic illness, disability and rehabilitation. Psychology becomes the study of a socially constructed being and sociology explores the social construction of society through the social practices of people. The recognition that language produces and constructs our experience of ourselves and each other has been reflected in the title of a popular topical media broadcast on disability issues – 'Does He Take Sugar?'. Names of rehabilitation units have been changed (e.g. the Hospital for Incurables in London) as well as staff titles (e.g. superintendent to manager) along with a restyling of uniforms.

In the late 1970s and early 1980s radical movements of people with disabilities in the USA (e.g. ILM, Movement for Independent Living) and in the UK (UPIAS, for example, Union of the Physically Impaired Against Segregation) led to important debates drawn from members' personal experiences. From these debates and in the context of the social constructionist movement a social model of disability emerged (e.g. Finkelstein 1981; Oliver 1983, 1990; Swain et al. 1993). This model takes the perspective that people are not disabled by their physical or mental impairment but by the attitudes and the built environment of non-disabled people. The subjective experience of those with chronic illness or disability (e.g. Campling 1981; Corker 1996; French 1993, 1994; Morris 1989, 1991; Slack 1999; Sutherland 1981) has become more evident in the literature of the last decade. This relatively recent development begins to redress the situation strongly criticized by those with disability that only the views of 'those credited with the responsibility for recovery i.e. the medical profession' (Oliver 1996) were recognized. These criticisms also attack models of psychological adjustment as being linked to professionally agreed criteria and 'non-disabled' assumptions of what it is like to experience impairment. Recognizing the subjective experience of people with chronic illness and disability begins to redress the balance in rehabilitation and demands new models of practice.

My story

In reclaiming subjectivity for 'valid and legitimate knowledge' (Hollway 1989), narratives in the form of reminiscences, life stories and oral histories become tools of research and methods of therapy (e.g. McLeod 1997, 1998). The emphasis has shifted from truth that is uncovered by the researcher or therapist to truth that is co-constructed between researcher and participant, or therapist and client. An implication of this shift is that 'the knower and the known cannot be unambiguously separated' (Henwood and Pidgeon 1995). So the context of my perceptions – my story – becomes a part of this story of counselling in rehabilitation.

My earliest experience of rehabilitation was watching my grandfather having physiotherapy treatment following a stroke in his eighties. Home treatment was unusual at that time (the 1960s) and the visits became focal points of the week. I remember his look of intense concentration as he tried to walk down the hallway and how we all kept quiet during his hour of treatment, somehow believing that this would help his progress. More significantly I remember how his disability changed all our lives. We (the children) had to be quieter and not play 'dangerously' in the garden, adults became tearful or abrupt and outings could be cancelled for no good reason. Later my brother underwent rehabilitation for several years following an accident where he nearly lost a leg and an eye. Then, as a teenager finding more independence I would go on long cycle rides in the school holidays. Suddenly remembering that my brother was sitting at home with crutches by his chair I would stop at a phone box to tell him news of the outside world, feeling slightly guilty and anxious that he was unable to walk more than a few feet without help.

These were the motivational experiences I cited at the age of 18 in my interview for physiotherapy training. The training itself focused on returning patients to physical functioning with little account of the emotional and psychological struggle needed to pursue a rehabilitation programme. Furthermore it neglected the profound impact which working intensively with people with chronic illness or disability can have on the rehabilitation staff. Many of the patients we met and worked with during the training were in crisis, perhaps following a recent injury or diagnosis. Some were recovering from operations which radically changed their body image and sense of identity such as a hysterectomy or leg amputation. As always, in a culture infused with the spirit of the armed forces, humour and a cheery smile often enabled people to cope with significant hardship. However, as Menzies Lyth(1988) had found in her pioneering research on nurses, difficult feelings were often expressed out of sight such as her example of nurses crying in the sluice room and then returning to their 'duty'. In the large London teaching hospital where I trained a tall bespectacled chaplain was evident one year in the staff cafeteria. He would quietly walk around the room and then sit with a member of staff who seemed tearful or quiet. Once he sat talking to a colleague of mine for an hour after one of her patients died unexpectedly. I realized that there was no one else who would have had the time or skills to talk with her during the highly structured and busy schedule of the hospital day.

Later, working in South Africa following the 1976 uprising, I treated many children and young adults with spinal cord injuries resulting from gunshot wounds or stabbing. Here I learnt more powerfully about the political, social and economic context of rehabilitation provision. We worked in a packed gym, with no air-conditioning and little room to move among the wheelchairs, parallel bars and treatment mats. This was the gym for the non-white Africans. Next door, in the gym for the white Africans, there would be one or maybe two patients. Cheers went up for those who took their first steps in long-leg braces. Walking was the main goal for those with low-level lesions and enormous efforts were put into achieving even a few steps. Those with lesions began to learn to use arm splints to provide some upper limb function.

Staff meetings reviewed patients' potential to return to work with little mention of any family context. Many did not receive visits from family as they lived too far away. On one occasion a patient was sent home to his wife for the weekend to 'see if the marriage still worked'. This was arranged in a matter-of-fact fashion during a ward round and I felt shocked at the lack of acknowledgement of the man's anxieties. I realized that there was no one on the team who could have helped with this patient's psychological and emotional understanding of re-establishing his relationship with his wife.

In subsequent jobs in the USA and the UK I experienced a range of instances during rehabilitation where the availability of sensitive counselling would have facilitated the programme. Some of these examples focused on the differing expectations of patient, rehabilitation staff and patient's relatives. I remember an elderly American woman who had recently lost her husband and soon after had a stroke while staying with her brother. At the end of one treatment she sobbed that her brother was telling her she was not working hard enough and 'should be walking by now'. In another example the parents of a boy with cerebral palsy would exhort him to 'hurry up and run around' as soon as I was out of earshot. In both these examples the relatives were given explanations of the condition and the limits and potential of treatment. However they still needed to stay with their own version and the difference in expectation was causing significant tensions which, in my view now, needed the skills of a counsellor with an understanding of the rehabilitation programme.

While living in the USA I became aware of the rehabilitation counselling courses and went to discuss the programme with staff at the local university. I also wanted to meet a rehabilitation counsellor in the work context and arranged to see a woman working in a Catholic residential home for the elderly. I was impressed with her opportunity to be close to the overall rehabilitation programme; for example, she was in the exercise treatment room moving around and talking to people to get a feel for how things were going, as well as attending multidisciplinary staff meetings. However, I was aware that this was not a facility available to all. At the time I was treating many patients in the community whose insurance could barely cover basic care and would certainly not extend to the provision of a counsellor. I read more about rehabilitation counselling provision in North America and Australia and found many of the papers to be orientated towards a return to work for the client. Although inspired by this provision, its focus on a return to work influenced by government economic policy appeared to be limited in remit.

On returning to the UK in the early 1980s I studied and researched the rehabilitation field (where this subject was now developing strongly at Southampton University) and found one or two publications on the counselling needs of those in rehabilitation (e.g. Stewart 1985). I discovered that district rehabilitation officers from the Department of Employment had a role to explore a patient's needs for returning to a job again, which had some overlap with the brief of some rehabilitation counsellors in North America. However, their responsibility appeared to be confined to assessment for work. I took a post lecturing undergraduate physiotherapists and worked on introducing a wider programme of psychosocial theory and relating this material to their current clinical placements.

It was a controversial area as several of the students thought that the sessions took away from their time on the 'important' subjects of anatomy and physiology. Gradually I found areas which seemed to meet their current concerns on placements: what to do when a patient has just been told some bad news by the doctor and does not want to do their treatment programme; how to cope with aggression from relatives; the death of patients; differing cross-cultural understandings; and problems of communication in the multidisciplinary team. The range of issues was not confined to patients of work age, 16 to 65, but extended to the elderly whom students saw as being ignored by staff on busy wards. However the physiotherapy students frequently formed strong attachments with these patients as they often had more time to talk during longer treatment sessions. Sometimes the lectures and seminars stimulated vigorous debates carried on into lunch and coffee breaks. At best they could stimulate enquiry and challenge established attitudes inherent in institutional practices.

At the same time I trained as a counsellor and psychotherapist. There was no course orientated towards the area of rehabilitation in the UK, but the course was an opportunity to explore my experiences in rehabilitation more fully. In the late 1980s I began to put forward a proposal for a course in rehabilitation counselling at the university where I was working. I explored the idea with managers in the health-care field and piloted a couple of one-day courses in hospitals. At the university I made contact with some interested colleagues with a view to setting up a part-time course for health professionals who wanted to develop their counselling skills and understanding of the psychosocial context of the rehabilitation setting.

The rehabilitation counselling course

The course commenced in 1990 at Brunel University (Griffiths 1993) and is now in its eleventh year. It is the only course of its kind in the UK, focusing on the needs of people in secondary and tertiary care as opposed to primary care. The course is designed for those with professional experience in the rehabilitation field. Most of the students are health-care professionals, including occupational therapists, physiotherapists, speech therapists, health visitors, mental health nurses, specialist nurses and social workers. All these students have had high-level communication skills training and at least basic counselling skills training in their undergraduate courses. A few students are from the voluntary sector, for example, charities linked to the rehabilitation field, and have usually had a basic counselling training with further practical experience. The course enables them to develop their understanding of the rehabilitation field, their knowledge and application of counselling skills and to carry out research in this area. In each cohort there have been one or two managers from the NHS, social services or voluntary sector who can additionally employ their counselling skills in the area of appraisals and staff support.

Rather than the 're-skilling', in a vocational or social skills sense, which can be a focus of North American or Australian models of rehabilitation counselling, our emphasis is on the 'process of change' which may be initiated by a chronic illness or disability. We explore this change within a systems context that considers the family, carers and work colleagues. Within this model a person with a disability, a carer or a health professional may consider having counselling to explore their position and responses. The counselling relationship may become the place to understand and develop new ways of relating.

Students are mature and experienced at the commencement of the course and already developing specialist areas of interest and expertise. These special interests are fostered in both their application of counselling skills and in their area of research. This development will often lead to changes within their current role or to a new role. The opportunity for specialism is similar to the American model. Examples of students' development following the course include: becoming the manager of a hospice day centre and initiating a creative arts project where time was provided for emergent themes to be talked about (Kennett 2000); instigating a counselling facility in a clinic where patients often received diagnoses of chronic illness (Ellison 1995); organizing a psycho-educational programme for parents of people with schizophrenia (Brenton 1997).

In other instances students have been able to develop their current roles. For example, one nurse specialist runs a facility to offer counselling support to head injury patients and their families; another nurse specialist has offered a similar facility in a coronary care unit. Physiotherapists in paediatrics and neurorehabilitation have particularly developed opportunities for relatives to receive counselling support. In some of these instances, links have been made with the psychology departments and joint posts for one or two days a week have provided a sharing of experience. The students' extensive background in rehabilitation environments means that they are at ease with the technology of the rehabilitation environment – heart monitors, oxygen cylinders, catheters, tracheostomies and wheelchairs – and can communicate their openness and understanding to the patients and their carers.

These developments are carried out through careful negotiation with managers and the multidisciplinary team. If a nurse specialist is counselling a patient she has no other nursing input with that person. Development of multidisciplinary teams may include workshops regarding the theory and practice of counselling. Safe and comfortable venues for counselling are sought. In a few instances, for example, with elderly who are no longer able to get up, this has been a cubicle with the curtain drawn around. Such sessions may have been shorter (e.g. 30 to 40 minutes) and are an example of sensitive adaptation to the context of the client. These clients raised issues of profound importance including longed-for reconciliation with children and fears of death.

Course organization

The course content is built around four key areas: rehabilitation counselling principles, sociological perspectives of chronic illness and disability, creative arts and research. A legal and ethical component is built into the counselling modules and students follow the BACP code of ethics. The students' personal development is central to the course and is fostered by personal journal writing, experiential group work in the creative arts and personal counselling. A sense of being co-responsible for their learning is encouraged with guided reading, peer presentations and opportunities to reflect on their individual learning.

The central model of the course is an integrated model with a focus on the humanistic approach, particularly the person-centred approach of Carl Rogers. The literature strongly supports a person-centred approach when working with people with disability or chronic illness. Lenny (1993), who has worked for the spinal injuries association, emphasizes the importance of the counsellor having a non-judgemental approach and not imposing meaning on the situation or labels on the person which may already have been part of the client's negative experience. For this reason she argues that a psychoanalytical approach is not appropriate. She suggests that the person-centred approach will more fully enable a client to make sense of the relationship between 'individually experienced impairment' and 'socially imposed disability'. Livneh (1986), an American rehabilitation counsellor and researcher, advocates more affective and/or insightful counselling approaches in the early counselling phases, with cognitive-behavioural and action-orientated approaches in the later phase. Both Livneh (1986) and Oliver (1995) concur in their research findings that counselling for people with disabilities needs to be flexible in approach and not to have just one theoretical orientation. We introduce a short series of sessions at the end of the first year on the cognitive-behavioural approach which a few students may utilize in short-term work. In the second year we also look at the work of other key figures in counselling and psychotherapy in the twentieth century for context and to stimulate wider reading in this area.

There have been several areas of change during the running of the course. The sociological perspectives of chronic illness and disability modules evolved out of a module called rehabilitation studies which looked at current sociological perspectives, autobiographical and biographical accounts of chronic illness and disability and media representation of this area. Creative arts broadened from drama and art exercises to experiential groups run by an art therapist and a drama therapist where symbolic meanings could be explored. The potential of this area to be significant for clients who may be unable to articulate their feelings and needs has been emphasized by students who have used non-verbal approaches effectively in their counselling work. For example, a physiotherapist working with children with disabilities has used storytelling and drawing to identify their feelings about the challenging physiotherapy rehabilitation programme (Watson 1998). Another student working in the area of neurorehabilitation used poetry in the counselling sessions as a means to communicate with a client from another culture. Cross-cultural counselling now has an increased emphasis on the course in response to our recognition that all students are working at some point in a cross-cultural context. The student cohorts are also multicultural, mirroring the ethnic profile of an urban rehabilitation setting and they provide an important context to explore cross-cultural perspectives.

Our research base

Since 1990 the databases available to us have expanded considerably. Enhancing computer literacy in order to access these resources is a key component of the first-year programme. We have continued to develop contacts with North American rehabilitation counsellors and have been invited to their national conferences to participate in panel discussions. Through the internet we have been invited to join email discussions with university programmes in North America where courses are established, and in South America and Europe where interest to develop similar courses is growing. Two students have received scholarships to the USA and one to Canada, to look at the place of counselling in rehabilitation and to share some of their research interests.

The increasing recognition of the importance of qualitative methodologies (e.g. Richardson 1996) is reflected in a growing emphasis on this approach in the course since 1990. Based on the key assumptions put forward by Gergen in 1985 (and discussed by Burr 1995), we encourage students to take a critical stance towards knowledge, to recognize that our ways of understanding are historically and culturally relative, that knowledge is sustained by social process and interactions and that our construction of the world may be linked to a particular pattern of social action. These are the key assumptions of social constructionism which contrast significantly with the approach of traditional psychology and medicine. For example, within social constructionism there can be no such thing as an objective fact. We each encounter the world from our own perspective and the research questions we frame will evolve from our particular viewpoint. Our involvement in the research process becomes something we can work with during the study and acknowledge in the results that we find.

This approach can be quite new to some students and may shake previously held assumptions. Seminar discussions, creative arts groups and research sessions are fora where the validity of differing readings of a text may be experienced. In this way the non-judgemental approach offered to clients is offered to peers. Reflexivity is a stance which develops in all students, particularly during the first year, and is demonstrated in journal writing and discussion. Sometimes students fail to find the words which express a shift of perspective taking place and resort to metaphor or a more tentative rephrasing of their experience. Their own story becomes central to their understanding of their motivation to work in rehabilitation and to develop research.

Following on from this approach, many students do use a qualitative methodology in their research. Some may use a combined approach (e.g. adding a standardized scale or test) and a few will use a purely quantitative approach (where a social constructionist perspective can still be engaged). Each year there are several action research studies which have change and intervention as an explicit aim. These have included earlier cited examples as well as exploring the counselling needs of partners of people who have had myocardial infarction (Shotter 1999); exploring the effectiveness of assertiveness training for mental health service users (Lim 1999); and an investigation of the use of co-counselling on the stress levels of staff in a specialized head injury unit (Gray 1996).

In other projects students have explored specific aspects of counselling in rehabilitation centring on the participants' experience which have also led to developments in practice or further research. A few students have themselves had disabilities which they chose to explore in their research. Others have used methods which involved participants in the planning of the research. This participatory research approach can lead to data, and later service development, which truly reflects the needs and aspirations of those who previously felt they had no voice and were being marginalized by society.

Examples of these studies include one on the expectations of stroke rehabilitation for patients and professionals (White 1997). The student found that explicit goals were linked to physical independence without a recognition of the 'trauma and loss of control experienced by the person on the outset of their ordeal'. This theme is echoed in several other studies where the 'devastation' for the person and/or their partner at the onset of the disability or chronic illness has remained unrecognized. In a linked study looking at the experiences of people with stroke at three months following discharge from hospital (Johnstone 1998), the researcher found a 'stuckness' and 'withdrawal from the world' in the participants which suggested 'a searching behaviour ... for the physical "state of life" that went before the stroke occurred'. This finding draws on grief theory and leads to a recommendation for counselling in the hospital setting prior to discharge planning.

Models of grief and loss are often rejected by disabled people as not according with their experience (Lenny 1993). However some students have found participants who expressed these emotions. One student studied the experience of chronic sorrow in parents of adults with learning disabilities (Robb 2000). She found evidence that all participants had experienced feelings related to chronic sorrow when their children were younger and that most of them continued to have these feelings. This experience of chronic loss was found to be periodic and recurrent. It was recommended that helping parents explore their perception of such a loss may be an appropriate role for a counsellor working in a rehabilitation setting.

Conclusion

This story has explored the context of the rehabilitation setting in the UK with particular emphasis on its changing ethos in recent years. The multidisciplinary team has now become the forum for organizing and evaluating rehabilitation provision within hospital and daycare centres. There is evidence from research to suggest that the expectations of the team and those of the patients often do not match and that the social and emotional experience of rehabilitation service users may be ignored. Furthermore the disability movement argues that rehabilitation professionals make assumptions about the experience of people with chronic illness and disability that are not valid, retaining power which needs to be shared between teams and service users.

The insights from the rehabilitation counselling course at Brunel University, gleaned from students' experience during and after the course, international research databases and students' research on the course, strongly point to a need for a rehabilitation counsellor to be part of the multidisciplinary teams in secondary and tertiary care. We see this position as offering counselling support to rehabilitation staff (similar to some hospice models), people with chronic illness and disability, their carers and relatives. Both short-term and longer-term provision needs to be available. Research suggests that a periodic provision over the longer term may be the model of choice for some people. Advocacy and psychoeducational programmes would be better effected if jointly operated between counsellor and client.

This development is different from primary care counselling promoted by the Counselling in Primary Care Trust since 1991. The trust promotes the provision of counselling in GP practices in the UK. Recent surveys of counselling in primary care (DOH 1999) indicate that mental ill health, particularly anxiety and depression, are extremely common in primary care. Mellor-Clark (2000, p.4) suggests that 'the most important factor' for the 20 per cent rise in primary care counselling between 1992 and 1998 is 're-stricted access to secondary and community mental healthcare services'. The focus of rehabilitation counselling, however, is not the mental health needs of the general population but specifically the counselling needs of those with chronic illness and disability. In moving away from the medical model to a social model of chronic illness and disability, we need to promote models of research which are participatory and where reflexivity is central to the process. The knowledge research base cannot develop if it is directed and 'powered' by professional interests. Reflexivity allows counsellors to undertake what Bryman (1988, quoted in Stevenson and Cooper 1997, p.160) argued was 'a crucial activity, the choosing of an inquiry position appropriate to the phenomenon to be researched'. An aspect of this 'reflexivity' for rehabilitation counsellors must be their exploration of their 'own responses to illness and disability' (Griffiths 1998, p.217), their motivation to work in this area (their 'story') and their specialist knowledge of the rehabilitation environment.

We participate in the Faculty of Healthcare Counsellors and Psychotherapists (FHCP), a subsidiary of the BACP, and take an active interest in moves towards government regulation. This development will be a part of the twenty-first century story. As we move on from nineteenth- and twentieth-century contexts into new societal and economic structures, and in this postmodern time recognize the effect of language on our understanding of ourselves and others, we need to continue to evaluate whether our provision meets the need of our time. The development of counselling in rehabilitation settings is the beginning. Ongoing participative development of our knowledge base with a reflexive look at our use of language and our motivations lead into the next phase of the story.

References

Barker, P. (1992) *Regeneration*. Harmondsworth: Penguin.

Barker, P. (1994) *The Eye in the Door*. Harmondsworth: Penguin.

Barker, P. (1996) *The Ghost Road*. Harmondsworth: Penguin.

Bernachon, P. (1972) 'In memoriam.' In P. Hopkins (ed) *Patient-Centred Medicine*. London: Regional Doctor Publications.

Brenton, K. (1997) 'The Chichester Project: Effects of group psychoeducational intervention in schizophrenia care.' Unpublished MSc Rehabilitation Counselling dissertation. Brunel University.

Burr, V. (1995) *An Introduction to Social Constructionism*. London: Routledge.

Campling, J. (1981) *Images of Ourselves*. London: Routledge.

Corker, M. (1996) *Deaf Transitions: Images and Origins of Deaf Families, Deaf Communities and Deaf Identities*. London: Jessica Kingsley Publishers.

DOH (1999) *A National Framework for Mental Health – Modern Standards and Service Models*. London: HMSO.

Drake, R. (1996) 'A critique of the role of the traditional charities.' In L. Barton (ed) *Disability and Society: Emerging Issues and Insights*. Harlow: Addison Wesley Longman.

Ellison, D. (1995) 'Coping with a chronic illness: An investigation of support following diagnosis.' Unpublished MSc Rehabilitation Counselling dissertation. Brunel University.

Finkelstein, V. (1981) 'To deny or not to deny disability.' In A. Brechin, P. Liddiard and J.S. Swain (eds) *Handicap in a Social World*. London: Hodder and Stoughton.

French (1993), S. (1993) ' "Can you see the rainbow?" The roots of denial.' In J. Swain, V. Finkelstein, S. French and M. Oliver (eds) *Disabling Barriers–Enabling Environments.* London: Sage Publications in association with The Open University.

French, S. (1994) *On Equal Terms: Working with Disabled People.* Oxford: Butterworth-Heinneman.

Gergen, K.J. (1985) 'The social constructionist movement in modern psychology.' *American Psychologist 40*, 266–275.

Glanville, H.J. (1977) 'What is rehabilitation? An inaugural lecture.' *Rehabilitation 100*, 13–25.

Goffman, E. (1963) *Stigma: Notes on the Management of a Spoiled Identity.* Harmondsworth: Penguin.

Gray, S. (1996) 'An investigation of the use of co-counselling on the stress levels among the staff in a specialised head injury and rehabilitation unit.' Unpublished MSc Rehabilitation Counselling dissertation. Brunel University.

Griffiths, P. (1993) 'Rehabilitation counselling: The development of a new course specialism in British counselling.' *British Journal of Guidance and Counselling 21*, 82–94.

Griffiths, P. (1998) 'Rehabilitation counselling.' In R. Bayne, P. Nicolson and I. Horton (eds) *Counselling and Communication Skills for Medical and Health Practitioners.* Leicester: BPS Books.

Henwood, K. and Pidgeon, N. (1995) 'Grounded theory and psychological research.' *The Psychologist 8*, 115–118.

Hollway, W. (1989) *Subjectivity and Method in Psychology: Gender, Meaning and Science.* London: Sage.

Johnstone, A. (1998) 'Living with stroke: Experiences of people three months after discharge from hospital.' Unpublished MSc Rehabilitation Counselling dissertation. Brunel University.

Kennett, C. (2000) 'Participation in a creative arts project can foster hope in a hospice day centre.' *Palliative Medicine 14*, 419–425.

Lenny, J. (1993) 'Do disabled people need counselling?' In J. Swain, V. Finkelstein, S. French and M. Oliver (eds) *Disabling Barriers – Enabling Environments.* London: Sage in association with The Open University.

Lim, K. (1999) 'An exploration of the effectiveness of assertiveness training for mental health service users.' Unpublished MSc Rehabilitation Counselling dissertation. Brunel University.

Livneh, H. (1986) 'A unified approach to existing models of adaptation to disability: Part 1 – A model of adaptation.' *Journal of Advanced Rehabilitation Counseling 17*, 5–16.

McLeod, J. (1997) *Narrative and Psychotherapy.* London: Sage.

McLeod, J. (1998) 'Listening to stories about illness and health: Applying the lessons of narrative psychology.' In R. Bayne, P. Nicolson and I. Horton (eds) *Counselling and Communication Skills for Medical and Health Practitioners.* Leicester: BPS Books.

Mellor-Clark, J. (2000) *Counselling in Primary Care in the Context of the NHS Quality Agenda: The Facts.* Rugby: British Association of Counselling and Psychotherapy.

Menzies Lyth, I. (1988) *Containing Anxiety in Institutions,* vol. 2. London: Free Association Press.

Morris, J. (1989) *Able Lives: Women's Experience of Paralysis.* London: Women's Press.

Morris, J. (1991) *Pride against Prejudice.* London: Women's Press.

Oliver, J. (1995) 'Counselling disabled people: A counsellor's perspective.' *Disability and Society 10*, 261–279.

Oliver, M. (1983) *Social Work with Disabled People.* Basingstoke: Macmillan.

Oliver, M. (1990) *The Politics of Disablement.* Basingstoke: Macmillan.

Oliver, M. (1993) 'Re-defining disability: A challenge to research.' In J. Swain, V. Finkelstein, S. French and M. Oliver (eds) *Disabling Barriers – Enabling Environments.* London: Sage in association with The Open University.

Oliver, M. (1996) 'A sociology of disability or a disablist sociology?' In L. Barton (ed) *Disability and Society: Emerging Issues and Insights.* Harlow: Addison Wesley Longman.

Richardson, J. T. E. (ed) (1996) *Handbook of Qualitative Research Methods for Psychology and the Social Sciences.* Leicester: BPS Books.

Robb, J. (2000) 'An exploratory study of chronic sorrow in parents of adults with learning disabilities.' Unpublished MSc Rehabilitation Counselling dissertation. Brunel University.

Ryan, J. and Thomas, F. (1987) *The Politics of Mental Handicap.* London: Free Association.

Sapir, M. (1972) 'On the diagnosis and the power of the doctor.' In P. Hopkins (ed) *Patient-Centered Medicine.* London: Regional Doctor Publications.

Shearer, A. (1981) *Disability: Whose Handicap?* Oxford: Blackwell.

Shotter, C. (1999) 'An exploration of the experience of partners of persons who have had a myocardial infarction.' Unpublished MSc Rehabilitation Counselling dissertation. Brunel University.

Slack, S. (1999) 'I am more than my wheels.' In M. Corker and S. French (eds) *Disability Discourse.* Buckingham: Open University Press.

Stevenson, C. and Cooper, N. (1997) 'Qualitative and quantitative research.' *The Psychologist* April, 159–160.

Stewart, W. (1985) *Rehabilitation Counselling.* London: Croom Helm.

Swain, J., Finkelstein, V., French, S. and Oliver, M. (eds) (1993) *Disabling Barriers – Enabling Environments.* London: Sage Publications in association with The Open University.

Sutherland, A. (1981) *Disabled we Stand.* London: Souvenir Press.

Watson, S. (1998) 'An exploration of physically disabled children's views of physiotherapy through stories and drawings and its contribution towards their perceptions of self.' Unpublished MSc Rehabilitation Counselling dissertation. Brunel University.

White, M. (1997) 'An exploration of the expectations of stroke rehabilitation: Patients and professionals.' Unpublished MSc Rehabilitation Counselling dissertation. Brunel University.

Whitehead, S. (1992) 'The social origins of normalisation.' In H. Brown and H. Smith (eds) *Normalisation: A Reader for the Nineties.* London: Routledge.

Whitworth, A.H. (1892) 'Accidents on the Ship Canal during the construction.' *Manchester Ship Canal News,* December.

Wolfensberger, W. (1987) 'Values in the funding of social services.' *American Journal of Mental Deficiency 92*, 141–143.

Chapter 2

Counselling People with Multiple Sclerosis

Julia Segal

Introduction

Counselling people with multiple sclerosis (MS) at the Central Middlesex Hospital (CMH) Multiple Sclerosis Unit began when people with MS and their relatives formed a self-help organization called Action and Research for Multiple Sclerosis (ARMS) to provide information and management strategies such as exercise groups, dietary advice, hyperbaric oxygen treatment and counselling, none of which were commonly available within the NHS at the time. The need for counselling was evident to some, though others were sceptical. John Simkins, the Chief Executive, was keen that help might be offered to the families of people with multiple sclerosis because he felt his own children had suffered from his lack of knowledge about how to handle their mother's MS in relation to them. Within the organization, there was discussion about the role of professional counselling vis-à-vis support from people with multiple sclerosis and their relatives. I took over the task of counselling people with multiple sclerosis in the ARMS Research Unit at the Central Middlesex Hospital and of overseeing provision of counselling around the country within ARMS branches. When the organization broke up in 1992, some branches continued offering counselling to their members, while the CMH unit was taken over by the NHS and is now part of the NW London Hospitals Trust.

I began working for ARMS as a counsellor in 1985. Referrals for counselling, which depended on other professionals identifying a need, had stigma attached to them and missed those who hid their anxieties and their difficulties. To overcome this, each new patient at the unit was offered an initial appointment with each professional – originally a doctor, a dietician, a physiotherapist, and a counsellor but now extended to include occupational therapist and nurse – and was then able to decide with them whether they needed further appointments or not. This had the further advantage for me as the counsellor in that I was able to meet people who lived well with their MS as well as those who found it hard.

People came at all stages of the disease: from those newly diagnosed and distressed by anxieties about the future to those who had had it 30 years or more, now retired after a lifetime's working and still active; from those whose problem was that nobody could see anything wrong with them, to those who were so disabled they could hardly move or speak. Some had minor difficulties in walking, with reduced stamina or disturbed eyesight, sensation or balance. Some had more serious problems with movement, with sexual functioning, fatigue, memory or perception. Some came at a time when there was not much change and they needed simply to make the most of the capacities they now had; others at a time when an unexpected change in circumstances, whether of their symptoms or their family life, brought distress and grief and perhaps a need for new ways of dealing with their thoughts and emotions. All brought anxieties and problems which had nothing to do with MS. Many also had troubles which were directly caused by their MS or by the management or mismanagement of their symptoms. Some had the additional burden of particular religious beliefs which were unhelpful in one way or another. Some had supportive social networks and others found themselves losing contact with friends, family or their religious community. Some came for one session and I never saw them again; many had at least five weekly sessions followed by regular check-ups for a while. Others have been seeing me for years on and off, returning when they felt the need for a further group of five sessions, staying for long-term weekly counselling, or coming two or three times a year to keep in touch. Some came with members of their families, partners or children; others came alone.

Effect of the counsellor's presence on other professionals

Before looking at the lessons I learnt from clients, I want to draw attention to the way the presence of a counsellor affected other professionals. Before I arrived they had often found that patients talked to them, sometimes at great length, about difficulties in their families or their lives. Once I was in post the other members of the team told me it was much easier to bring these confidences to a halt, saying 'perhaps you would like to talk to the counsellor about that?' This meant they could spend more time doing the job – as physiotherapist, dietician, doctor – which they had chosen and which they did well. Clients also became less likely to unburden themselves to others when they knew that a counselling session was imminent. Those who wanted to maintain the role of confidante were able to keep it within manageable limits, but all were glad to be able to hand over responsibility for the emotional turmoils of some patients. Often there were, of course, patients who were unable to use counselling: people who found it impossible to keep boundaries and were experienced as 'all over the place', intrusive, disturbing, full of distress they could not contain and could not allow others to contain. Counsellors can help a multidisciplinary team to retain a professional capacity for caring in such difficult circumstances.

By helping clients feel better about themselves or their circumstances, counselling also at times helped them to begin to participate in exercise groups, to take more notice of the food they ate or to listen to the other professionals and try their suggestions. In these ways the rehabilitation task of the team was made easier.

One client came to me from another rehabilitation service where there was no counsellor. He had been so angered by various events connected with a badly handled admission procedure that he had been quite unable to take in and use the service they offered when he eventually arrived there. After I had facilitated the working through of his complex emotions and enabled him to write a letter (which he did not eventually send), he was able to begin working constructively with professionals.

I would like now to look at some of the lessons I have learnt from clients directly.

Everyone is different

This seems to me the most important lesson to learn. After counselling more than 400 people with MS and their relatives, I can still be surprised by people's reactions to their own and others' MS. I cannot predict how people will react to MS, though much of what they tell me resonates with the stories others have to tell. The meaning given by the individual patient to their MS is the first focus of the counselling work. It has to be teased out of their verbal and nonverbal communications, examined, taken seriously and perhaps challenged. To some clients MS means they are useless, impotent, unlovable. To others it is a challenge, it means they have overcome something, cheated death. To some it means life is ended; for others it means a new possibility for a good life has begun. For some it means the end of a marriage; for others it means the marriage cannot now be ended. Others find love survives and may even grow. MS can also bring a couple to the decision to marry. Some are angry, some are not. Clients' interpretations of the diagnosis and experience of MS depend on their own past experience (particularly of dependence and of illness) and their observations of others. They, like counsellors, tend to generalize from one or two experiences of people they have known with MS – or any other illness. In the desire for certainty people often make false assumptions or connections which do not stand up to scrutiny. Teasing out the similarities and the differences, the true and false lessons to be learnt from past experiences, can be important. The counsellor's understanding can influence the meanings a client gives to MS and may help them discover new meanings and consequently a new direction for their life.

Anxieties about the effects of emotional stress on MS

People with multiple sclerosis often express anxieties about the effect of stress on their condition though there is no scientific evidence that it makes the prognosis for MS worse. My own observation suggests that stress affects the way people handle their MS, but does not determine whether the underlying condition gets better or worse over a long period of time. I have seen people with very stressful lives living with MS for many years hardly affected at all. I have also failed to discover any correlation between life events and relapses in my clients.

Unfortunately I have seen lives made considerably harder by fear of stress. For example, one man sent his children to boarding school because he was afraid that they would cause him stress and make his MS worse if they stayed at home; another constantly accused his wife of threatening his health when she objected to anything he did or said. Another couple constantly fought because the wife was terrified her husband was doing too much when he lived for his work and loved pressure.

Stressors such as heat, exercise or anger can make MS symptoms show up temporarily but the symptom is always one which has been experienced before and it goes away again after a few hours. MS can only be said to be getting worse when new symptoms appear or old ones get worse than they have ever been before, over a period of weeks. This is related to the physiology of the condition. Over time, the myelin sheath around nerve fibres in the brain and spinal column breaks down sometimes causing what is known as a relapse but sometimes more gradually. During the period of breakdown the nerves do not work properly and new symptoms may appear. A relapse generally lasts about six weeks, but each client will have his or her own experience of this process and may find it useful to think about how their own body reacts. Over this period a scar replaces the myelin sheath (the 'sclerosis') enabling the nerve to begin working again, but it may not work so well. Symptoms get better, though they may not disappear completely. Once such a scar is there the body learns to accommodate it. Stressors (such as heat or extreme cold) can make this accommodation process harder so an old symptom may show up again, but this does not mean that the myelin sheath is breaking down again. The MS is not getting worse.

It can be important for people to know this. People sometimes give up activities (such as sex, parenting or exercise) because it made their MS symptoms show up and they confuse this with the MS getting worse. People can lose mobility because they have given up exercise rather than for any other reason to do with MS. Exercise can sometimes improve stamina, for many people with MS as well as for others. Even those who suffer from MS fatigue may find their stamina – and their lives – improved by exercise. How people define stress varies enormously. A certain amount of stress is essential and unavoidable for life. People with MS must live with it; they cannot simply take time out until they are better.

Relationships are vital

Where relationships are good, which they can be, coping with MS is easier. It can change lives without destroying them. Counselling can play an important role in helping to facilitate good relationships. Many people fear they will lose their relationships as a result of MS; others who live alone often fear they will now never find anyone. In my experience MS does not usually mean the end of a relationship. In addition, quite disabled people can find new partners and may marry. Although some relationships do break up, MS may not be the primary cause. MS can also keep couples together who otherwise would probably have broken up. MS can put a strain on relationships, but it can also create situations in which relationships can flourish.

A man who gave up work because of his MS said his relationship with his daughter had improved and now gave him great pleasure as he was now there when she came in from school and he fed her, whereas previously he had only seen her late in the evening. His wife found it a bit hard to begin with but she also appreciated coming home from work to cooked meals and the family diet had improved.

Counselling often focuses on past relationships, particularly with parents or lovers. In my experience, forgiveness of parents for past wrongs, real or imaginary, can enable people to feel more loved, better supported internally and more able to handle their current lives and their current relationships. This applies just as well when MS is part of the current life as when it is not.

Loss

MS may cause losses of many kinds: loss of certain hopes for the future; loss of a job or the capacity to work as before; loss of the ability to walk or to run; loss of sexual functioning; loss of cognitive functioning; loss of friendships; sometimes a sense of loss of the self. This is complicated by the fact that nobody knows which losses will affect any particular person, which adds a further loss – of the illusion of knowing what the future will bring. Any loss has meaning attached to it and an apparently minor loss may have huge significance. People can feel angry when other people do not appreciate the magnitude of their losses. They can also feel guilty for being upset about losing the capacity to play tennis, for example, when they know others have lost more. In addition, any loss brings up feelings and memories, conscious and unconscious, related to past losses. Previous losses re-experienced can cause difficulties in current relationships: for example, if a husband is treated as if he were an abandoning father or mother from the past. The feelings of falling apart and being useless and unlovable which often accompany significant losses can spread into all aspects of life.

Each loss caused by the MS has to be grieved individually. People do not come to terms once and for all with MS. They have to face many separate losses which may follow in quick succession or may be spread over many years. The diagnosis itself may represent a loss of belief in a healthy body – whatever that means for the person concerned – but it may not. It can be reassuring for some who have had years of mysterious symptoms interpreted in a more frightening way (Am I going mad? Have I got a brain tumour?). It generally takes two years or more before each loss is incorporated into a new view of the world. Within this time people often seem to deny the loss. The meaning of a denied loss may be conscious, half-unconscious or quite unrecognized. For example, one woman talked as if she had only a few years left to live although her MS seemed to give little cause for concern. Two-thirds of the way through the session I asked her if she was expecting to die soon and she realized, apparently for the first time, that she had assumed she would die at the same age as her mother, which meant in five years' time.

Massive denial can arise when people are very afraid of what it would mean to accept 'reality' – but this 'reality' they fear is seldom actually realistic. Denial can be an automatic process which prevents fears being looked at properly and leaves them exaggerated and often attached to primitive 'monsters' – very frightening fantasies from childhood which an adult would know were untrue. The conviction with which these frightening fantasies, beliefs and assumptions are held and a fear that 'if I say it, it will come true' can make it hard to uncover just what it is that is being denied. However, naming such fears helps to make them more realistic and to lose their monstrous quality. For example, desperate attempts to 'think positively' may be caused by a fear that thinking negatively will lead to total breakdown for ever, rather than realistic time-limited grieving. Equally, a desperate clinging to medication which is known to bring only minor benefits may be used to stave off fears that having untreated MS is a terrible sentence of death-in-life. Naming and understanding fears can relieve people of a pressure to behave in a way which feels forced and false.

The main difficulty may be for the counsellor to persuade him or herself that it is safe and important to touch these sensitive areas, since clients can be very persuasive that there are some issues which are too frightening to explore. A counsellor who is afraid that living with MS is equivalent to a death sentence, or that nobody could love or marry someone with MS, may not be able to challenge a client with such beliefs. I once had to face a family with their evident belief that the mother was going to die of MS because her husband did not love her enough. At the moment when I said it, I also believed it to be true. It was only after we had sat with it that we all realized it was not true. However much anyone loved her, she would still die. If we cannot put these terrifying thoughts into words our clients are left alone with them, with possibly serious consequences. In this case two children, as well as the husband himself, had been living with this fear for a long time and it had affected their day-to-day relationships, leaving the children with no hope of comfort from their father for themselves, either before or after their mother's death.

Mourning past losses

MS may eventually force people completely to rebuild the basis upon which they live their lives; basic assumptions may have to be abandoned and new ones developed. This painful process is the essence of mourning and requires a certain amount of hope and faith in the future for people to feel it is worth the effort. Living with the uncertainties of MS may require a quite new way of approaching the world; refusal to accept uncertainty can cause many difficulties. Attempts to control the uncontrollable may be quite destructive of daily comfort or relationships and may lead to unnecessary losses. For example, alcohol may be used to control unwanted feelings of grief, but bring more trouble in its wake. Attempts to prevent a relative with MS from making his or her own decisions about treatment may be intended to control the uncertainties of their condition but in fact lead to serious friction within the family, rather than improved management of the MS. Commonly people refuse help in an attempt to retain control in spite of the fact that accepting help – perhaps for the first time they can remember – would actually lead to more control. Clearly the issue of uncertainty and control is closely tied up with dependence, an issue which is extremely fraught for many people. When childhood experience of dependence has not been happy, adult dependence can be feared enormously. Many people talk as if it were possible to be entirely independent of others, particularly where they have felt unable to trust those who should have taken care of them. The concept of independence can be set up as a denial of the painful uncertainties of dependence on unreliable others. People may need help to grieve for the loss of previous ways of living which were based on illusions of certainty, control and a childish view of 'independence' which denies the interdependence of adults. I often find myself discussing a concept which some clients find quite new – that of 'adult mature dependence'. Recognizing that adults can find pleasure in mutual dependence may involve grieving for failures in earlier relationships where dependence was a source of pain.

Counselling can help people to acknowledge and assess their actual losses and to disentangle what they have to lose from what they could actually keep or even gain. With an understanding counsellor who will hold and take seriously their sense of loss without needing to minimize or exaggerate it, clients may gradually find the capacity to let the past go and rebuild a new life which takes account of the realities of MS. For some people the sense of being understood is a new experience which can enrich their lives.

Parenting issues

Professionals sometimes seem to ignore the fact that some of their patients are parents; people who are ill themselves sometimes forget this too. I find it distressing that many people do not believe those with MS can be good parents. (They can of course also be bad ones, just as anyone else can.) MS can take away parenting functions, particularly if it affects people cognitively so that they can no longer listen to or understand their children, but this does not affect everyone with MS and there are other functions of parents which may not be lost. Just being there can be important. Parents who are loved can be of vital importance to growing children, even if they are not capable of doing much or even showing much love themselves. Sometimes parents who are ill become very self-centred; this may be a reaction to their illness or it may be a sign of early cognitive difficulties. But parents whose MS forces them to give up work may be more available for their children at a significant time in their lives, and this may be more important than any loss of income. The slowness of the development of MS means that children may have a chance to grow up before their parent's MS becomes seriously troublesome.

Children often have anxieties about their parents' illnesses which their parents may not have recognized. I often focus with parents on their beliefs about their children in relation to the MS and its disabilities. Once alerted, and with their own guilt and anxieties relieved a little by counselling, they often find new ways to observe, communicate with and help their children. The children themselves then show signs of relief, reduction in anxiety and improvements of behaviour, both in relation to the parent with multiple sclerosis and the other parent.

> I asked a mother if her teenage son had reacted to her husband being in hospital. She said she hadn't noticed anything much. I said children are sometimes afraid it's their fault, but they don't usually tell. She then said she had noticed he had stopped whistling around the house and she wondered if this was a sign of something. She came back the next week saying she had told him I had asked if he thought it was his fault his father had been taken ill. Predictably, he scoffed – but she noticed he had begun whistling again after their conversation and she thought he seemed less tense than previously.

Carers/partners

Partners of people with MS share many of the losses although they have a different view of them. They can be helped to observe and think about what is happening and perhaps to understand better how the MS is affecting both them and their partners. MS may not be the root cause of difficulties in relationships, and counselling which focuses on the relationship itself rather than on the MS may sometimes be appropriate. If the relationship can be retrieved, the MS may be easier to manage.

Occasionally someone with MS who was previously emotionally supportive loses this capacity. In this case their partner has a serious loss which needs to be recognized. The partner may need help to handle their anger and grief about this before they can maximize the remaining capacities of their disabled partner and value what they can still give. Ultimately they may need to seek support elsewhere and counselling may be important in facilitating this in the face of anxieties about betrayal, 'survivor guilt' or fear of the other's envy of their own capacity to live.

Issues of sexuality can be important at this point as sexual feelings can be aroused in emotionally supportive relationships. Maintaining some form of sexuality within the primary relationship can be significant in determining whether life is bearable or not. Sexual betrayal can feel like betrayal even if one partner has lost sensation or sexual functioning. People vary in their capacity to tolerate sexual infidelity or to see it as a trade-off for the continuance of other forms of caring. Although Viagra gives limited sexual sensation to the man himself, it may have a place in maintaining a relationship – or in threatening it if a man who has lost his erection feels he needs to demonstrate his potency and power by sleeping with another woman.

Violence/abuse

The frustrations of loving and caring for someone with MS if they are cognitively affected or denying some of their disabilities can be enormous. In addition, muscles can tense up at awkward moments and instructions be apparently ignored, though at other times they may be followed. People often do not recognize just what is happening and may interpret behaviour as deliberately obstructive when in fact the person cannot avoid it. Even deliberately awkward behaviour can sometimes be differently understood as a means of conveying the frustrations and irritations of MS nonverbally. One man seemed to make his wife angry when he was angry himself but was unable to express it directly.

Both women and men who care for a partner with MS may find themselves reacting to an infuriating situation with violence of a minor or major kind. These situations need to be handled carefully. Clients can feel terrible about confessing to hitting, thumping or roughly handling their partner, but they need to be helped to let the GP know. Fear of judgement and punishment may be accompanied by excruciating guilt. Unfortunately none of these may be sufficient to prevent a recurrence. The GP may need to be allowed to determine whether real damage has been done. The carer may need help to see what they have actually done since they may either exaggerate or minimize the damage. Clearly dangerous violence would require the person with MS to be taken into care immediately, but milder forms of marital abuse may be better handled at home. Someone who loves their partner and normally takes very good care of him or her, but who occasionally loses their temper, may provide a happier home for someone with MS than a residential home, some of which have low standards of care and may even subject residents to abuse. (I am reminded of a client who told me he had been removed from the care of an alcoholic mother as a child and put into an orphanage run by an alcoholic matron.) As with any marital abuse, these situations can be difficult to assess and the well-being of the patient and the family as a whole may be extremely difficult to judge. People with MS who are being abused may not tell; they may not remember, they may want to stay with the partner and feel the abuse is their fault, or they may be quite comfortable with the level of abuse. One husband knew he provoked his wife and was proud of being unhurt by her occasional thumps. He would certainly not have agreed to be removed from home because his wife hit him. Social services, however, alerted by the wife and counsellor together, increased the level of support offered to the family and kept a closer eye on the wife's needs.

Once the situation has been acknowledged and any necessary safeguards put in place, counselling can focus on the situations which give rise to the abuse and the context in which it happens. The counsellor and client together may be able to recognize danger points and take steps to reduce them. A client who feels too guilty to ask for sufficient support from social services may begin to recognize the necessity of this support. The role of alcohol or other drugs may be important. A discussion with a specialist physiotherapist can help the carer to understand muscle spasms and minimize them. A sympathetic neuropsychologist may help both partners to recognize and acknowledge the ways in which MS is affecting the capacity to think and act. A continence nurse may help with bowel or bladder management; a speech therapist with eating or speaking difficulties; a GP may provide antidepressants temporarily for the carer or the person with MS. Fears that a loved partner will be removed and put into a nursing home may have to be dealt with, as well as anxieties about their death – or about their continuing to live for ever in a state which causes misery to themselves and those around. The complex and contradictory feelings involved need to be explored. In my experience, people sometimes struggle against all the odds to keep their severely disabled partners at home in spite of enormous difficulties and great ambivalence. Counselling can play a significant part in this process, enabling a stressed carer to accept sufficient help to cope at home or to let their partner go elsewhere.

Unbearable fears are bearable and can be shared

I touched earlier on the difficulty of naming some terrifying fears connected with MS, particularly those concerned with living and dying, with wanting the self or other people dead, with failures of love. The psychoanalyst Hanna Segal taught me that in counselling reality is safer than pretence; that protecting people from their own fears means leaving them alone with them and is not a good idea; that reassurance does not work; that it is better to look at people's anxieties; to stay with their fears; to face their terrors. In spite of my respect for her knowledge and experience, faced with people with MS I found it very hard to put these principles into practice. However, I found that people tended to come back feeling better when we had done this and feeling worse if I had avoided something which was clearly troubling them. I often went away feeling exhausted and a bit worried about what we had discussed, but repeatedly painful and difficult sessions seemed to bring relief to the client. They said things like 'I feel a weight has been lifted off my shoulders' or 'I feel as if I have woken up after a long time'.

I think that people with MS, just like any others, need recognition of their real concerns and worries. MS can make people feel they no longer belong to the human race; that their experience is now totally different from anyone else's. Working with a counsellor who is not afraid to share upsetting feelings can bring a sense of shared reality and re-establish a feeling of belonging in the real world.

Cognitive effects of MS

I have mentioned cognitive difficulties before in different contexts. Many people with MS have no cognitive symptoms, or no more than mild memory loss, but some are affected more severely. In general it can be helpful to locate cognitive or perceptual problems, though it can be distressing for the counsellor as well as the client. I struggled with the awkwardness and embarrassment of telling one client's relative how his mind had been affected by the MS, only to find that the client was very pleased indeed that the relative at last understood. Difficulty in making decisions, assessing the speed of traffic, reading a map, responding within a normal time to a question such as 'would you like a cup of tea?' or 'what did you do this morning?' may be extremely irritating and misunderstood as wilful awkwardness by relatives. The person with MS may know something is wrong but not know what it is or how to handle it. Recognizing and naming the difficulty, perhaps with the help of a partner or carer or in their presence, can sometimes bring surprising relief to all concerned. Anger is often a sign of resistance to painful awareness: carers may get angry with their partner's cognitive disabilities while they cannot bear to accept the nature, significance, reality and permanence of evident changes. They may even provoke a situation in which the disability is evident and infuriating, partly out of a desire to find out if it is there or not. Once the change has been fully acknowledged, including the unpredictability of it, new ways of behaving may develop which circumvent the problem rather than exacerbate it.

Those who live with people who are unable to think clearly and normally, for whatever reason, may find their own capacity to think affected too. Counselling may provide a time in which normal good sense can return. Those who have given up work to care for disabled partners may sometimes find themselves unable to think clearly and to make sensible decisions in the presence of their partner. This, I think, is a normal consequence of the identification processes which accompany close relationships. These processes also allow the carer to have a very powerful sense of what it is that the person with MS wants or wishes to say. Thinking about the reality of this with the counsellor may be useful as it may be based more on past experience and less on acknowledgement of the current situation, particularly if there have been recent distressing changes.

Driving

Cars have powerful significance in our culture, both for men and women. They represent a safe means of getting about in an unsafe world, protecting the occupant from the external environment; they represent independence where dependence may be scorned or feared; they make life easier in hundreds of small ways. They enable the owner to be a 'giver' rather than a 'receiver'. Cars stand for power and potency as well as body armour. Where disability in general signifies weakness, vulnerability, something slightly distasteful, a good-looking car commands respect and makes the owner feel not only safer, but also on more equal terms with the world. Hopes of finding a new partner may also be consciously or unconsciously influenced by having a smart car. The motability scheme which provides and cares for cars has helped increase the self-confidence of many people with disabilities.

Where people with MS can no longer walk as they did, they may become dependent on their cars. If they lose the capacity to drive this can be a serious blow. Often there is a long period during which people are aware that there are times when they are not safe to drive and other times when they are. Relatives may disagree and it can be useful to help the client to tease out the reasons why, which may be realistic or may arise from prejudice. The task of telling someone they cannot drive any longer often devolves on to a partner, who may be blamed and accused unreasonably by the distressed driver. Doctors cannot talk to partners behind their patient's back, so partners have to be able to face the patient with their belief that the patient is unsafe before they can even discuss it with the doctor. This may be very difficult and distressing for everyone.

The counsellor's point of view

For several years I ran a discussion group for counsellors around the country who worked with people with multiple sclerosis. We pooled many thoughts. We found, for example, that we were often under pressure to see people in their own homes although our normal practice was to see them in a consulting room. We each tried this once or twice and most of us decided it was not a good idea. All the usual reasons why clients go to counsellors (rather than vice versa) apply just as much when clients have a disability. We also found that the effort of getting clients to us was itself worthwhile. If transport could be arranged for counselling it could be arranged for other journeys too, and this could be as important as the counselling itself. Sometimes it emerged that the pressure for counselling came from others and failure to organize transport was a sign that a potential client was not really interested. In other parts of the country where counselling services are less accessible and transport less well organized, some counsellors do offer a home counselling service. The training required, costings and clients' experience of such counselling would differ from the service we are able to provide.

We found that the feeling of uselessness was common and we linked this with the feeling that people with multiple sclerosis often have, that they are now useless. This fitted. We did not feel useless with everyone and it made sense as a countertransference experience when we did feel it. We also found a tendency to generalize. The fewer people with multiple sclerosis we had seen, the more likely we were to make generalizations. Once we had seen more than four or five, our generalizations failed and we learnt to take each person as he or she came. This tendency is related, I think, to a desire to be better prepared; not to be constantly taken by surprise by the MS and our clients. We wanted to know. So did clients, of course. Some of our work involved watching for clients' attempts to control uncertain situations which in fact made them worse (for example, one man said he was told to sell his house and buy a bungalow when he was diagnosed with MS, when there was no evidence that his MS would ever force him to move). The uncertainties of MS are often mentioned as the worst thing about it by professionals in training groups.

Counsellors can also share the feelings of carers. Carers often feel guilty for not having MS. One counsellor said she felt so bad about this that she was giving up because she felt the job should go to someone with MS. There was no counsellor with MS available to take the job. Though most people with multiple sclerosis who come for counselling are not particularly disabled, some are. One counsellor working privately had a client who fell in her house; without backup this was difficult to handle. There are also general difficulties to do with lack of exposure to people with disabilities. Counsellors did not always know whether, when or how to offer help, what kind of advocacy to offer or to refuse, or how to keep to the role of counsellor when the pressure to step outside the role was huge. It helped to remember that these pressures can arise in any counselling and the reasons for resisting are the same with people with multiple sclerosis as they are with anyone else. If someone is really unable to run his or her own care, he or she needs a care manager. If the counsellor becomes a care manager the client loses his or her counsellor.

Boundaries around working with people with physical difficulties may have to be worked out. Recently (after 13 years) I have had to make clear statements about when I allow someone to transfer to a different chair from a wheelchair when I cannot tell if they may fall or not and they may not be able to tell me truthfully either. Somewhat earlier I had to decide whether to insist on using a wheelchair to bring a client to my room when the client didn't want to admit needing it but I was afraid they would lose their balance. I had to develop clear policies with the help of the physio-therapist manager of the unit, attempting to reconcile clients' sensitivities with issues of safety and potential litigation.

Our group of counsellors also found we experienced some symptoms ourselves and all had the fleeting anxiety 'have I got MS?' more than once. (We did not.) Other than this I would say that we found ourselves stimulated to look at our own lives and make changes and forced to challenge our own ideas of what makes life worth living. Issues of suicide and euthanasia, our own envy of others' better fortune and the capacity to enjoy whatever life brings were also discussed as a result of our work with clients.

Conclusion

Counselling people with multiple sclerosis can be very satisfying. I am the team member who sees people getting better. Whatever happens with people's bodies, counselling can sometimes enable them to live more fulfilled lives, more at peace with past relationships and less anxious about the future. Some people with multiple sclerosis do not need counselling. They have satisfactory lives with supportive friends or families and they have found their own ways of handling the emotional aspects of the illness. Others who felt it was a sentence to a partial death blossom under counselling as they lose some of their unrealistic anxieties and learn to hope for and work towards a good life with MS.

Further reading

Morris, J. (ed) (1989) *Able Lives. Women's Experience of Paralysis.* London: Women's Press.

Parker, G. (1993) *With This Body. Caring and Disability in Marriage.* Oxford: Oxford University Press.

Robinson, I., Neilson, S. and Clifford Rose, F. (2000) *Multiple Sclerosis at Your Fingertips.* London: Class Publishers.

Segal, J.C. (1991) 'Use of the concept of unconscious phantasy in understanding reactions to chronic illness.' *Counselling 2,* 4, 146–149.

Segal J. C. (1996) 'Whose disability? Counter-transference in work with people with disabilities.' *Psychodynamic Counselling 2,* 155–166.

Segal J. C. and Simkins J. (1996) *Helping Children with Ill or Disabled Parents: A Guide for Professionals.* London: Jessica Kingsley Publishers.

Chapter 3

Counselling in a Head Injury Unit

Diane Aronson

In this chapter I wish to share some of my experience of the first two years in a newly created counsellor post within a head injury unit. I am employed part time as member of a multidisciplinary team in an NHS hospital. In the absence of a statutory framework or guidelines for practice within this field, I have spent much of my time on developmental issues. The role has needed to be defined, a process made more difficult by the small number of precedents for this type of work within Britain.

Within the first few months in post, I met with a small number of other counsellors who worked within specialist hospital units. I have been struck by the similarities in aspects of our practice, even when the setting and the client group are quite different. I hope that by sharing some of my own learning about the nature and structure of the work, it will be of use to others who might be looking at establishing a counselling role within a hospital setting.

My own background prior to counselling training was as a mental health occupational therapist. I also work within a medical centre at a university and am well acclimatized to health service culture. Despite further training which might have enabled me to move away from the health service, I continuously find myself drawn back, probably because of a fundamental belief in individuals' rights to live as satisfying a life as possible within the constraints of mental, physical and emotional limitations. These limitations are all evident amongst those who have suffered brain injury and their relatives, and I continue to strive to enable them to find their own maximum potential despite the traumas they have suffered.

Background to the post

I work in a rehabilitation unit for people who have suffered brain injury through traumatic head injury, severe stroke or illness such as meningitis or encephalitis. The concept of rehabilitation fits with my personal philosophy that underpins my work, which is a belief in the value of facilitating individuals to achieve their personal potential. 'Rehabilitation' is not the same as 'recovery' which suggests a return to the individual's previous level of health and functioning. I believe that rehabilitation requires that I recognize the individual as a whole person, who is part of a number of broader systems, especially their families or close relationships, and that counselling needs therefore to be inclusive of the people who form a significant part of the patient's life.

The rehabilitation unit includes a small unit for children aged 5 to 18. Patients usually stay on the unit for several months. The anticipated stay when admitted tends to be four months, but many have had to stay considerably longer due to difficulty in finding a further placement if they are not able to return straight home. It is a transitional time between the early stages following the event and their future life. It has long been recognized that the patient group and their families have high emotional needs, but it had been difficult to provide structured support. A research project entitled 'Who uses a rehabilitation counselling service, and why?' was carried out by Sue Gray (1997). A pilot counselling service was offered as part of a research project and its effectiveness was evaluated. The results demonstrated that patients and their relatives felt there was a need for counselling and a recommendation was made that a part-time counsellor be employed to work with the staff, patients, relatives and friends of the head injury unit.

It is of note that within the pressurized economic climate of the health service, research is often needed to justify new positions, as finance is a scarce commodity with plenty of contenders for its use. The result is that most research within counselling in secondary care has been to establish the credibility and need for counselling with very little definition of the role itself. Isabel Menzies Lyth (1997) argues that further research in counselling in medical settings should aim at looking at the development of the function of the counsellor, rather than the effectiveness of the counselling (see Carroll 1996). This has been reflected in my experience where I have found I have had to work on developing the role. In my meetings with three other counsellors in hospital units, I have been struck by the synchronicity of our experiences of both the nature and the structural aspects of the work.

This post required a counsellor with previous health service experience, as it was felt this would facilitate an easier transition into the team. The unit has a strong emphasis on multidisciplinary teamwork and my own background as a mental health occupational therapist was considered advantageous. It has facilitated my ability to blend into the health service culture, but it also has its disadvantages, especially in terms of establishing boundaries, which I will come on to. The nature of counselling work usually means that the counsellor remains a little separate from other staff when working in an institutional setting. It can feel a very fine balancing act to be a full member of a team whilst holding different boundaries from the others. I shall go on to describe some of this tension.

Development of the service

The team in the unit consists of a large number of nursing staff, qualified and unqualified, physiotherapists, occupational therapists, speech and language therapists, a clinical psychologist and doctors. Emotional support of patients and their relatives has always been provided by members of the team, especially since the instigation of a 'co-ordinator' system, which names a key member of staff as the person responsible for ensuring the co-ordination of a patient's treatment, care and future plans. It has been essential for me, as the first counsellor in the team, to establish a position which respects the work that others do in providing emotional support, whilst clarifying the added professional dimension that counselling can bring to that aspect. Part of health service culture is to be busy, with clearly defined (and visible) tasks and as such it can be easy for a counsellor to feel deskilled in comparison with the rest of the team. It is a unique position within the team and needs definition and clarity in order to be fully valued and utilized. The main issue has been in establishing boundaries, which may relate to the actual and perceived role of the counsellor: boundaries between the work of the counsellor and that of other professionals; contractual boundaries with the clients; and boundaries of time and space, such as in the use of rooms and making and keeping appointments. I shall examine some of these issues in further detail.

The client group

There is an organizational limit to defining my client group, in that I am employed to work with people who are patients on the unit and their relatives or close friends. This immediately prevents me from working with people once they have left the unit, which is an area that has potential for development. Other than that, I have had to develop ways of accessing potential clients. With reference to terms, I define someone as a 'client' when I am working with them in a counselling relationship, although they may be a 'patient' on the unit. There was an initial rush for me to counsel members of staff. That is a separate issue, but I make it clear that I do not see staff for counselling as such.

The expectation within the unit has been for me to work with patients' relatives. Their need for emotional support is often apparent. They are having to cope with distressing circumstances that could never have been anticipated and are learning to adjust to an unknown future with a person they love possibly changed irrevocably. They may show their distress, either directly or indirectly. Sometimes anger is expressed about dissatisfaction with aspects of care. This has an emotional impact on the staff working with them, which is often the time I will be asked to see someone.

However, emotional needs are not always so overt. This can be especially true for the parents of children, who may work very hard to seem positive in front of the child, and the staff. I was working with one mother who had suffered multiple losses when a nurse commented, 'I didn't know you were seeing her – I thought she was all right.' This remark suggested a belief that only relatives overtly displaying distress needed counselling. I am trying to introduce a protocol that ensures all parents are given an initial appointment with me. There is still a need to overcome the stigma of 'being sent to see the counsellor'. For some relatives there may be a sense of shame in being seen as 'not coping'. I have found it useful to visit the ward areas when I am not busy. I talk with the nursing staff, who may refer someone to me, and also meet informally with visiting relatives and friends. One relative, after leaving the unit, commented, 'For all sorts of reasons it can be very hard to actually ask for help, even if you know it is there, whereas a chat in passing opens doors.' She recommended that I visit out of hours, at evenings and weekends when relatives may be visiting. I am sure this is much needed and reflects one of my dilemmas, which is how much I am able to give of myself to the work. I am only contracted for 13 hours per week and I have to set some limits. I find that one of the most difficult aspects about the work is the continuing need to promote myself and to accept that constantly changing staff groups need information repeated regularly.

The client group that has been least clearly defined is the patients themselves. They are receiving intense nursing, therapeutic and medical attention. They often have communication difficulties and cognitive deficits, such as short-term memory problems, which can lead staff to believe that they do not have the articulation or intellectual capacity to benefit from counselling. There is also a tendency to refer someone to me only if they are expressing distress, rather than understanding that counselling can make an important contribution to facilitating a positive outcome from such a major life transition. Prigatano (1986, p.95) refers to the need for psychotherapy, stating that 'psychotherapy after brain injury can be vital if reasonable adaptation to a severe illness is to be accomplished'. The clinical psychologist may work with patients to assess their cognitive and perceptual abilities and then extend this to include emotional needs. In these circumstances I would not duplicate the work, so I always check to find out whether the psychologist is already working with the patient, if so in what capacity, and whether we both agree that counselling is appropriate.

I have struggled most to work with clients who have severe communication difficulties. It can be easy to overlook the emotional needs of someone who has difficulty in expressing himself. As Arthur Frank states: 'The voices of the ill are easy to ignore, because these voices are often faltering in tone and mixed in message' (1995, p.25). Sometimes I will use approaches that do not require the use of speech, such as drawing, or choosing pictures or other items. I need to be creative in order to bridge any gulf in communication: it can prove invaluable to give someone undivided attention who is not often listened to. I would therefore like to develop this aspect of my work further.

Practical issues

Room space

Room space has been one of the most critical factors in ensuring my ability to work effectively as a counsellor. For over a year I worked without a separate office, booking rooms only to find them double booked. It is difficult to create a 'safe place' for counselling when there is no concrete confirmation of where that is. Hospitals are always short of space and someone in a new role has to vie for space with existing staff. Theoretically, a counselling service should not exist without the appropriate space to house it, but that is not how the health service works. Usually a need must be demonstrated to determine priority for one member of staff over another. It can feel as if sibling warfare is breaking out when there is competition for room space and, whilst I am now satisfied with my own tiny office, this has meant displacing others. It is an area where the counsellor has to be clear and determined about professional needs.

Counselling contracts and appointments

I work with people according to need, which is usually agreed between the client and myself, whilst the patient remains on the unit. I have not found it appropriate to offer fixed numbers of sessions, although I do usually offer an initial session without any commitment. Flexibility is an essential requirement of a counsellor's role within a hospital setting, especially when working with distressed relatives who have to travel long distances. However, this does not preclude the necessity of making appointments and the expectation that they will be kept, or other arrangements made. It can help relatives to cope with the chaos in their lives if normal expectations are made of things which are still under their control, such as keeping appointments. Appointments with clients who are patients on the unit can be more frustrating. I have to fit in with the timetabling system for other therapies and, even if I have booked a session a week in advance, things can happen to prevent me seeing clients, such as an appointment elsewhere or other aspects of their care which have to be attended to.

Role definition

This relates to service provision and what I actually do as a counsellor in this setting. Apart from the counselling, I have received increasingly frequent requests for teaching. Some of this relates specifically to counselling or counselling skills and some is part of an in-service training programme for team members, with counselling input in areas related to interpersonal communication. In such a specialized role, it seems important to disseminate some of the learning. It also creates an opportunity to talk with other staff about their perception of the counsellor's role, to clear up any areas of role confusion and to demonstrate the value placed on the work of all staff who offer emotional support.

Emotional support may be given to relatives without them needing to agree to a formal counselling relationship. I have a relationship with some relatives whom I meet on the ward but who would never come to my office for 'counselling'. I see this as part of my role, but it is not formal counselling. The other area of support is for staff. I will see staff members for brief 'feedback sessions' to support them in their work with some of the patients and their relatives. However, the team has its own systems of support and I have been careful to maintain a fine boundary so that I do not become too involved in this area. Staff support is vital, but it can cause role confusion if a counsellor works with staff from within the same unit too intensively in this way. I also remind staff of access to an employee assistance programme that is available to us.

Aspects of working within a multidisciplinary team

It is unusual for a counsellor to be a full member of a team within a hospital as I am, rather than someone who visits the hospital from another post elsewhere. As a health service professional used to multidisciplinary teamwork, I have experienced myself feeling pulled to join in with the familiar sense of shared experience and camaraderie that can exist in a hospital unit. However, in a unit where information is freely shared it feels important that counselling retains some sense of separateness. I am a lone professional, perceived as different by the rest of the team, offering a safe place for clients to express themselves without fear that the content will be shared across the unit. It is a continuous balancing act. It is important to work in partnership with the team, aiming for mutual respect for our different areas of expertise.

Nursing staff may easily feel deskilled, especially in a rehabilitation unit where therapy staff are given such kudos for their work and achievements with the patients. A nurse on the children's ward complained to me one day that the therapists came in and did what she considered to be the important work and she was left wondering what they, as nurses, really did. That led to a discussion on how the arrival of a counsellor could further devalue the work they did by suggesting that the talking should be left to me. The work of the counsellor structures support for patients and their relatives, but does not replace the continuous process of support and communication that occurs with the nursing and other care staff. A good working relationship with the team comes from respect, education and a willingness to learn from each other. As the sole representative of my profession, it is inevitable that much of the impetus for this must come from me, as others may cling to their professional groups. It is therefore essential to arrange adequate support for myself elsewhere.

I have found it helpful to acknowledge the organizational context within which I work. In *Workplace Counselling* Michael Carroll (1996) comments on the significant impact of organizational contexts on the counselling relationships within them. He also refers to Isobel Lyth Menzie's hospital study (1960) which looked at the way that nursing tasks are organized to deflect anxieties concerning pain and death. Working in a unit that contains such depths of human pain, it is important to ensure that my role does not become part of that deflection. Carroll (1996) refers to 'splitting' in organizations, a psychoanalytic term to describe the process which appears to separate a person or organization into two parts: the good and the bad. This avoids the anxieties of integrating the two and is apparent in organizations where one person or department is applauded for excellence, whilst another may become the scapegoat.

This has been important for me to recognize in my role within the team, where it may be possible for my position to become polarized into one that is useless, scapegoated, or where I am viewed as a saviour. The client group may also demonstrate aspects of splitting and relatives often express anger with the organization. This may be rational and reality-based and they may need help in developing strategies to communicate their worries to the appropriate personnel. It may also be connected with their own feelings of helplessness and loss. Part of my task is to enable them to integrate their feelings and to recognize those times when feelings may become displaced or projected on to dissatisfaction with the organization. This may lead to splitting when a staff member is being blamed for poor care of the relative, etc. The counsellor's role is to remain neutral and to hear the distress and concerns of the client, which can sometimes feel at odds with allegiance to the team. Carroll states:

> The [workplace] counsellor plies his/her trade at the interface between the individual and the organisation, while himself/herself being a member of that organisation. Boundary problems can become a nightmare, loyalties a major concern. (Carroll 1996, p.153)

My own supervision is essential in that it provides a space for my gaining an understanding of some of these processes and for me to express some of my inner turmoil.

The area most in need of clarification in relation to multidisciplinary teamwork concerns issues related to confidentiality. Teams share information about patients or clients, sometimes quite personal, intimate information. In counselling, absolute confidentiality, except in extreme circumstances related to safety, is traditionally deemed to be an essential part of the process. The BACP Code of Ethics (1993) states: 'Confidentiality is a means to providing the client with safety and privacy. For this reason any limitation on the degree of confidentiality offered is likely to diminish the usefulness of counselling.' This clear statement becomes muddied when applied to working within a team. Tim Bond (1993) reflects that 'counsellors working in medical settings and social services experience particular challenges over establishing good practice with regard to confidentiality' (p.131).

Teams are used to sharing information, a practice intended for the patient's best interests. The head injury unit has shared notes in which all the other team members write. There has been much discussion amongst counsellors in health-care settings as to whether the team may represent a 'net' of confidentiality, with positive benefits from collaborative working. Mearns (1998) states that 'some counsellors are not only precious about confidentiality, they even make an icon out of it and positively generate problems where none need exist'. He advocates a 'confidentiality net' where it is possible to refer in general terms to a client's progress, the appropriateness of the referral or future expectations for the client without disclosing any details. This has been my own experience, where it seems inappropriate to work with a patient on the unit as part of the rehabilitation team without sharing some of the information about their progress. However, caution is needed to avoid becoming too carefree with details. There is also a difference in working with a client who is a patient on the unit and a client who is a friend or relative of a patient, when the confidentiality is the same as when working elsewhere as a counsellor.

I return to the counselling principles of congruence and integrity, aiming at being clear and honest with all my clients. I have not encountered any difficulties if I tell my clients what the boundaries of confidentiality are and agree with them any information to be shared with the rest of the team. I keep my own separate, confidential notes, but will occasionally make a comment in the medical notes, which may be broadly to do with my perception of a client's mood level, or recently because I believed a patient on the unit to be a potential suicide risk.

Confidentiality is about sharing information, but I also receive information. Patients and their relatives see me as a team member and are surprised if I do not know basic facts about their condition, progress and plans. I receive all information and occasionally attend meetings about patients' progress. However, there are disadvantages as sometimes I may receive information before a client does, which inhibits the counselling process, as it is impossible to be fully congruent in these circumstances. I try to avoid this happening by explaining to other staff how impossible it is to work with the sense of an honest relationship if I have been given information that the client is not yet able to have.

The nature of the work

This is a client group that has been ravaged by trauma, disease or disability. The event which has brought the patient into hospital has not been foreseen and at the time of admission the eventual outcome in terms of levels of recovery cannot usually be predicted. I work with people who are involved in a continuous process of adjustment and living with uncertainty. Hospital treatment programmes are usually for specific, clearly identified problems: for example, a person will be treated for his heart problem or her arthritic knee. When we are working with people whose brains have been damaged, the complexity of the resulting problems means that any aspect of the person's being may be affected. There can be a sense of fragmentation, with the speech and language therapists working on communication, the physiotherapists working on physical function, the psychologist looking at aspects of cognitive function, etc. One of the challenges for staff on the unit is the recognition that the whole of the individual's life must be taken into account, especially when making future plans. The counsellor is able to work with the whole person, not only in terms of future plans, but also with acknowledgement of the life that preceded the incident. I work with people who had a life, with all the trappings that go with daily life, including family, work and leisure. For many, that life will never be the same again. One of the joys of my work is the intense respect I have developed for the strength and resourcefulness of human nature. I meet with courage, determination and despair on a daily basis.

Patients are on the unit for one part of a journey, which started with the accident or illness and leads to a point of relative stability when they are settled into a new life in the future. The clients, their families and friends have stories to tell, which need to be heard. The patients may have large gaps in their memories and may be unaware of the original event. However, those close to them will have lived through the anguish of facing the possibility of their death and all the turmoil that goes with experiences of intensive care. A large part of my work is to listen to people's stories. In *The Wounded Storyteller* Frank (1995) describes the need to narrate. He states that 'stories have to *repair* the damage that illness has done to the ill person's sense of where she is in life, and where she may be going' (p.53). Trauma and major illness interrupt the flow of expectations of life. It is part of human nature to feel invincible. We begin each day with an expectation that we will be home for supper, to put the children to bed and to return to work the next day, etc. Not to come home, or not to have your partner come home because they have been hit by a car or fallen down from a stroke is devastation indeed. This is a story that may need telling and retelling before any sort of sense or acceptance can begin to emerge. Arthur Frank refers to holocaust stories, which at times resonate with the stories of my clients. He describes these as 'chaos stories' where 'troubles go to bottomless depths'. It is the capacity to hear these stories which may differentiate the counsellor's role from that of others. This capacity is facilitated by addressing some of the more structural elements of the role. For instance, being able to take clients to a separate room away from the ward area may give them a sense of safety and sometimes a sense of permission to speak.

The need or ability to tell stories may happen at different stages of the process. A mother of a child on the unit had lost two close members of her family in the car accident that had caused her child's head injury. She seemed very positive and was always encouraging to her child. It was only with me (in hospital at least) that she began to talk about and give some expression to her grief. It felt as if this could truly go to bottomless depths. It took some time before she felt able to begin to look at her profound sense of loss and to tell the story of what had happened. She described it as opening a door on to a black hole, which she peeped into from the safety of our counselling sessions. This was a story that could not be rushed into or hurried along.

Stories from the patients themselves can be fragmented. Some people are deeply disturbed by their memory loss and several have described to me the sense of putting a jigsaw together, but with various parts missing. They may need to gather information from others to complete the jigsaw and even then feel dissatisfied, because they are replacement parts and not from their own original memories. It can be difficult to hear the stories of people who have communication difficulties and yet their stories may need to be heard as much as those with full verbal abilities. *The Diving Bell and the Butterfly* is a beautiful reminder of this (Bauby 1997). The book is an eloquent and often witty memoir of a man paralysed by a brain-stem stroke, and a testament to the life within, despite external disability. Dominique Bauby dictated the book with the use of one eyelid. He describes how the life he once knew was 'snuffed out' on one fateful day. His eventual progress to a wheelchair was a moment of great excitement for the staff and serves to remind us of the despair which may be felt each time a patient is confronted with reality: 'I had graduated from being a patient whose prognosis was uncertain to an official quadriplegic ... I was too devastated by this downgrading of my hopes to take much notice' (p.16).

The need to narrate is often linked to experiences of loss. Most of my clients have experienced loss of some sort, whether of physical function, mental ability, lifestyle, or future hopes for any other part of everyday existence that we usually take for granted. I have found it helpful to read some of the literature on bereavement and grief, such as Worden (1983), acknowledging the stages that people may go through as part of a grieving process. However, it is complicated to work with loss without a death. Another complication in participating in a unit where improvement, if not full recovery, is aimed for is to maintain a sense of hope alongside the losses. The following example illustrates this.

Amanda was a 41-year-old woman with two children aged 9 and 6. She led a normal, busy life that would be expected of a mother with young children until she suffered a sudden brain injury. She came to the unit for rehabilitation about two months after the accident. During her time in the unit, Amanda progressed from total dependency in stages: from recovering her speech, to being able to eat again, to being able to transfer herself from her wheelchair to the toilet and eventually to walking independently. She also progressed from suffering severe short-term memory loss to almost normal function. Her excellent recovery was cause for celebration, although she was left with some residual difficulties, such as almost no function in her left hand.

Amanda appreciated how well she had done and at the same time, at every stage, also became increasingly aware of what she was not able to do and of how much she missed of her normal life. She missed her son's sixth birthday and he was distraught because she did not make a promised cake for his party. When Amanda was unable to do anything at all she could accept her situation, at least for the time. However, as she improved she regularly came to me and cried, after therapists had told me how well she was doing. One day her tears were because she had found she couldn't carry a breakfast tray back to the kitchen since she only had the use of one hand. She gave me a list of all the things she couldn't do and we looked at the fact that a week before they hadn't been an issue, because she couldn't even walk unaided then. Progress also made her realize her limitations.

In a hospital situation which celebrates progress, it can be very difficult to give space to the accompanying sense of loss. Sometimes, what can't be done needs to be grieved for in order to move forward and recognize what can be done. Relatives will usually endeavour to be positive with the person who is a patient. They often find it helpful when I acknowledge the sense of paradox that many of them feel, holding the joy in progress at the same time as the grief. Parents of children will encourage the child, celebrating first steps, and come to me and weep. They are thrown back to a different, earlier stage of parenting with an older child who should be heading towards independence. I have also known times when parents have said, 'I wish she had died.' This may be a thought that is torturing them and it can lose some of its terror by being expressed. I feel privileged that someone will express such inner thoughts and feelings with me. There are also times when joy can be expressed and laughter is often a part of counselling sessions.

Along with the grief are reactions to coping with crisis and managing transitions. I sometimes draw Hopson's transition curve (Hopson and Adams 1976), which demonstrates how self-esteem may rise as an initial reaction to a crisis, only to plummet as reality hits. In working through the transition and coping with the new challenges it presents, a person may eventually end up with a greater sense of self-esteem as a result of their learning and coping. Clients often find it useful to relate this practical description to their own situations. Sometimes I will see pairs of family members or couples together, to help them to adapt to some of the massive changes they are going through together and to re-establish their relationship within the context of those changes.

I worked with one couple, Alison and Peter, after Peter's admission to the unit following a motorbike accident. Peter had learnt to walk again, but was distressed by his memory loss and his difficulty in making sense of what had happened due to amnesia. I worked with Peter to start with and he used counselling to express some of his internal distress and confusion. Alison had been a loyal and supportive wife, who had helped him through the first few months after the accident. The experience of seeing Peter in hospital in the early stages, unconscious and possibly going to die, had been a major trauma for her. It was only as Peter improved that problems in their marriage appeared. It turned out that Peter had behaved badly in the weeks preceding his accident and they had agreed to separate just days before the fateful motorbike ride. Alison was left with the anger she felt towards him for actions of which he had no memory.

I met with them weekly to enable them to come to terms with the impossibility of ever fully clearing this. Peter was changed and they needed help in learning to be together in a different way. There was a strong sense of love and respect underneath the difficulties and they were able to reconnect with some of this, but they needed to continue the work after he returned home.

A counsellor needs areas of particular expertise in working with this client group, or knowledge of where to access that expertise. For people who have been affected by trauma, it is important to be alert to the possibility of post-traumatic stress reactions, or even full-blown disorders. When there has been a major accident, the ensuing memory loss may provide the patient protection from this. However, hospital experiences may be equally traumatic.

When working with one client, the mother of a young man on the unit, it emerged that she was plagued by visions of him being carried screaming through the hospital. That was the last time she saw him active and she found it very difficult to let go of the image.

Sexual function is an area that is often neglected in the rehabilitation of people with disability. It can be helpful gently to raise the topic if there have been some hints. Leaflets may be useful as they can be read in privacy. There may be fears of impotence, difficulties in the practicalities of sexual activity and sometimes brain injury can cause increased or inappropriate sexual behaviour which may be disturbing for partners, for friends or family, particularly when there is disinhibition. Sex can be a sensitive subject and other staff members may refer patients to the counsellor if it seems to be an issue. A recent referral to me concerned a woman in her mid-forties who was asking for overnight leave to meet an ex-boyfriend in an hotel. The staff were concerned about her vulnerability, the possibility that she might get hurt as the man had not seen her since the accident and risk of pregnancy. She was aware of the reason for the referral and quite indignant. She told me 'I know about condoms!' and related the tale of her very long-standing relationship with the man. Another client might have been at risk, but I was convinced that she was not and we had an enjoyable session with plenty of laughter.

A specific knowledge of the effects of brain injury can be helpful, but it is possible to learn about this through working with the client group and open enquiry with other staff. The area that still causes me most confusion is whether it is appropriate for me to work with people with cognitive damage. My experience has been that it is possible to make contact with clients in the moment, without putting value judgements on the quality of that contact. This may mean, for example, that a client with severe short-term memory problems may quickly forget the content of our session, but that does not mean the contact we made during the time was unhelpful. However, it is important to acknowledge the effects of cognitive damage and try to understand whether emotional reactions are a genuine emotional response, or one that is heightened by the effects of the cognitive impairment. This can also reflect the confusion of relatives who may find the patient has developed 'inappropriate' emotional responses.

This is an exciting area to work with, as I have found that some clients retain emotional memories from week to week but have no knowledge of what had been discussed. This happened with the client Amanda, who would remember that she had cried and felt better for it, but could not remember for some time the things she had cried about. Working with the emotions seemed to help reactivate some mental capacities and she slowly became more consistent in her short-term memory, as if she was emerging out of a fog back into the real world.

Personal support

This is hugely demanding work and at times I am touched on a very deep, personal level. The clients' stories are extremely powerful and can raise existential questions for anyone working with them. I need not state the necessity for supervision, as this is always a professional requirement in counselling. However, I have found it essential in helping me to maintain my personal boundaries and avoid becoming too overwhelmed. There have been several clients who have been at the same life stage as myself, such as Amanda who is a similar age, with similar aged children. My supervision can help me to be truly present for the client, separating out my own issues. I am fortunate that supervision was contracted into my post and I believe that it is something which should always be funded as part of any such position.

In addition to the required hours of supervision, informal links are important to prevent a sense of isolation. I have become part of a local network of health-care counsellors and I also use support from colleagues on the unit. Ongoing professional development is also part of my support.

Conclusion

There is much more that could be written about counselling this special client group. I have not referred to my counselling orientation, but attempted to look at some of the issues of practice. These relate to practical areas, ethical issues such as confidentiality and something of the nature of working with people who have lived through sudden, life-changing experiences that have left them, or someone they love, changed. The sense of contact that I sometimes experience is a very real privilege. The depths of human nature which are touched can bring about a real sense of beauty: 'the saddest things fill you up – like in a big way and you feel so full as in no happiness can bring such'. (Hall 1997, p.2)

References

BACP (1993) *Code of Ethics and Practice for Counsellors.* Rugby: BAC.

Bauby, J.-D. (1997) *The Diving-Bell and the Butterfly.* London: Fourth Estate.

Bond, T. (1993) *Standards and Ethics for Counselling in Action.* London: Sage.

Carroll, M. (1996) *Workplace Counselling.* London: Sage.

Counselling in Medical Settings (1995) *Guidelines for Staff Employed to Counsel in Hospital & Health Care Settings.* Rugby: CMS.

Frank, A.W. (1995) *The Wounded Storyteller: Body, Illness and Ethics.* Chicago: University of Chicago Press.

Gray, S. (1997) 'Who uses a rehabilitation counselling service, and why?' Unpublished research project carried out at the Royal National Hospital for Rheumatic Diseases, Bath.

Hall, L. (1997) *Spoonface Steinberg.* London: Methuen.

Mearns, D. (1998) 'Managing a primary care service.' *CMS Journal 57,* 1–5.

Menzies Lyth, I. (1997) 'Recorded by Myriam Petit-Cannels at the International Conference: Counselling in Health Care, Cambridge.' *C.M.S. News 53,* 17.

Prigatano, G.P. (1986) *Neuropsychological Rehabilitation after Brain Injury.* Baltimore: Johns Hopkins University Press.

Worden, J.W. (1983) *Grief Counselling and Grief Therapy.* London: Routledge.

Chapter 4

Counselling Young Stroke Survivors During Rehabilitation

Sally Lockwood

Introduction

This chapter is about younger people whose lives have been affected by stroke. It has been written by a non-disabled practitioner and is dedicated to Jane, Diana, Geraldine, Alan, Bob, Dave and Neal, who have shared their experience of stroke so generously in the hope that other younger stroke survivors may gain insight and some comfort from hearing their stories.

I became involved with stroke in the mid-1980s when employed as a medical social worker in a geriatric hospital. I remember feeling appalled at the insensitive way in which younger stroke-affected people were placed on general geriatric wards. I still cringe when I think of those ward rounds where patients were spoken 'to' and not 'with'. The professionals held the power and the patients were their subjects. Critical and cynical remarks were frequently made about the patient's behaviour or lack of response. The patients, often still in shock following their trauma and confused or bewildered by professional jargon, had little choice but to remain passive. Their feelings were rarely taken into account or, for that matter, ever sought. The period of rehabilitation had started, although this often seemed a meaningless word, offering false hope and expectations when everything had become chaotic with the sudden onset of stroke and life had lost its meaning.

My interest in stroke remains but I have moved on, both personally and professionally. This chapter stems from the individual and group work and research that I have been involved in over the past four years with stroke-affected people. My role as manager and senior co-ordinator for the Bristol Area Stroke Foundation is multifaceted, offering information, guidance, education and counselling. It is the counselling aspect of this role which has stimulated my interest in the exploration of practical and emotional needs experienced by the younger stroke-affected person during the recovery period. It has become apparent through my counselling work that there is a lack of professional emotional support for patients during their period of hospitalization and the transition to home. This is not surprising when there is a dearth of professional counsellors in hospitals, or indeed in the community, with a special interest in and knowledge of chronic disability. In the Bristol area there is limited counselling provision in hospitals and (at the time of writing) throughout the UK there are only three counsellors for those with severe speech and language difficulties (Corker and French 1999). There is a general consensus amongst clients that, whilst physical and practical needs are mainly met, there is little opportunity to discuss the psychological impact of a sudden stroke upon their lives, and the fears of facing life with a disability. As a consequence of this, I have wanted to learn more about the psychological implications of having a stroke from the survivor's point of view.

The aim of this chapter is to raise awareness of the emotional and practical issues for the younger stroke survivor, with particular emphasis on the need for counselling as part of a multidisciplinary approach to rehabilitation. My focus is on the psychological process during the different stages of rehabilitation: the onset and period of hospitalization; the transitional period of returning home and the present; and the search for meaning. I have drawn on the personal experiences of seven individuals who participated in my research project. This was a qualitative study, based on a focus group methodology, which used narrative analysis to represent the research findings. As a counsellor I have been given privileged access and permission to share these stories, which I believe have enhanced both my personal and professional life. In writing this chapter I am grateful for the opportunity to share my practice and knowledge. In doing so I hope that other professionals involved in stroke care and rehabilitation may also better understand the experiences described by the participants, so that they may begin to explore their own empathic understanding and attitudes in addressing the psychosocial effects for the survivor, as well as the medical consequences.

A narrative approach is used to give voice to the feelings and emotions of those affected by stroke throughout the different stages of rehabilitation. Narrative offers an opportunity to explore the teller's story and provides an analysis of how it is put together. A combination of narrative analysis in the form of stanza and 'snapshots' of dialogue have provided a means of presenting material in its natural form and have offered a powerful way to represent experiences and describe emotions (McLeod 1997; Riessman 1993).

Background to stroke

> The Doctor said, 'I think you've had a stroke.' Immediately my thought was, I'm too young to have a stroke. I suppose really, until it happened to me, somebody having had a stroke meant they were an old person, and I didn't feel like that.

It is a myth that stroke only affects the elderly. Stroke can affect anyone of any age. A stroke happens when the blood supply to the brain is interrupted. This can result from either a blood clot in one of the arteries serving the brain, or from a haemorrhage which causes bleeding into the brain, resulting in damage or, as Robert McCrum (1998) prefers to call it, 'an insult to the brain' (p.23).

Stroke can cause physical, emotional and social devastation for the affected person and their family. There is often no warning prior to the onset. The person may be leading a perfectly normal life one minute and suddenly find himself incapacitated the next. For the affected person and his or her family, this can represent a major trauma. Schlossberg (1984) terms this the 'unanticipated transition', when a crisis erupts unexpectedly and is not part of the expected life-cycle transition. For the younger person the psychological effect can be dramatic as they have their whole life in front of them. Following the trauma, on return home, the person has to face the reality of the consequences of the stroke and this may initiate a period of grieving for what they have lost and fear about the future. Basic daily tasks and practicalities such as eating and using the toilet, which were once a matter of routine, become major events, taking hours and using excessive amounts of energy, causing frustration and distress. The effects of stroke are unique to the individual, as indeed are needs and responses following the stroke, and the level of support they needed during the rehabilitation period.

The Trauma

It sounds stupid
I was due to take
A tap-dancing exam
I'm thinking
This doesn't happen
To people like me.

On Monday 6 am
Sat up
In dressing gown
Just went down
Telephone rang
I couldn't speak.

I'll never forget that day
It was Christmas Day 1996
I used to say 1966.

I think I heard her say
'She's had a stroke
Let's get her straight to the hospital'
And it was funny, as though
It wasn't happening to me.

In order to understand the impact of trauma and the related reactions, which are associated with loss, it is necessary to refer to the literature on trauma, theories relating to loss, transitions and life-span development. Although reference is made to trauma and crisis, there is a subtle difference between them. A traumatic event is unpredictable and totally uncontrollable. What may evolve from the onset of trauma is a state of crisis and chaos. In other words, a crisis is not necessarily a direct reaction to what has happened to the individual but rather his or her interpretation of the event which involves the feelings, thoughts and behaviour towards that event (Kfir 1989; Kfir and Slevin 1991).

Stroke, like many other traumatic incidents, has elements of uncontrollability. The onset is unpredictable. There is nothing a person can do to stop it happening, although there are preventive measures which may be taken. As Dave says, 'It is like a bolt out of the blue.' Seligman (1975) describes the parallels between uncontrollability and unpredictability in the sense that when an unpredictable event occurs, such as stroke, the controllable elements of safety transfer to feelings of fear and uncontrolla-bility. Bearing this hypothesis in mind, it is therefore understandable that the sudden onset of stroke may be followed by periods of shock and denial with associated feelings of helplessness, hopelessness, frustration, fear and despair. This is even more pertinent for the younger stroke sufferer who is under the impression that stroke is an illness associated with the elderly. As Geraldine says, 'I'm too young to have a stroke.' This trauma has occurred outside the normal expectation of life stage development and will require major adjustment (Erikson 1980; Levinson 1978). The onset of stroke in younger people interrupts the normal chronological sequence of life stages and they may be forced to retire from work much earlier than anticipated. This retirement has not been planned and therefore no prepa-ration made to fill the work gap. Unplanned retirement due to ill health, together with the disability and the need to use aids for mobility, make the younger stroke-affected person feel older than their chronological age. As a result of stroke the individual's plans are often turned into chaos and he or she will need to reorganize their sense of self and life (Epstein 1989). This transition will take time and cannot be effective until the person has had the opportunity to revisit the trauma and begin to make some sense and meaning of what has happened (Herman 1992). It is important that debriefing work is paced and the client is ready to face the reality. Revisiting the trauma too soon may be damaging, particularly for the person who has suffered cognitive impairment as a result of the stroke. In the early stages of rehabilitation the survivor's emotions need to be contained within a safe and trusting relationship.

Post-traumatic stress disorder (PTSD) often follows a violent incident and a stroke-affected person may feel the victim of a violent attack to the brain, or that he or she has received a punishment for a previous wrongdo-ing. The trauma of the stroke and the hospital experience may remain fixed in the brain and, according to Goleman (1996), become 'emblazoned in the emotional circuitry' (p.201). The memories of the onset of the stroke, together with the hospital experience, are often as vivid whether the stroke occurred six months or several years ago. Some clients have described the hospital experience as being as traumatic as having the stroke. The attitude of the professionals, both positive and negative, can affect the psychologi-cal state of the stroke patient. In the counselling relationship it is important to enable clients to explore their feelings about the illness, their hospital experience and fears for the future, rather than deny them.

The focus group

This section focuses on the interaction of a group of younger stroke-affected people. Discussion in the group demonstrated many similarities in the content of their stories, but what makes those stories unique to the individual and the reader are the nuances behind them, the hidden and personal meanings and the challenges of living with a new self. The telling and sharing of the self-story can provide a cathartic and therapeutic experience, particularly when feelings and emotions are explored (Grafanaki 1996; Kleinman 1988).

The participants in the focus group had all experienced their strokes within the last six years and were advanced in their recovery. Their ages ranged from 37 to 58. All seven had been employed prior to the stroke and three have since returned to work, albeit in a different capacity. Five of the seven participants have separated from their partners since the onset of their stroke. The range of impairment in the group varied, covering many of the problems related to stroke. These included severe speech and language problems, paralysis, cognitive difficulties affecting memory and behaviour, emotional outbursts of crying or laughing, fatigue and depression. They talked about the initial onset of the stroke and their period of hospitalization, their return home and their current lives.

The onset and period of hospitalization

During the morning of 29 July 1995, a powerful storm struck overhead. It was an unusually hot summer with temperatures in the high eighties. Dave awoke suddenly but by the time he had fully come round it was all over. Well, not all over. This was really the beginning. Dave had suffered a stroke. It was like 'a bolt out of the blue'. He had no warning. There was nothing he could do to stop it. The situation was out of his control. Dave was in shock. His life was in crisis. It was unanticipated. It would mean major change.

Most clients in the group felt it was easy to avoid the reality of their situation whilst they were in hospital. They were encouraged to focus on the less threatening aspects of rehabilitation, such as mobilizing, as opposed to the emotional issues. In addition they were given anti-depressants. This appears to be common practice for all stroke patients in some hospitals, whether they are depressed or not. Anti-depressants can have a dulling effect on the patient and add to their denial by suppressing strong feelings, often delaying the grieving process

(Hammersley and Beeley 1992). The participants felt that social workers in hospital tended to address practical and emotional issues in terms of problem solving, which often caused confusion and further anxiety rather than offering a safe and trusting environment where feelings could be shared and contained.

Alan felt he would have benefited 'from counselling of some sort' in the first few days. 'All I had was a visit from the social worker who was adamant that I should go into respite.' He described his confusion: 'Respite meant going into a home. This was very frightening. What I wanted was to get back home. So the talk of respite made me feel even more depressed and anxious. What I wanted was to talk to somebody about my feelings and frustrations.'

The lack of information about the causes and prognosis of stroke increased the frustration, fear and uncertainty for the future. This uncertainty, together with the lengthy time span involved in stroke recovery, added to feelings of powerlessness. Bright (1996) suggests that uncertainty in itself can delay the grieving process and keep the person in denial. It is difficult to face reality and rebuild life when the facts are unclear and no sense can be made of the situation. Most young stroke survivors felt that bad news was better than none. The sense of being uninformed added further anxiety and confusion about the ability to make future plans, together with the fact that patients often associate an illness with pain. As it is rare to feel pain following stroke, it fuelled the belief that they were not ill and added to their denial.

Denial

You're in bed, I'm thinking
What am I doing lying in bed?
There's nothing wrong!
I had no pain, no nothing.
It was strange, although I knew
This side was gone
I felt no pain
I couldn't imagine why
This brain haemorrhage
Had caused this, I just couldn't
Believe it.

To a certain extent the hospital professionals tend to collude with this denial, as it feels more comfortable than dealing with the pain of reality (Kleinman 1988; Segal 1991). The danger of this is that it suppresses the real meaning of loss and deprives the person of an opportunity to grieve, perhaps creating deeper emotional wounds which may cause internal chaos and lack of confidence. This can create emotional as well as physical paralysis which may be equally disabling as the outside world does not see it and therefore has no way of knowing about it (Frank 1995).

In addition to the trauma surrounding stroke are the physical, psychological and cognitive consequences, which can cause the affected person to feel dissociated and detached from the person they were before. Jung (1934, quoted in Kalsched 1998) explains how the psyche's normal reaction to a traumatic event is to withdraw from the situation; the person distances and separates the mind and body from the reality. Laing (1965) describes this splitting in terms of the 'embodied and unembodied self', whereby the affected person does not recognize himself and feels quite detached from his body. Although Laing's work was related to the schizophrenic personality, it has relevance for those affected by brain injury, particularly when behavioural changes occur. As one of my clients said after his stroke: 'You mourn your own death. I don't know this person any more and what's more I don't like him.'

The change of personality can cause distress to the partner, particularly when this is accompanied by speech and language problems. One partner shared with me: 'I don't know this man I'm married to any more. It's like living with a stranger. I miss my husband.' Apart from the loss of self, other losses identified by clients during their period in hospital included dignity, self-respect and hope.

Self-respect

I had a bad experience with one of the Physios
I was feeling very emotional; I used to cry myself to sleep.
This one particular day I'd fallen asleep on the bed
The Physio woke me up and said
'We're going to walk up and down the ward today'
I said I can't do it today
'Don't be stupid, you can get out of bed and do it.'
I took three steps and crumpled on the floor.
It wasn't the fact that I'd crumpled
I felt humiliated in front of everyone else on the ward.

No Hope

My worst nightmare was
The fact I had my own wheelchair
With my name on it
I kept thinking I don't want that.
I couldn't see a future with
This blasted chair at the side of my bed.

Both these examples raise the issue of the importance of empathy in the hospital experience. Spiro *et al.* (1993, p.7) suggests: 'Empathy underlines the qualities of the humanistic physician and should frame the skills of all professionals who care for patients.' Unfortunately, this is not always the case as medics often choose not to engage with the person but rather focus on the condition, thus separating the mind from the body (Goleman 1996). This avoidance is often due to the fact that medical professionals are afraid to get too close to their patients in case it interferes with their medical judgements (Melosh 1982). In certain circumstances, I would suggest that the practitioner is more at risk of misunderstanding or even misdiagnosing the illness as he or she fails to consider the patient as a whole. Talking to patients, hearing their illness story from their perspective and what that illness means to them can enhance diagnostic skills through building a relationship of trust, respect and holistic care (Greenhalgh and Hurwitz 1999). In the case of stroke survivors their condition may not be cured but their rehabilitation may well be encouraged by helpers who listen empathically, have a positive approach to care and an understanding of the patient's medical, social and emotional needs. Neal sums this up when talking about the medical professionals involved in his care: 'They look at it from the professional perspective and not the patient's perspective. I really think they need to change that around.'

The transitional period: going home

The transitional period is often the time when the true meaning of loss becomes apparent (Kennedy 1991). Bridges (1995) describes transition as being the psychological process which people undergo in order to come to terms with the new situation. Change is the external process that follows the internal process of transition, which means letting go of the identity prior to the change. The implications of the condition, together with the practical difficulties, may evoke feelings of fear, frustration and despair.

The grieving and mourning process often begins when reality sets in and the person feels alone, away from the safety of the hospital. The prospect of months of rehabilitation can be overwhelming and exhausting. Anxiety about the future may lead to depression, particularly if the person has doubts about his or her own coping resources and feels isolated (Trower, Casey and Dryden 1988).

Alone

I needed someone to talk to
To guide me in the right direction.
I'd been dumped
It was only then that the problems
Reared their ugly head, such as
Having a relationship with someone
When you're disabled.
I couldn't walk any more
Do normal things like
Help around the garden
Round the house; things like that
Things you did before.
I couldn't contribute
Towards the relationship
In any way.

Jane expresses her deep sadness at the loss of friendships, role, status and body image. These losses were not apparent until her return home.

Loss

Sue, no
Chris, no
The car
Driving
Job
Friends
Travelling
Stockings
High-heels
No.

Prior to the stroke Jane worked as a senior manager for a large commercial organization. She was divorced but had a steady relationship which ended during her hospitalization. Jane was a successful woman in a man's world. She was at the peak of her career when the stroke struck. She worked from 5 am to 8 pm daily, work being the major part of her life. Due to her severe physical, speech and language impairments she lost everything. Her grief was immense and, not surprisingly, depression set in soon after her return home. Her losses, however, were not centred on the physical losses of her bodily functions but on her position in life. Life to Jane had lost its meaning. Jung (1934) connects trauma to meaning rather than to the stimulus related to the trauma. When relating this to Jane's case, the true meaning of her trauma was not the stroke, with the physical problems incurred, but rather the loss of her self-identity and purpose in life. So going home for Jane meant facing reality, searching for new meaning and purpose.

Returning home following stroke can be another point of crisis and is often the most vulnerable time when depression can occur. Many clients feel 'let down' or 'dumped' by the supporting services through lack of follow-up or after-care. Practical difficulties such as having to wait several weeks for appropriate adaptations to the home compound the emotional problems. Feelings of poor self-esteem and despair are exacerbated by the lack of practical or emotional support. Male clients affected by stroke often mourn their perceived loss of masculinity. The emotional lability following stroke may cause embarrassment for men – 'big boys don't cry' – especially if they were not emotionally expressive prior to onset of the stroke. A flood of uncontrolled emotion can be overwhelming and, as Rowan (1997) suggests, anything to do with emotions can feel like a threat to masculinity.

For Alan and Dave the stroke meant that they could not fulfil what they perceived to be their manly functions. This not only lowered their self-esteem but also reinforced the victim role. Hunter and Gerber (1990) point out that recovery from a traumatic event cannot begin until the male has acknowledged the word 'victim' as being the result of a traumatic event which was out of his control. Victim implies powerlessness and to gain a sense of control may mean engaging with and accepting the true nature of victimization (Etherington 2000). This extract demonstrates how Dave begins to move from helplessness to hopefulness, from victim to survivor.

Transition

Something just clicks
I thought
I'll go to the toilet
I can do that
There's a toilet upstairs
Christ knows how I got up
Got to that toilet
Sat on the pan.
I tell you what
I got out of the wheelchair
Stood in front of the toilet
With my dick out
With my hand
Where it belonged.
Going to the toilet makes you cry
I thought, I'm now going to the toilet
How you should go, I thought
I'm going properly.

These extracts show us a glimpse of some of the psychological processes that have been experienced by young stroke survivors during the transition of returning home and I will now move on to how people describe their current situation and their search for meaning when the old life has to be left behind and the search for the new begins (Bridges 1995).

The present: the search for meaning

Dave has begun to take control of his life again. His 'chaos story' slowly transforms into a 'quest narrative' (Frank 1995). According to Frank, quest stories are the beginning of restoring the 'body-self' (Kleinman 1988). It is an attempt to 'meet suffering head on; they accept illness and seek to use it' (Frank 1995, p.115). The quest becomes the journey and the search for meaning when the affected person begins to focus positively on the future and considers making some changes following the trauma of the stroke. The quest story is the 'triumph over medicine' and gives the teller a voice (Frank 1995, p.115). This voice offers empowerment, encouragement and hope to other victims, promoting a sense of advocacy, power and healing.

This does not assume that all sufferers are able to tell a quest story. For some the devastation is too great and they remain in chaos, locked into their trauma. Alan is stuck in his chaos story and struggles to regard himself as a survivor. The group differs in their view of themselves. I join the conversation where Alan feels doomed and is just waiting for the next thing to happen: 'I would argue with you. I'm not a stroke survivor. I'm a stroke casualty or a sufferer.'

Geraldine:	There are different ways to look at it. I see myself as a survivor, not a victim.
	Alan tells the group he feels his stroke is a punishment.
Dave:	So what are you being punished for?
Geraldine:	Yeah, why do you think you are being punished?
Alan:	One was leaving my wife and daughter. I suppose I left them because I was thinking of what's best for me. I got what I wanted out of life, so this is my way of bringing you down to earth, you're gonna get what you deserve.
Geraldine:	So how long are you going to go on punishing yourself?
Alan:	Probably forever, probably forever.
Geraldine:	You don't deserve that.
Bob:	But even the people who've been saints all their life still get strokes!
Diana:	Yeah, so you shouldn't blame yourself for those sorts of things.

Alan's feelings of self-retribution are strong and the group attempts to put them in perspective. Disability and chronic illness is often linked with punishment and the act of God. The result of this false perception of self, as in the case of Alan, can serve to reinforce negative and destructive feelings, forcing the person to remain a victim (Segal 1991).

Others in the group described themselves as survivors and had taken the opportunity to review their pattern of life and make some changes. This seemed to depend on the level of professional and family support they had received on return home. Emotional and physical recovery was influenced by the individual's social support systems; the opportunity for receiving professional psychological help; partner and family support; feelings of self-worth and self-identity. Most important was the opportunity to meet with others affected by stroke to share the experience and gain mutual support.

Rediscovering self

I enjoy every day I'm about now
I really do.
When I came out of hospital
What I wanted was
Someone to encourage me
Not my family, they were too close.
They would say
'Don't worry Mum,
Everything's gonna be alright'
I just wanted to scream inside of me
No it's not.
Then I had counselling.
I'm still on my happy pills
But they are being reduced.
But the turning point
In my life
Was when I met Nicky
Who'd been through the stroke.
If only I could have met somebody
Like her in the beginning.
I thought, if she can do it
So can I.
I've got a lovely partner now
I've gotta lot of friends
That I've only had
Since I had the stroke.
They like me as I am
I'm not trying to be
The person I was
Anymore.

Diana no longer perceives herself as a disabled person but rather a person living with a disability. She has given 'testimony' to the group and those who have received it have borne witness (Frank 1995; Herman 1992).

Faith, courage and hope in her own self have been renewed. The 'disabled self' is no longer a threat. She has mourned her losses and reclaimed part of what she thought was lost. Restoration begins with an awareness of not being alone. Group support with a shared commonality can be invaluable (Herman 1992). This was demonstrated in the group when Alan shared his feelings of loss of manliness. Dave had been given permission to unlock his feelings on this subject, feelings which he has previously been too afraid to admit: 'I understand what Alan says. I find it helpful for someone to tell me how he felt. I thought I was the only one. I understand exactly where he's coming from.'

Similarly, the group shared intimate feelings of loss, fear and their deepest despair, but out of those deep and sensitive feelings came signs of hope and optimism. All shared their intense fear of having a further stroke and wondered whether they could cope again. They felt that a sense of humour was essential and at times even the most poignant comments were defused with laughter.

The participants have shared with me their myriad feelings during the different rehabilitative stages of stroke. They have demonstrated the difficulties of letting go and seeking a new meaning to life. Rehabilitation following stroke is a long journey which has a beginning and middle but no end, because the end of this story is really the beginning. As Bob concludes:

> *I've been running a marathon*
> *I'm just coming to the last mile*
> *I've gotta give myself a real push*
> *To get to the next mile*
> *I'm running out of breath*
> *But I've gotta do it*
> *I'm fairly optimistic, really.*

Personal reflections

Counselling young people whose lives have been affected by stroke has been a humbling and rewarding experience. Seeing people when they are in the depths of despair, offering containment and a safe place to share these feelings, observing over time how some manage to work through these difficulties and seek major change is, indeed, rewarding. I cannot begin to imagine how I would cope if I were struck by stroke. I would hope that as a patient my emotional needs would be considered alongside my medical requirements. I know I would want the professionals involved in my rehabilitation to adapt to my needs and not the other way round. As a client I expect that whatever I bring to a counselling session should be treated with respect and understood in terms of my view of reality. I would want the counsellor to help me explore what was not understood, to enable me to develop and move on, if that was my goal. I would want to feel valued, heard and understood and then maybe I could pursue achievable outcomes. As a non-stroke-affected person and practitioner, I hope that I have learnt from these stories some of the 'real' problems faced by my clients living with the effects of stroke.

Working in the voluntary sector has given me the opportunity to utilize and develop my practice skills whilst maintaining a management role. Group support, following a period of individual counselling, offers encouragement, understanding and a shared experience, which can in itself be healing. The group's experiences have not only given me personal insight for my counselling work but have offered direction for wider practice issues in stroke rehabilitation, particularly concerning the understanding of the psychological problems connected with stroke by all professionals involved in stroke care. Most importantly clients have raised my awareness of the value of what they can offer to enhance service delivery and development. As a manager, I have been encouraged to readdress the power imbalance and decision-making process within my organization. As a result, a service user committee has been established to function as an advisory panel and this will take a key role in the organization.

As a social worker and counsellor, I feel it is important to share my client work and personal experience publicly in the hope that other practitioners may be challenged to develop their knowledge and experience. As a practitioner it is sometimes hard to face up to many of the issues raised by my clients, but if I am to learn through experience, good or bad, I will gain from facing those challenges. To deny the voice of the lived experience is a retrograde step in practice. Theory provides the foundation for practice but is blind if it does not open its eyes to others' experiences. I have learnt the power of language with its influences and innuendoes, the silent words that are felt but locked away. Every word Jane speaks requires great effort and concentration as she is aphasic, and yet she has so much to say and makes an important contribution to the group. Her facial expressions, body language and the written word have replaced her spoken voice, but her 'voice' has been heard and, I hope, accurately represented.

Recommendations

1. Counselling should be an integral part of a multidisciplinary approach to stroke rehabilitation. Professional counselling should be available in hospital to address psychological need and emotional support.

2. Counselling, information and guidance are important at each stage of rehabilitation – hospitalization, the return home and in the longer term.

3. Whilst it is recognized that some health-care personnel use counselling skills as part of their role, the difference between counselling skills and professional counselling should be clarified.

4. Hospital personnel would benefit from counselling skills training.

5. Ideally, stroke patients should be cared for on a specialist ward or unit where staff are particularly dedicated and trained to the needs of their patients.

6. Information, support and guidance should also be made available to partners and carers.

7. The person's total needs should be considered with an holistic approach to rehabilitation.

8. Therapeutic groups, following individual counselling, offer continued support, a social network to help rebuild confidence, a forum to share up-to-date information on stroke and the opportunity to explore the trauma, loss and search for new meaning in the telling and hearing of stories.

Conclusion

The application of a focus group interview as a means of identifying needs proved valuable in obtaining in-depth data on a practical and emotional level. Whilst focus group interviews do not appear to have been widely used in counselling research, I found it an innovative technique to interview a minority group with shared commonality. The collaborative nature of the group balanced levels of power and control, which offered a collective voice to those involved.

The exploration of the practical and emotional needs of young stroke survivors has indicated the need for counselling together with improved communication and guidance, throughout the different stages of rehabilitation. Counselling, information, guidance and group support provided by the voluntary sector are vital services in the professional care during rehabilitation and should be recognized as valuable contributions towards a multidisciplinary approach to rehabilitation.

Rehabilitation following stroke is a frustrating and exhausting journey, both physically and psychologically. The participants have enlightened me and will I hope enlighten all those who read this chapter.

References

Bridges, W. (1995) *Managing Transitions: Making the Most of Change,* MA, USA: Addison-Wesley Publishing Co.

Bright, R. (1996) *Grief and Powerlessness: Helping People Regain Control of Their Lives.* London: Jessica Kingsley Publishers.

Corker, M. and French, S. (eds) (1999) *Disability Discourse.* Buckingham: Open University Press.

Epstein, R.S. (1989) 'Post-traumatic stress disorder: A review of diagnostic and treatment issue.' *Psychiatric Annals, 19,* 556–563.

Erikson, E. (1980) *Identity and the Life Cycle.* New York: Norton.

Etherington, K. (2000) *Narrative Approaches to Working with Adult Male Survivors of Child Sexual Abuse.* London: Jessica Kingsley Publishers.

Frank, A. (1995) *The Wounded Storyteller: Body, Illness and Ethics.* Chicago: University of Chicago Press.

Goleman, D. (1996) *Emotional Intelligence.* London: Bloomsbury.

Grafiniki, S. (1996) 'How research can change the researchers: The need for sensitivity, flexibility and ethical boundaries in conducting qualitative research in counselling/psychotherapy.' *British Journal of Guidance and Counselling 24,* 3, 329–337

Greenhalgh, T. and Hurwitz, B. (1999) 'Narrative based medicine, why study narrative?' *British Medical Journal 318,* 48–50.

Hammersley, D. and Beeley, L. (1992) 'The effects of medication on counselling.' *Counselling,* 162–164.

Herman, J.L. (1992) *Trauma and Recovery.* London: Pandora.

Hunter, M. and Gerber, P.N. (1990) 'Use of terms "victim and survivor" in grief stages commonly seen during recovery from child sexual abuse.' In *The Sexually Abused Male.* Lexington: Lexington Books.

Jung, C.S. (1934) 'The relations between the ego and the unconscious', Collected Works 7. In D. Kalsched (1998) *The Inner World of Trauma.* London: Routledge.

Kennedy, P. (1991) 'Counselling with spinal cord injured people.' In H. Davis and L. Fallowfield (eds) *Counselling and Communication in Health Care.* Chichester: Wiley.

Kfir, N. (1989) *Crisis Intervention.* Verbatim. New York: Hemisphere Publishing Corporation.

Kfir, N. and Slevin, M. (1991) *Challenging Cancer: From Chaos to Control.* London: Tavistock Press.

Kleinman, A. (1988) *The Illness Narratives.* New York: Basic Books.

Laing, R.D. (1965) *The Divided Self.* London: Pelican.

Levinson, D.J. (1978) *The Seasons of a Man's Life.* New York: Knopf.

McCrum, R. (1998) *My Year Off: Rediscovering Life After Stroke.* London: Picador.

McLeod, J. (1997) *Narrative and Psychotherapy.* London: Sage.

Melosh, B. (1982) *The Physician's Land.* Philadelphia: Philadelphia Temple University Press.

Riessman, C.K. (1993) *Narrative Analysis.* London: Sage.

Rowan, J. (1997) *Healing the Male Psyche.* London: Sage.

Schlossberg, N. (1984) *Counselling Adults in Transition.* New York: Springer.

Segal, J. (1991) 'The use of the concept of unconscious phantasy in understanding reactions to chronic illness.' *Counselling,* 146–148

Seligman, M.E.P. (1975) *Helplessness: On Depression, Development and Death.* San Francisco: Freeman.

Spiro, H., McCrea, Cumin, M.G., Peschel, E. And St. James, D. (eds) (1993) *Empathy and the Practice of Medicine.* Yale: Yale University Press.

Trower, P., Casey, A. and Dryden, W. (1988) *Cognitive-behavioural Counselling in Action.* London: Sage.

Further reading

Bauby, J. (1997) *The Diving Bell and the Butterfly.* London: Fourth Estate.

Parr, S., Byng, S. and Gilpin, S. with Ireland, C. *Talking About Aphasia.* Buckingham: Open University Press.

Stroke Association (1999) *Stroke Care – A Matter of Chance. A National Survey of Stroke Services.* Report by Shah Ebrahim and Judith Redfern. University of Bristol and Royal Free and University College Medical School.

Useful contact addresses

Bristol Area Stroke Foundation
The Gatehouse Centre
Hareclive Road
Hartcliffe
Bristol BS13 9JN
Tel: 0117 964 7657

Different Strokes
Sir Walter Scott House
2 Broadway Market
London E8 4QJ
Tel: 020 7249 6645

The Stroke Association
Stroke House
Whitecross Street
London ECIY 8JJ
Tel: 020 7490 7999

Chapter 5

Counselling in Stroke Rehabilitation

A Client's Account

Diana Sheppard

I would like to dedicate this chapter to my son Shane and my daughter Stacey for their love, care and patience (which I know I pushed to the limits sometimes). For inspiration I would like to thank Nikki. For giving me the will to live and not give up – my granddaughter, Kali Louise. God bless you all. I would also like to thank all those who I believe helped in my rehabilitation, friends and professionals alike.

Monday, 6 October 1997 at 8.20 am, a day and a time I will never forget. Not some happy anniversary or a special person's birthday: that was the day my life ended, the day I died. Let me take you back. I was born in 1957 an only child. For the first nine or ten years I remember being quite happy although my Mum and Dad divorced when I was about 7 years old. From birth I mainly lived with my maternal grandparents as both my Mum and Dad were working full time. They had bought a house and I suppose it was a necessity for my Mum to work. Growing up in those early years I never had many friends; my Nan and Popper (granddad) were my best friends. When I was about 9 or 10, my Popper, whom I loved dearly, died of a brain haemorrhage. Not long after this my Mum (who later died when I was 30 years old and she was only 52) met a man and soon all three of us lived together in a new house. My Dad, whom I had contact with every Saturday from round about 10 am to 6 pm on the dot, was soon to marry someone who is only twelve or so years older than me. Happy families all the way around – I wish it could have been.

Over the following years I suffered emotional, sexual and physical abuse from all of these people, as well as having to be part of and witness domestic violence between my Mum and the man she lived with. I am not going to name names or apportion blame. The people who afflicted these horrible things on me know who they are and to what extent they did it. On my sixteenth birthday in 1973, I moved out from my Mum's and this man's house and returned to live with my best friend, my Nan – the only person, along with my Popper, I truly believed loved me.

In 1987 I lost my Mum, who had a heart attack and died: I lost my Nan who died of pneumonia in 1992. In 1997 I had my faithful dog Brandy put to rest. He had been my strength on many occasions over the ten years since my Mum died – he had previously suffered a couple of fits and was in pain, he no longer enjoyed life. It broke my heart to lose yet again something I loved that was important and very special to me.

I also had three marriages and three divorces – I do pick 'em don't I!!! The first was a womanizer, liar and drinker, but he gave me two beautiful, caring children and we did have some wonderful years together. The second was a compulsive gambler and liar – a mistake from the beginning – and last but not least, another womanizer and liar who was fortunate enough to have a great excuse for leaving me – I had a stroke! These years were not all bad. There were also good fun times, times when I laughed and enjoyed life with family and friends. There were also sad times and times of despair, dealing with other episodes of my life and my children's lives, but at least I had what kept me sane and battling on – my children. Had I not had these two wonderful human beings, I think I could have quite easily ended up as an alcoholic (as my Mum unfortunately did) or turned to drugs or something equally destroying. So as you can see, my life so far was certainly not a truly happy one.

August 1997: my husband and I moved back to Bristol after living in Portsmouth for three years (he was a petty officer in the Royal Navy). I was happy to be returning to my home town where all my friends and family lived, especially my children. My son Shane was 21 years old and my daughter Stacey, 19, was expecting her first baby – my first grandchild. On 29 August my former husband moved me into the new house and two days later he was gone – up to Scotland where he was based in the Navy and also had a girlfriend in situ. Nothing much had changed! So there were problems between us and life was not rosy, but hey I was back with my kids, I was back in my home town where I felt secure. I was going to be happy!

The day of my stroke started as any other normal working day. I got up, got ready for work, which took about two hours as I have always prided myself on my appearance, and off I drove. I had no feelings of being unwell and looked forward to the week as I was working for an agency and was placed in a human resources team at a major airline company. The personnel manager had asked the previous Friday if I would consider working full time for the airline direct. I was overjoyed; that Monday morning I was going to say 'yes', but it wasn't to be. I arrived at 8 am, made myself coffee and sat at my desk waiting for my manager to give me instructions for the day. I planned to go and see the personnel manager in my official coffee break later that morning. The phone on my desk started to ring and I picked it up, started to speak – and whoa, nothing I said was comprehensible: in fact it was gobbledegook.

The day I died

I can remember the paramedics arriving. I was laid on the office floor, everyone standing around. I felt no pain, I couldn't speak. My right side felt very heavy and I could not move any part of it; my face felt numb. I remember thinking, 'Why don't they all go away, let me get some air and I will feel fine.' Then I heard the female paramedic say to someone, 'Let's get her to hospital, I think she has had a stroke.' Those words put the fear of God into me. I thought, 'No, I'm too young to have a stroke, only old people have strokes. I am going to die.'

I can remember the ambulance journey well; no sirens, so I thought perhaps I was not going to die – they had made a mistake. Straight into the trauma room at the hospital, loads of tests, questions (which I had great difficulty in answering because of lack of speech), my daughter arriving, my son arriving, someone telling me my husband was on his way down from Scotland; then the MRI scan. Whilst in the scan I thought a miracle had happened. I could feel my right hand, I could move my leg. I was going to be OK. I was removed from the scanner and a nurse was waiting for me. I said, 'Look I can move, I can speak, I am going to be all right.' With that I lifted myself from one stretcher bed to another. Then it hit me once more. I started to lose feeling down my right side again, felt numbness in my face and tried to speak but nothing came out – only an overwhelming sense of fear that I would never see my children again, never know my grandchild, and tears that I could not stop falling: the thought that yes, I might die. I was scared.

I have only one recollection of the next three or four days. At one point I came to: I was lying in a hospital bed, connected by tubes in both arms and wires to machines that were beeping or dripping fluid into my body. My son was there with his girlfriend of over two years, Sarah. My daughter, together with my unborn grandchild, was there with my Dad, Step-mum and my friend Bev. They stood round my bed, looking at me. They were all crying or very close to tears and I thought, 'Oh well, this is it, I am dying.' I wasn't frightened: it felt like a nice place to be, wherever I was. I was just sad at leaving my children behind but I thought, 'Well, I will soon see my Nan and Mum again.' I have since been told that all this happened on the first day of my hospital stay, my children being told later by the doctor that he didn't know if I would survive or not.

My hospital stay lasted for nearly four weeks. By the end of the first week I could stand aided. I then progressed to 'shuffling' with help. My speech came back quite well. I could raise my arm slightly, but could not use my fingers independently. Then I was told by the professionals that this could be as good as it gets, although most improvement takes place in the first six months and then slow progress for up to two years. You cannot imagine the pain, anger and frustration I felt inside at being told this. Why didn't I die – I don't want to have to live like this – I want the old me back. I cried and cried, went into depression but could not speak to my children, family or friends about it – I didn't want to upset them. I couldn't. I felt they had been through enough. The nursing staff didn't want to know or didn't know how to deal with it. Medically they looked after me well, but as to how I was feeling and emotional/psychological support – they didn't have a clue. Do you know I received more empathy from one of the domestics on the ward who came and sat on my bed one day because she saw I was crying, put her arms around me, gave me a cuddle and just let me cry. That meant more to me than anything in the world that precise moment and I shall never forget her.

My husband visited, but not very frequently. When he was there he would sit by the bed, not speaking; there would be no holding of hands or offer of support and encouragement. One day I found the strength to tell him to leave, that I did not want him there – and he went! My daughter was the one who visited day in and day out, from 10 am to roughly 8 pm or 9 pm every day. My son visited when work permitted, although he did take one week's leave the very first week and was there constantly. His girl-friend Sarah visited as often as she could – I am glad she was there, not only for me but also for the support she offered Shane and to Stacey. My

Dad and Step-mum came in three times a week – I had never felt so close to them but I still could not talk of my fears or how I really felt to any of them.

Going home

The day came when I was being allowed home on the condition that there was somebody there to look after me. My husband would not take time off work so my daughter who was five months pregnant moved in with me to help. She lifted me in and out of the shower, she saw to my toilet and hygiene needs. She cooked, when I could be bothered to eat. She was my parent, my nurse, my cook and cleaner: I could not have survived without her. I was even more depressed, just sitting watching TV in the same four walls, day in day out – I wanted to die. In fact I wanted to die so much that one evening I drank a bottle of wine and got all my tablets out on the coffee table. The hospital had prescribed me with antidepressants: I was going to take them – I wanted out. I felt as though I was a 'thing' who couldn't even wash herself. I couldn't walk. I couldn't use my right arm. I wanted to be the 'me' I was before the stroke but that was never going to happen, not now, not ever! Time passed and I still sat there with tablets on the table (no wine left) and my thoughts went to my unborn grandchild and my two children. I couldn't do it but I had to do something.

I decided that the next day I would phone the Bristol Area Stroke Foundation (BASF). I had been given one of their leaflets at a session with the hospital social worker (who was about as useful as a pair of running shoes would have been to me at that time). She thought that they might be able to offer counselling, help or advice. May I add that this session was three months after I had my stroke in the previous October. Somebody at last thought I might need to talk to someone about what had happened to me. I must admit, I did not phone straight away. I am stubborn and strong willed and thought that I should be able to sort this out on my own. Besides, counselling was for people who couldn't cope, couldn't manage their lives. I'd managed all my life, hadn't I? I did eventually phone towards the end of January. I told no one. I thought they would see me as a weak person, a failure, but I was desperate. My counselling started at the beginning of February. I shall now try to put on paper my feelings and how the following months went.

A struggle to find me

First, this lady called, a very well presented, smartly dressed person. I thought, 'What does she know about stroke? A lot of good this is going to be.' I can see now why I thought like that. She reminded me of how I used to be, how I wanted to be again and there was I in my everyday wear since returning home from hospital – tracksuit bottoms and a sweatshirt, no make-up and hair not styled. It is hard to style hair when you have only one hand to use. More to the point, it was even harder because I had lost all feeling of worth and no longer respected myself. I just didn't care. I cannot remember the exact content of our first meeting, but I know she was friendly, showed empathy not sympathy and was not condescending. She was actually interested in what I had to say and encouraged me without making me feel threatened or under interrogation. It was my personal time. I also felt comfortable and safe as the sessions were in my home and I knew I had the safety net of asking her to leave. A session for the following week was planned and when she had gone I thought how nice it was to have had a visitor. Boy did my views on these sessions vary during the next couple of months.

Although my counsellor was never intrusive or directly challenging, she certainly had a way of encouraging me to talk, never asking challenging questions but using minimal prompts (which I later learned about when I took a counselling course). I am a talker anyway. If there is somebody there to listen I will talk for ages, but I found myself telling her things I could not even tell my own mother/children/best friend. Oh, it was such a relief to be able to be angry, to rant and rave, to tell her of my frustrations and fears about the stroke without being judged or being told 'don't be silly, you will be all right'. Deep down I knew I would never be the same again and that frightened and upset me.

During one of the earlier sessions, I remember showing every emotion I am capable of, from tears to laughter, from fear to hope, but most of all the underlying feelings of anger and pure hatred. I was angry that it had happened to me, that I had had the stroke; because of this I now only had one side of my body functioning. My memory was very scattered, I could not control my tears and my speech was affected. My husband had left me because he couldn't handle the situation and the commitment that would be needed from him. I wish I could have left me! It was down to me to cope on my own – as I felt I had all my life. That session really took all my emotional and physical energy and, although my counsellor always ended the sessions on a positive note, I can remember on that occasion, after she left, I was beside myself. I couldn't cry enough tears, the hurt was unbearable; I was inconsolable. I wished I had physically died in hospital. From what I remember, that was the session that had the worst after-effect on me. These feelings lasted for days, not diminishing until one morning when I woke up after again seriously contemplating taking my own life the night before. My daughter was there – then eight months pregnant, carrying a tiny little life that I so much wanted to be part of and to love.

I told my counsellor how I had considered taking my own life with alcohol and tablets. I felt comfortable enough to share this with her. No angry shouts, no accusations, just an acceptance that I had very nearly ended it all. We talked about the situation and my feelings and I felt immediately relieved inside. I felt as though a burden had been taken away from me. (My children never knew this, but they will now.) The next couple of sessions were hard for me but, funnily enough, around that time was the beginning of my acceptance of the stroke and what I could expect my life to be in the future. I didn't like it, I still did not want to be this disabled person, but I was learning to accept it had happened.

It was also round about this time that my counsellor introduced me to Nikki. I had expressed a wish to meet somebody who had gone through a similar experience. My counsellor took me to meet her on a Wednesday morning. We sat, drank coffee and talked along with the counsellor and then, very discreetly, the counsellor offered to leave us for a while so we could talk on our own. I immediately thought, no don't do that, I don't know this lady, we will have nothing to talk about. That couldn't have been further from the truth. She sat opposite me and just said, 'Ask me anything you want.' So I did and she was very honest about her experiences – there were many similarities in our lives. Well, turning point number two, I walked, well shuffled, out of her house after giving her a big hug and decided there and then I was going to get through this. I was going to learn to walk as normally as possible. I was determined to get my life back – not as it was before the stroke but a damn lot better than it was at that time. Thank you Nikki, you will always be remembered.

March 1998, my granddaughter was born, Kali Louise. After this event I changed for the better. Now I was more determined than ever to live a relatively 'normal' life. I treated my counselling sessions more positively and used them to their full extent. I had even begun to explore the earlier years of abuse and clear them from my mind with the guidance of my counsellor. Yes, the sessions were still hard. Yes, there were still tears, anger, hatred and all the emotions I've mentioned before, but now to me there was a purpose. Over time my confidence slowly returned, sometimes with knock-backs. It was like taking two steps forward and one step back – but I was getting there.

What also helped during those months were the group meetings I attended (and still do) for younger stroke survivors where I made many good friends. We all had something in common: we'd had a stroke (or an illness that can cause the similar devastation on the body and mind). I classed it as group counselling. We all confided feelings, hopes and fears that I would find hard to share with just anybody. Even as I write this chapter I still look forward to the next meeting. As my confidence and the feeling of actually liking myself grew I became more adventurous. I started going out socially and met more new people. One evening I went to a nightclub in Bristol and met a man who over the next couple of months fuelled me with confidence and a sense of living. This, combined with my counselling sessions, gave me a thirst for life. Yes I had a limp and my arm would get tired sometimes for no reason at all, but I was enjoying life so much that I wanted to return to work. My counselling sessions had reduced to once a fortnight and I felt really capable of returning to full-time employment. By October 1998 I had met a new partner, Andy, who was a very different type of person from those I had previously been attracted to, because I was different from how I used to be.

At this time life was great, I had settled every thing legally with my former husband, my home was secure and Kali Louise was doing grand. I started work in late August 1999. By the beginning of October 1999 I had collapsed in my bathroom one morning whilst getting ready for work and just cried and cried. I felt emotionally and physically drained – my body could not cope with working. Needless to say depression hit again, big time. I returned to my counsellor and over a matter of a couple of months I again came to accept that my life did not include full-time work. Once again there were painful sessions when I wanted to give up, but not quite as badly as before. I even felt the same sense of loss as I did when I first had the stroke and again felt very resentful about having had the stroke in the first place. My counsellor actually asked me to jot down on paper and describe, in a colour, how I felt on a good day and a bad day. This is what I wrote:

I feel a deep grey
Don't want to get up – sleep
Can't be bothered – just mope around
Don't want to talk or see anyone
Sometimes even Kali.
I get angry with myself and cry

★★★★★★★★★★★★★★★★

Sunshine day – it's yellow
Kali is here, she makes me feel pink
It's a smiley day
Where all the problems are hiccups
Even the puddles from the deep grey day sparkle

As time progressed, so did I. I took up voluntary work with the Bristol Area Stroke Foundation, visiting younger stroke survivors and, at a later date, was recommended to be part of the liaison committee for the BASF. Spending a lot of quality time with Kali Louise and my children has always meant so much to me. Andy's always around. He has helped me along (and still does) more than I have given him credit for. Shane is a personal trainer and spends some of his time at a local private gym which I also joined and haven't looked back since. My strength on the right side has greatly improved and now I can even walk most days without a limp. I have also gone back to a love of my early years – horse-riding – and I take my very first dressage test in a couple of weeks. I did have a setback just a month or so ago concerning personal relationships which stemmed from abuse in my very early teens, so once again I had counselling. The first couple of sessions were not any easier than when I first had counselling three years ago. But I dealt with it. I can now truthfully say there are no ghosts who can haunt me from my past – for whatever reason. My body and my mind are in my control and that is the way I like it. One positive thing can be said of my stroke. If I had never had the misfortune to be struck by it, I would never have considered counselling and I doubt I would have ever sought counselling to deal with my past and find the real me.

The new Me

I now like Me
Me, Myself and I
Life after the death of Me
Life, I died, I am living
Knowing Me
Knowing the hidden Me
Life is for living
My life turned inside out
Life after stroke
Living for Me.

Monday, 6 October 1997 at 8.20 am: a day and a time I will never forget, not the day I died – the day I started to learn to live!

Chapter 6

Counselling after Hearing Loss

Ruth Morgan-Jones

Introduction

The latest statistics about hearing loss suggest that today 7.5 million or one in seven people in the UK have a hearing loss (RNID 1990). This number is expected to rise dramatically as the growth of numbers of elderly people in the population increases and the number of people suffering from NIHL (noise-induced hearing loss) escalates. With regard to the latter, the number of people exposed to potentially dangerous sound levels has tripled since the early 1980s (*Evening Standard* 1999).

This chapter is an exploration of some of the psychosocial counselling issues which may be present when working with people who have acquired their hearing loss either suddenly or gradually. Although reference will be made to work with people who are prelingually deaf, the main focus will be on people who have lost some or all of their hearing as they are seen as being lost between two worlds, the deaf and the hearing.

After a general discussion of medical/audiological factors, the specific psychosocial issues that will be explored are counsellor and client attitudes, bereavement and mental health issues, belonging and continuity, and autonomy and normality. The chapter will then focus on couple relationships in particular when one partner is hearing and the other is hearing impaired. Problems in this area will be illustrated by a case study. The chapter will end by looking at what rehabilitation services are available in the UK today and how it may be possible to revision the communication strategies required, specifically the 'looking' and 'repeating', so that they may be seen as mutually beneficial for both hearing and hearing impaired people.

Personal journey

Before examining these issues, I believe it would be helpful to share a brief review of my own journey. A special concern for counselling people with acquired hearing loss was triggered by the acknowledgement that my own hearing loss diverged from the family pattern and had become much worse. It might be said that there were two phases of acknowledgement and adjust-ment (Jones, Kyle and Wood 1987). In the late 1940s some rather primitive tests were given. The fact that I could not hear a loud ticking watch through a closed door convinced the ENT consultant that, by the age of four, I had inherited the family's mild/moderate deafness which had preceded me for five generations. A combination of factors meant that I coped with it excep-tionally well. Because I was a confident, extroverted, optimistic child who liked people and seemed to know what she wanted in life with a propensity for getting it, the hearing loss was simply a situational nuisance. Occa-sionally, I did feel excluded. An example of this was during the ritual telling of secrets amongst my female friends, as I could never hear their whispers. Closeness to my parents at this time helped to compensate for this (Mor-gan-Jones 1984). My excellent lip-reading skills also meant that my hearing loss did not hold me back in any way until I reached mid-life when the unforeseen happened.

My hearing loss exceeded the family pattern and became severe/profound. At this point, I did experience surprise, shock and disbelief. While I had a hunch that my hearing had been deteriorating, I had little understanding of how it would impact on my counselling career until the Tavistock Marital Studies Institute rejected me for training as a marital therapist. They considered that my excellent lip-reading skills were not suf-ficient to be a good therapist. I could not trust my hearing enough to hear clearly the nuances of English speech, especially when strong or subtle emotions were expressed. It was recommended that I 'cash in' on my deafness in some way. While initially resistant to this idea because I consid-ered hearing loss a morbid subject to study, it gradually began genuinely to interest me. I eventually obtained my doctorate by studying the impact of hearing impairment on family life at the London School of Economics. It has now been published as a book (Morgan-Jones 2001) and I find that I have thus become a family sociologist as well as a counsellor.

Doing the research brought me face to face with other people who had experienced varying degrees of hearing loss. I began to assess the kind of provision and care they had received and to reflect upon my own. Professional counselling was never given to either the people in my study or to myself. I also discovered that there was a profession, Hearing Therapy, established in 1978 by the DHSS, whose purpose was to look after the well-being of people with acquired hearing loss within the NHS. They had, however, very limited professional training and even less in the specific development of counselling skills. Because of this, I founded my own counselling service for hearing-impaired people and their families, HearSay, in 1990.

Simultaneously, I had to decide whether or not to learn British Sign Language for both my research and counselling work. All around me people seemed to assume that it was only logical that I would do so if I wanted to help hearing impaired and deaf people. One cautioning voice was that of Michael Harvey, author of *Psychotherapy with Deaf and Hard-of-Hearing Persons, A Systemic Model* (1989). He implied that the Deaf community could actually be very rejecting of people who tried to join it on the basis of their acquired deafness alone. This was because membership is actually based upon a total commitment to the welfare of profoundly deaf people, a commitment which I gradually discovered I did not have. My commitment was much broader than this and focused more generally on the rehabilitation of people with disabilities more generally, with a special interest in people who have acquired deafness. It is for this reason that I am most pleased to be writing this chapter.

There were many other factors that made me very reluctant to consider learning British Sign Language. The most significant was my gradual awareness of the statistics involved. I eventually discovered that for every one person who is prelingually deaf and uses signs, there are approximately 150 people who have acquired hearing loss. While the professionals in the Deaf field know these statistics, the neglect of people with acquired hearing loss is very rarely fully acknowledged as the injustice that it is. What this means is that a spectrum has developed with the hearing world at one end and the signing Deaf community at the other. In between these two worlds are people with acquired hearing loss who may often not know where they belong and have very little in the way of 'voice' or platform from which to present their concerns and needs.

Helping the client to develop an appropriate identity is one of the major tasks when working with people with acquired hearing loss. In the Foreword to my book about the people in the sample, Martin Bulmer wrote: 'The experience of hearing differently and learning to negotiate one's unique journey, stands out from her matter-of-fact descriptions.' What is meant by the term 'unique journey' is in fact one's developing identity as it evolves through life. Similarly, Erikson defines personal identity as 'the ability to express oneself as something that has continuity and sameness and to act accordingly' (1965, p.37).

From my own experience as well as in helping others, I know that the process cannot be hurried and has to be patiently worked at as factors which facilitate these fledgling deaf/hearing identities and those which inhibit them are identified. I will now move on to examine those factors.

Medical/audiological factors

Before discussing how counsellors can help with the forming and forging of healthy deaf/hearing identities, I wish to look at some basic medical/audiological factors which are descriptive of the kind of hearing loss a particular person has: for example, the time of onset, type, degree of loss, aetiology, rapidity and nature of residual hearing.

There are two main kinds of hearing loss: conductive and sensorineural. The latter type is considered more serious because medical intervention to date is unable to correct its imperceptible onset and insidious progress. The parts of the ear which are affected are the tiny hairs which line the part of the inner ear called the cochlea. They lose their resiliency and cannot respond effectively to different sound frequencies. Causes of this kind of hearing loss are varied and complex. Some aetiological factors are noise, genetic inheritance, illness with accompanying high fever and toxic drugs. But without any doubt, the commonest cause is the 'wear and tear' of old age. For example, a retired headmaster recalls:

> I used to go up to this church, All Saints…but I don't go now…not because I have any difference of [religious] view, but I can't sit in that church and hear a good sermon! I know that's not the only thing you go to church for, but I can't hear a single sentence…it's such a lovely church and I like to go but it doesn't seem worthwhile.

A second man in his seventies who had recently been deafened by Ménière's disease, which has a sensorineural component, talked about his frustration when around his adult children:

> Our…children…will forget… They start talking together and I just cannot follow what they're saying… So there I am standing in a group… but not of the group. Maybe they don't want me to…[be there]. If I could

hear what they're saying, I'd know whether I was part of the conversation or not…so there's difficulty, although…on the whole they are pretty good.

The use of hearing aids and other assistive devices providing mere amplification or refinement of sound is insufficient to compensate for a sensorineural loss because of the distortion which takes place. With the exception of the cochlear implant operation, there is still no effective medical or surgical treatment which may be offered to people with sensorineural loss.

Conductive loss is not considered as serious because it can usually be treated surgically and medically. This is an inherited condition and genetic counselling is recommended for family members. It affects the bony capsule surrounding the inner ear. As the disease gradually destroys the healthy bone, a soft highly vascular bone develops resulting in the stapes (stirrup bone) becoming stuck in the oval window. In this position the stapes can no longer vibrate and a conductive hearing loss occurs. Otosclerosis and other conductive losses respond well to the use of a hearing aid, which means that if the inner ear is normal, there is usually little difficulty with distortion. However, this is not without frustrations, as Rachel, a social researcher, conveys as she thinks about what life will be like after her operation:

'I was very excited to think that without aids, I could go swimming, you know…could run around…outside they whistle…yes, yes, they're a nuisance… [How I would] love to get rid of these awful things.'

The medical profession is generally able to give more hope to people with conductive loss than those who suffer from sensorineural loss as both hearing aids and surgical intervention have been known to be effective. While rarely mentioned, medical intervention has been known to cause total deafness rather than restore it. One of my saddest cases was that of a young midwife who had to give up her profession because the operation to correct her otosclerosis condition had been so unsuccessful that she had lost rather than gained her hearing. It was also pointed out to me by Dueck (1984) that the restoration to more or less normal hearing can sometimes bring about the deterioration of a relatively healthy partnership if it is unable to adjust to the new circumstances resulting from surgical intervention. So far I have not experienced this problem directly in my own counselling practice in relation to the restoration of hearing, but I have seen it in operation in couple relationships more generally when the balance between them is disrupted. Counselling help was not offered in either of the two cases above and had to be sought outside the NHS.

The degree of hearing loss is another significant audiological factor to be aware of as it indicates how well a person understands human speech. Assuming the loss is equal in both ears, a very rough guideline will now be described. A mild loss will cause the person to begin to strain, ask for repetition occasionally, need the TV a bit louder and give some wrong answers. For example, one of the people in my study described how it felt to have a mild/moderate loss:

> There are times when I haven't heard something and I should have heard it and I've said [to myself] 'Oh, I feel sorry that I haven't heard it' and in that sense I feel a bit frustrated... On the other hand, what's the point of being frustrated all the time...it won't help me.

With a moderate hearing loss, the person will need frequent repetition, much louder TV volume, make frequent wrong answers and misunderstand words in group conversation and noticeable fatigue from listening intently. A severe loss is evident to everyone and usually requires a hearing aid. The person with a profound loss hears only very loud sounds if anything.

While one might conclude from these medical/audiological factors that people who have suffered the most profound hearing losses for the longest periods of time would be the worst off, my own experience (Morgan-Jones 2001) suggests that this is not necessarily the case in that psychosocial factors may be as important, if not more important, to ongoing adjustment. We will now explore what some of these factors are and how they may be dealt with in counselling.

Psychosocial factors

In order to facilitate the rebuilding of a life after severe or profound hearing loss has struck, counsellors need to help their clients to identify those areas where they feel a sense of loss and to develop compensating strategies. As people with hearing loss are just as varied as any other group, their feelings about areas of loss will also vary. Nevertheless, hearing loss does predispose individuals and families to problems in some specific areas. We have already touched on finding one's 'identity' in the introduction to this chapter. Closely connected with identity is one's life style or 'the enduring patterns of living, loving and working in the world' (Wax 1989). Four possible life-style choices have emerged in the literature. Those who choose the Deaf community are described as maintaining a life style which segregates them partially as a social minority group from the larger hearing world (Glickman 1986). This group has a strong sense of belonging and a platform for their demands with their own special language. However, like all minority groups, they become objects of discrimination and have thus developed a deep suspicion of professionals. This is exemplified in the remarks of one of my respondents, Arthur:

> I am always suspicious of the motives of professionals who work with deaf people. Two professions in particular...doctors and teachers...are strongly anti-sign language... I think deaf people themselves do not help by relying on social workers for help...and in many ways...social workers subconsciously encourage [dependency]...[in order to] safeguard their jobs... That's my opinion.

For counsellors who are interested in specializing in this area, please see the work of Mairian Corker (1994, 1996)

Working with attitudes: the counsellors' and the clients'

The hard of hearing, the second life-style grouping, are usually 'mainstreamed' into the larger hearing world and tend to become part of the same cultural framework as most service providers. Assimilationists is the name sometimes given to members of this group. They choose to preserve an illusion of equality by 'passing' (Goffman 1963) in the majority hearing culture, but may experience some sacrifice of self-identity in that their hearing impairment is not always considered (Harvey 1998). The third category consists of deaf and hard-of-hearing people who are 'biculturals' in that they can move between Deaf culture and mainstream society. These people tend to be bilingual and have a broad range of social skills learned in both worlds. The fourth group could be considered 'marginal' in that they do not fit well into either deaf or hearing worlds. Because this group tends to be withdrawn, they are often lost to service providers unless some significant event such as hospitalization or involvement in research brings them into contact with the outside world (Wax 1989).

Most of the hearing-impaired people I worked with and myself belong to this 'assimilationist' category which means that we are not isolated. The fact that we are happy in this category appears to depend much more on attitude rather than degree of loss, as found in my research (Morgan-Jones 2001). This is explained by Anthony, a migrated, deafened Nigerian:

I never took deafness lying down. I was still aiming at the top. But many or most deaf people tend to become withdrawn...so it discourages even the kindest helpers...[as dependency is feared]... In my own case, I was succeeding...[everything] I touched turned to gold! ...so my helpers stuck by me.

Helping clients to develop more positive ways of thinking about their disability can only happen if the counsellor has also done this work and they are not projecting their own negative fantasies on to their clients (Romano 1984). This also brings forward another point about the counsellor's attitude. Because initially the deafness appears to be so central to the communication between counsellor and client, it is very easy to fall into the trap of feeling that it is an all-consuming disability affecting every aspect of life in the same way that it is affecting an interview. Counsellors who don't counter this attitude are guilty of falling into the 'reductionist' trap where their clients are seen as disabled first and people second. My experience suggests this attitude is extremely common on some level even among experienced professionals, exemplified in the use of such phrases as 'the hearing impaired' rather than hearing-impaired people. If the counsellor is patient, they will be able to find the client's strengths. In building on these, more strengths will be forthcoming as the client feels he or she is accepted, trusted and believed in.

Bereavement and mental health issues

I have always found it difficult to find the right place for bereavement and mental health issues when discussing counselling help given to hearing-impaired people. This is because until recently this was the only area dealt with in the deaf/counselling literature. Again it was Michael Harvey (1989) who articulated what many researchers and clinicians had believed all along: that negative behavioural and emotional characteristics presented by deaf and hearing-impaired clients have emerged and are supported as a function of the interaction within and between systems. By systems it is meant that people are considered as part of an overall context, not simply as individuals with a personal problem. Although not always the case, Harvey's statement implies that the majority of mental health problems of deaf and hearing-impaired people are rooted in context, not personal pathology. Harvey (1989) argues that such problems are often the result of interactions with people who have generally negative attitudes about deafness and hearing impairment, although these attitudes may be disguised as concern.

This is certainly the case in many instances, as can be seen in the following account that Henry gives of how he escapes from the condescending hearing world:

> When I'm studying, I take my hearing aids off my glasses and try to lose myself in what I'm doing...so I'm escaping from the hearing world... [In this way, the outside of myself and] the inside [are] in tune with what I'm doing...[with no disturbing background noises].

While escaping in such instances can partly solve interactional problems for short periods of time, there are very real bereavement issues which need to be addressed with some people, especially those who have been suddenly deafened, in that they must grieve for what has been lost. Stages from disability and bereavement theory have been borrowed to describe the journey taken initially by deafened people such as feelings of denial, anger, guilt, depression and adaptation (Kubler Ross 1970). Further explanation is given for understanding these stages by adding the following points: the stages do not always happen in this order; there is no time limitation on any one stage; not everyone experiences all these stages; some never experience any of these stages.

Progressing from bereavement theory, Burfield and Casey (1987) suggest that mental health for deafened people circulates around the answers to three questions:

- How do you feel about yourself?
- How do you feel about other people?
- How are you able to meet the demands of life?

Casey discussed his own experience of being deafened:

> 'When I first became deaf, I lost everything that I was. I couldn't use the phone and other people literally did everything for me and I let them. I couldn't figure a way out so I gave up my independence and control.'

The loss of independence and control is particularly poignant for men as these qualities are so closely identified with their socialization. It also sounds as if Casey may have experienced what Heinz Kohut (1971) termed 'fragmentation of self'.

Wax (1989) argues that some constructs for evaluating the mental health of hearing-impaired people are inadequate since they are measured against mainstream hearing norms and standards. A more effective paradigm is to examine psychological and mental health norms so as to perceive what constitutes appropriate cognitive, affective and behavioural standards and norms for deaf and hearing-impaired people. Sussman (1986) has identified ten 'overcoming skills' or key characteristics of the psychologically healthy deaf person. Wax (1989, p.155) has modified them to read:

- positive psychological acceptance of hearing impairment
- positive self-concept/self-esteem
- ability to cope with negative and/or patronising attitudes
- assertiveness
- ability to place speech ability in perspective
- positive attitudes toward communication devices
- socialization with other hearing-impaired people
- ability to survive 'misguidances'
- philosophical and unhostile sense of humour
- *Gemeinschaftsgefühl* (feeling of belonging).

Although primarily developed in relation to members of the Deaf community, this list is also relevant for people with acquired hearing loss.

Belonging and continuity

Because many people in this hard-of-hearing group have no 'reference group' (Hyman 1942) unless they happen to be near a congenial self-help group in their area, they are very dependent on hearing relations and friends for a sense of belonging. Often counselling help is needed for all the family of a hearing-impaired member so that they are able to perceive how they can increase this 'belonging' sense, especially in such places as around the dinner table. It is well documented that if this is not done 'the dinner table', the symbol of family togetherness and the primary forum for the socialization of children, may become a symbol of isolation and even alienation for many hearing-impaired people (Morgan-Jones 2001).

In my study the problem was beautifully illustrated in Max's family. He was an elderly widower, formerly a distinguished educator, who ate supper every evening with his daughter's family and their teenage children. This family was very aware that Grandpa was often left on the outside of family conversations. His son-in-law, Colin, recounted this:

> [Max] likes to know what's going on like most of us do... He feels excluded because you're not always conscious of his deafness...because when [we're] having a conversation, we tend to...drop our voices...and we talk about something that has happened between the two of us, which really isn't for his ears anyway...[maybe something quite trivial]...but then he says, 'What is happening?'...[or] 'Am I missing out on something?

Although Max's family did amazingly well in caring for him on a practical level and to some extent on an emotional one, these examples highlight the problematic and paradoxical heart of the matter with many English families and their elderly, hearing-impaired relations. Max knew implicitly that English middle-class domestic norms dictate, by way of their conversational style (Tannen 1986, 1989), that the feelings of 'belonging' are generated by unstated meanings and being privy to the mundane details of everyday domestic life. When a hearing loss prevented their absorption, the situation became even more complex because of the traditional English dislike of 're-peating' unless a subject is truly important.

A family's awareness of such dynamics around the dining-room table may be crucial for the happiness of hearing-impaired elderly members. A counsellor with some understanding of these dynamics could discuss with the whole family their differing perceptions of conversation during family meals. While at first this could make everyone feel a bit self-conscious, their grandfather's need for repetition, even when discussing apparently trivial matters, could be gradually integrated so that he would no longer feel himself to be an irritation or a burden (Barry 1995), which can be so destructive to the self-esteem of many hearing-impaired elderly people.

A sense of continuity before and after the hearing loss is also important. This can best be illustrated in the case of Anthony and his attitude towards noise generally. Although he doesn't actually hear noise, it still bothers him if he makes any extraneous noises:

> I am a very sensitive person when it comes to noise. I don't like noise... anywhere... There are little noises I make which I don't know I'm making...I usually find that when I eat I make a noise.

Another man in the study insisted on developing his record collection and appeared to find considerable enjoyment in doing so. This was a hobby he had begun earlier in his life and, despite his decreasing hearing, he wished to continue it. I myself play the French horn and enjoy participating in duets, a wind ensemble and French horn festivals (Morgan-Jones 1998). As the notes of the horn are deep and rich, my hearing aids allow me to hear the sound clearly and pitching and intonation are only difficult in the higher register.

Autonomy and normality

Issues of autonomy and normality very much bothered some people. It particularly worried one woman, Joy, that she had to depend on her husband to arrange social outings. This was an area of her life where she had full autonomy before she was deafened from meningitis at the age of 38. She reflected:

> My friends call and of course Mike has to answer...it's not like having a [proper] telephone conversation...you can't have any secrets...yes, I do miss the telephone...it's just [that] other people don't like writing...I don't belong to the RNID telephone exchange. It's very useful if you have got a business...but for ordinary chat, it hardly seems worth it...no privacy.

Nearly all the couples in my study complained of the loss of normal spontaneous conversation. One severely deafened man who worked as a designer put it this way:

> I quite like to forget...that I can't live a [completely] normal life and although I keep on saying 'Let's keep it normal'...it's not [always] possible.

His hearing wife, Sarah, also felt a great loss in connection with spontaneous conversation and blamed this on Joe's deafness and a number of his more formidable mannerisms:

> Well, it [his deafness] stops you talking...[and] making remarks about what's in the papers and [you] think, 'Oh, I cannot be bothered'...but I haven't got the energy sometimes.

This indicates that both the severely deaf husband and his hearing wife, although managing communication between them very well most of the time, did at times miss what they would probably call normal conversation in that it flowed freely without any worry about whether it was lip-readable or not.

We will now look in more depth at difficulties which can arise when hearing loss develops once a couple relationship has become established.

Intimacy and hearing loss

I have spoken with a number of hearing-impaired people who are now divorced from hearing partners. It has intrigued me that they initially see their hearing loss as a major contributor to the breakdown of their relationship. After further questioning, it has always emerged that there were, in fact, many factors which caused the breakdown. In such instances, the hearing loss of one partner has simply been an exacerbating factor in that it makes ordinary everyday communication a little more complex. In working with couples where there is hearing impairment, I found it extremely important to help them discriminate what in fact truly belonged to the hearing impairment and what belonged to other aspects of their relationship. Second, it is also important for couples to see that the special strategies which have evolved in order to cope with a hearing loss are actually enhancing of all couple relationships.

In exploring the first point, a very important distinction has to be made between difficulties related to the physical process of not hearing and those related to the emotional/intellectual process of not hearing properly. Before we look at a case example, we need to look very briefly at what it is about intimacy that can make people fear it. Put succinctly, Feldman (1979) suggests that fear of intimacy arises from four reasons: fear of merger, exposure, attack and abandonment. To expand, a person may fear that merger with a partner would mean the loss of personal boundaries or identity. This occurs when the sense of self is poorly developed or when the sense of the other is very powerful, as in some enmeshed relationships. People may fear exposure because those with low self-esteem may be threatened by being revealed as weak, inadequate or undesirable. Being physically or verbally attacked may be a third intimacy fear if people's basic trust in themselves and the world is low. Lastly, people may fear abandonment or feel overwhelmed and helpless when the person they love is gone.

Because in most circumstances lip-reading requires a certain physical closeness, hearing and hearing-impaired partners who fear intimacy may find their difficulties in communication multiplied enormously. As this is such an important point, I will illustrate it with a conversation which took place during a research interview.

A conversation with Paul and Sarah

Paul and Sarah have been married for eight years and it is the second marriage for both. Because Paul believed that his first family never understood about his severe hearing impairment, he felt that fate had brought him together with Sarah. She came with a ready-made small family and was a trained nurse. Without having to explain, Paul felt that she already seemed to understand him. However, as the research interviews progressed, one of the problem areas mentioned was this couple's inability to sit down at the same time so that lip-reading could take place. Although Sarah claimed it was Paul who would never sit down, further discussion revealed that Sarah also had difficulty surrendering herself to an exchange.

Sarah: And I was just thinking about [how] I said to Paul 'Stay here!' because otherwise he goes and does things; and I have to wait until he sits down again. And I get so frustrated because I can't talk...and I will even go into his workroom when he is working...and walk out again because it is too difficult to turn the radio off and to get him to turn around and listen to me. And I think: 'Who takes responsibility for lip-reading?'

Here Sarah begins on her basic theme that getting through to Paul is like an obstacle course. He replies with stereotypical male defensiveness.

Paul: She starts it all the time. I want to get on with my work or whatever I am doing...so in the normal way, if I wasn't deaf, we could carry on working and doing things ...which ordinary people can get on with...but we...no way.

Here Paul reveals his strong resentment in not being more 'normal' and able to get on with his work while still talking. Research on gender suggests that this is a specific resentment which would be felt by traditionally socialized men who normally could talk and work at the same time. Sarah continues to reveal other obstacles.

Sarah: I don't think that was really the point I was trying to make... I'm very pleased that you are as active as you are. I mean he [talking to the interviewer] is very lively...bang, bang, crash, crash and everything...so you know he's around...but it's almost as if you are living with someone who won't stop for anything.

Paul: Her grandfather's the same; she has a deaf grandfather who is the same.

Another obstacle acknowledged by Sarah is Paul's forceful and lively manner. She likes it, but also finds it inhibits communication. In order to cope, she has adopted a policy of waiting. Paul seems to have found a comfortable role model in Sarah's deaf grandfather and reassures himself about his own behaviour.

Sarah: My point is that I always seem to be the one waiting around for my husband to sit down and listen to me. I think if somebody was less patient and less willing to sit and wait, it would be quite a disaster area really.

Sarah makes it very clear that communication would not take place with any regularity if she were less compassionate than she is. Paul has become quieter and is at last listening to her. Perhaps because she has made her point and would like to embellish it, she now has difficulty listening to Paul.

Paul: Talking about communication from my point of view, Sarah has said that she has to wait while I settle down. I've found it frustrating when Sarah is doing something…and I'm sitting down and I want to say something to Sarah. I can't talk to her when she's moving around. Now it's not a question of Sarah not being able to hear. It's I not being able to keep my mind on what I want to say to her when she's got her back to me. I'm saying something and I say, 'Sit down.' She's just as bad.

Sarah: Yes [*aside to the interviewer*] he doesn't understand that I can hear without seeing him.

Since Sarah has not understood Paul, he repeats himself. Sarah fails a second time to hear the deeper meaning of his request. He needs her to sit down and face him so that he can think clearly and perhaps reassure himself that a misunderstanding has not taken place. The hearing- impaired interviewer intervenes in hopes of clarifying the situation.

Interviewer: [*speaking to Paul*]: You want the facial feedback, you want to see the face and body?

Paul: That's why I get frustrated with the telephone.

Interviewer: Right yes, it's these times when you initiate a conversation?

Paul: Yes.

Sarah does not respond to this exchange, but refocuses on her virtues which she feels, understandably, have not been fully appreciated. Although she does not seem to understand Paul's needs here, she does give him the reassurance he requires at other times. From this conversation, it seems as if both Paul and Sarah have a fear of intimacy with each other which is most likely to be the legacy of their childhood relationships along with their failed marriages. From additional material not presented, I believe that Sarah most feared being attacked, while Paul feared engulfment.

On the positive side, Paul and Sarah are learning to live productively with their many differences such as gender, age, religion, personality, sensitivities and deafness. They are learning to be a little more tolerant of these differences at a deeper level. Counselling intervention could encourage Sarah to relax her helper/expertise role which she has a slight tendency to overplay making her vulnerable to 'burn out' (Elliott, Glass and William Evans 1987). Simultaneously, Paul could come to grips with some of his fears about taking initiatives.

To return to the initial point, the couple's major problem is a fear of intimacy. Paul's hearing loss has a tendency to exacerbate it. In this way they are joined by most people in that there are very few individuals who do not experience fears of intimacy at some point in their lives.

We will now move on to a second important point when working with couples which is an awareness and understanding that many of the coping strategies used by hearing-impaired people are in fact beneficial to all intimate relationships.

Rehabilitation

After my hearing deteriorated, I remember hating the word 'rehabilitation' and did not want it applied to anything in connection with myself. Then I was introduced to the word 'reconfiguration' (Padden 1989), which felt much more congenial as it suggested a reshuffle on a horizontal level rather than some sort of restoration to normality, which the term rehabilitation suggests.

What actually happens to people who become hearing-impaired in the UK once their hearing aids are given to them? What sort of follow-up service is available? Before reading the following comments, it might be of interest to know that I am an American. Although I have lived in the UK for over 30 years, my double marginal status has left me with a sharp awareness of injustices in this country, especially those related to the fact that English people have not been known for putting their energy into intimate, emotional and personal communication (McGill and Pearce 1982). I will expand on this point by a brief review of the development of the Hearing Therapy Profession.

In 1978, a new profession came into being (DHSS 1978) called Hearing Therapy. The role of the Hearing Therapist was to assess the extent of the disability and to formulate a rehabilitation strategy. Initially, the aim was to raise the patient's communication performance to the maximum possible and to maintain it at this level. This was seen as a very complex process because of the multiple factors involved. For example, what were the patients' levels of residual hearing, innate lip-reading ability, communication life style, social needs and their motivation to make the adjustments involved? It was further suggested that the assessment would be designed to elicit the patients' own definition of their communication problems; for example, what the patients regarded as difficult situations and in what circumstances they arose (Hegarty, Pocklington and Crowe 1983).

While contemporary hearing therapy does go a long way towards reaching some of these aims, it is my view that a great injustice was done when the DHSS failed to adopt the original recommendations of its sub-committee (DHSS-ACSHIP 1975) which stated unequivocally that Hearing Therapy Training should begin at graduate level. While some Hearing Therapists do have degrees, the decision to 'dumb down' Hearing Therapy training by substituting experience and lip-readability for a graduate degree has meant that the profession lacks the full standing of other therapeutic professions and fails to give hearing-impaired people the highly skilled help they truly deserve. In deciding to provide only one year of training beyond secondary level, the DHSS lost sight of the multifaceted nature of hearing impairment in that it is not just about the physical process of not hearing, nor the frustrations experienced in losing information and social control; it strikes at the very heart of all human communication. Seen from this perspective, the problem is much deeper and more encompassing in that the ability to hear is a primary component in all relational processes, especially those within the family.

I argue that if Hearing Therapists are to be truly effective, they must receive a much more rigorous training, specifically in counselling theory and practice along with more opportunities for self-development and evaluation, than they currently receive (Morgan-Jones 2001). Moreover, in Britain to date only a little over 100 Hearing Therapists have been trained out of the 300 originally recommended (Attwell and Watts 1987). While the training of Hearing Therapists is continually developing, the current deficiencies in the profession with reference to counselling leave the door open for rehabilitation/reconfiguration work to be done by many voluntary bodies as well as counselling services which have knowledge of the needs of hearing-impaired people. The people in my study listed the following as having given them significant help: a psychiatrist, a psycho-therapist, a speech therapist, a homeopathic doctor, a singing teacher, a marital therapist, a head teacher and a Methodist minister.

If funding were available, the ideal way forward would be to establish an institute where a multidisciplinary holistic approach could be employed and counselling, training and research into acquired loss take place. However, until such time as this might be feasible, there remains the possibility of transforming some current understandings of the help given to hearing- impaired people so that there is more reciprocity and equality. We will continue to focus on the couple relationship.

Communication strategies

Couples where one partner is hearing and the other is hearing-impaired can be made to feel like outsiders and as if they don't fit in completely to either the Deaf or hearing worlds. It might be helpful to mention at this point that my husband and I have not had this difficulty. This is most likely because he is a Church of England vicar and parish life tends to contain us both at a basic social level. By this I mean that in enlightened Christian circles, all disabilities and differences are accepted in time and there is encouragement to make use of them in any way appropriate.

However, as counsellors, it can be helpful to know some basic information about the communication strategies used to help hearing-impaired people so that they feel more integrated into the hearing world on an equal footing, if that is their wish. For relaxed conversation to take place between a hearing and hearing-impaired person, a number of processes usually need to take place. I have called one of these the ETTA factor – the Effort, Time, Thought and Attention required. This concept draws attention to the fact that some hearing people must think very carefully about the requirements for lip-reading. The ETTA factor is about taking the trouble to accommodate to what does not feel normal. It is about having the energy for the Effort, Time, Thought and Attention required to help a hearing-impaired person take his or her rightful place in both formal and informal conversation. The provision of access to conversation follows the same principle as the provision of a ramp for wheelchair users so that they may enter and leave buildings. ETTA can initially feel like a very self-conscious activity, but in time it becomes integrated.

Revisioning the communication strategies of 'looking' so that lip-reading can take place and repeating so that clarification may be obtained are two other important processes to consider. For example, sociologists (Allan 1989), social psychologists (Noller 1984) and linguists (Tannen 1991) suggest that 'looking' or gaze behaviour facilitates the development of intimate relationships generally. There is clear evidence for a looking-liking connection of the following type: the more you look at me (the more attention you give me), the more I will like you. This connection is confirmed in Ellyson's (1974) study which shows a correlation between 'looking' behaviour and husbands who are adjusted in their marriages. Ellyson observes that these husbands both looked at and listened to their wives when their wives spoke to them. The 'looking' behaviour required as a communication strategy for people with acquired hearing loss does in fact facilitate intimate relationships much more generally.

In a similar way, 'repetition' has been discovered to be of greater value than conventionally realized (Ree 1999). Tannen (1989) argues that repetition is a pervasive, fundamental, infinitely useful conversational strategy. It has varied purposes, for example, production, comprehension, connection and interaction. In addition, it gives poetry its rhythmical character and has been highly valued and studied in literary texts. Gertrude Stein said: 'Repeating then is in everyone, in everyone in their being and their feeling and their way of realising everything' (1935, p.214).

While resistance would be expected to requests for behaviour change along with the above interpretations of looking and repeating, the mere existence of the interpretations can be reassuring and hopeful to people who are hearing-impaired and their spouses.

Concluding remarks

This chapter has been an introduction to counselling people who have acquired hearing loss. On closing I would like to say something about what it is like for someone like myself who is a woman with an acquired hearing loss to work with people with a similar problem. Some time after my hearing loss became more of a major issue in my life and I began my research at the LSE, I decided to return to part-time work as a counsellor. I had previously worked for ten years as a Relate counsellor and knew I enjoyed working with couples. Now I sought to specialize in the area of problems experienced by people with hearing loss and their families. As mentioned earlier, I established HearSay to do this. For five years I worked exclusively in this area. In hindsight doing this appeared to be a way to re-root myself in a career that gave meaning to my own problem. My own hearing loss loomed very large at this time in that its existence was shaping my life in a way that it had never done before. Initially, to be honest, I had to work quite hard at identifying with my hearing-impaired clients as most of them had very different personalities and life styles from my own even though the disability was in common. I believe that some good and interesting work was done during this period and that I was particularly helpful as a role model. However, in saying this, there is no way of objectively measuring the part played by my own hearing loss in healing my clients. Also because I was experienced in general counselling before developing in a specialist area, I could discriminate much more clearly how some problems were the result of hearing loss, while others resulted from altogether different factors.

As my counselling experience and research developed, my empathetic range and confidence also grew. Even though my hearing loss was gradually getting worse, it appeared less and less of an issue on every level. During this process, which I will describe as a gradual reclaiming of my extrovert personality, I found myself counselling people who responded well to my more warm interactional counselling style. I recall a particular turning point was attending the 1994 British Association for Counselling annual training conference at the University of Keele. I felt comfortable attending this meeting along with the accompanying workshops. One on disability led by Julia Segal comes particularly to mind. For the first time I was invited to become a member of what is now called BACP (British Association for Counselling and Psychotherapy) and to register in their directory.

Unfortunately, because most hearing-impaired people cannot afford my current fees, I see very few people with acquired hearing loss. My experience suggests that my empathetic range, lip-reading ability and fee are the three factors guiding the parameters of my private practice at the time of writing. My disability and gender appear to come through as third and fourth factors of importance. I hope that my disability will become more useful once again when I acquire the funding for my hoped-for institute.

I would like to emphasize once again that this chapter is introductory and makes no attempt at presenting an exhaustive account of the issues involved when counselling people with hearing loss. It is, I feel, a very interesting and exciting area to work in as both counsellor and researcher since many of the issues are subtle and complex and not necessarily, at first sight, what they appear to be.

References

Allan, G. (1989) *Friendships: Developing a Sociological Perspective.* London: Harvester Wheatsheaf.

Attwell, N. and Watts, F. (1987) 'Hearing therapy and hearing loss.' In J. Kyle (ed) *Adjustment to Acquired Hearing Loss.* Bristol: Centre for Deaf Studies, pp.231–237.

Barry, J. (l995) 'Care-needs and care-receivers: view from the margins.' In R. Edwards and J. Ribbons (eds) *Women's Studies International Forum – Special Issue ,18,* 245–383.

Burfield, D. and Casey, J. (1987) 'Psychosocial problems and adaptation of the deafened adult.' In J.G. Kyle (ed) *Adjustment to Acquired Hearing Loss.* Bristol: Centre for Deaf studies, The University of Bristol, 176–182.

Corker, M. (1994) *Counselling – The Deaf Challenge.* London: Jessica Kingsley Publishers.

Corker, M. (1996) *Deaf Transitions: Images and Origins of Deaf Families, Deaf Communities and Deaf Identities.* London: Jessica Kingsley Publishers.

DHSS-ACSHIP (l975) Services for hearing-impaired People. *Report of a Sub-committee Appointed to Consider the Rehabilitation of the Adult hearing-impaired.* London: HMSO.

DHSS-Circular HC(78)11) (1978) Department of Health and Social Security, Health Services Development. *Appointment of Hearing Therapists.* London: HMSO.

Dueck, E. (1984) Interview with author at Guys Hospital, St Thomas Street. 10 May l984.

Elliott, H., Glass, L. and William Evans, J. (1987) *Mental Health Assessment of Deaf Clients: A Practical Manual.* San Diego: College Hill.

Ellyson, S.L. (1974) 'Visual behaviour exhibited by males differing as to interpersonal control orientation in one- and two-way communication systems.' Unpublished master thesis. Cited in R.G. Harper, A.N. Wiens and J.D. Matarazzo (1978) *Nonverbal Communication: The State of the Art.* New York: Wiley.

Erikson, E.H. (1965) *Childhood and Society.* London: Paladin Grafton Books.

Evening Standard (1999) ' Deaf Before Her Time.' 20 July 1999.

Feldman, L.B. (1979) 'Marital conflict and marital intimacy: An integrative pschodynamic-behavioral systemic model.' *Family Process 18,* 69–78.

Glickman, N. (1986) 'Cultural identity, deafness and mental health.' *Journal of Rehabilitation of the Deaf 20,* 2, l–l0.

Goffman, E. (1963) *Stigma.* Harmondsworth: Penguin.

Harvey, M. A. (1989) *Psychotherapy with Deaf and Hard of Hearing Persons.* London: Lawrence Erbaum.

Harvey, M.A. (1998) *Odyssey of Hearing Loss, Tales of Triumph.* San Diego: Dawn Sign Press.

Hegarty, S., Pocklington, K. and Crowe, M. (1983) *The Making of a Profession: A Study of the Training and Work of the First Hearing Therapists.* London: Chameleon Press.

Hyman, H.H. (1942) 'The psychology of status.' *Archives of Psychology 269.*

Jones, L., Kyle, J. and Wood, P. (1987) *Words Apart: Losing Your Hearing As An Adult.* London: Tavistock.

Kohut, H. (1971) *The Analysis of Self.* New York: International: Universities Press.

Kubler Ross, E. (1970) *On Death and Dying.* London: Macmillan.

McGill, D. and Pearce, D. (1982) 'British families.' In M. McGolderick, J.K. Pearce and J. Giordano (eds) *Ethnicity and Family Therapy.* London: Guilford Press, 457–479.

Morgan-Jones, R. (1984) 'Playing it by ear.' *Marriage Guidance,* Autumn, 24–31.

Morgan-Jones, K. (1998) 'Increasing the challenge.' *Horn Magazine 6,* 3, 18–19.

Morgan-Jones, R. (2001) *Hearing Differently: Impact of Hearing Impairment on Family Life.* London: Whurr.

Noller, P. (1984) *Nonverbal Communication and Marital Interaction.* Queensland: Pergamon Press.

Padden, C. (1989) Interview by author with Professor of Communications, University of California, San Diego, 28 August.

Ree, J. (1999) *I See a Voice.* London: HarperCollins.

Romano, M. (1984) 'The impact of disability on family and society.' In J.V. Basmajian (ed) *Foundations of Medical Rehabilitation.* Baltimore: Williams and Wilkens.

Royal National Institute for the Deaf Research Group (1990) *Statistics Relating to Deafness.* October.

Stein, G. (1935) *The Gradual Making of 'The Making of Americans' Lectures in America.* New York: Random House.

Sussman, A. (1986) 'Psychotherapy and deafness.' Course at Fremont School for the Deaf, Fremont, California.

Tannen, D. (1986) *That's Not What I Meant: How Conversation Style Makes or Breaks Relationships.* New York: Ballantine.

Tannen, D. (1989) *Talking Voices, Repetition, Dialogue, and Imagery in Conversational Discourse.* Cambridge: Cambridge University Press.

Tannen, D. (1991) *You Just Don't Understand.* New York: Ballantine.

Wax, T. (1989) 'Assessment dilemmas of late-onset hearing loss.' In H. Sloss Luey, H. Elliott and L. Glass (eds) *Mental Health Assessment of Deaf Clients.* Proceedings of conference, San Francisco, 12–13 February.

Chapter 7

Counselling People with Ulcerative Colitis Choosing an Internal Pouch

Rehabilitating the Hidden Self

Gillian B. Thomas

Introduction

I have been involved in counselling people with inflammatory bowel disease for nearly 15 years, about half as long as I have had the disease myself. I chose this area of work in answer to my own need to comprehend and mitigate an experience which would otherwise have been wholly negative (would still be wholly negative as, after three decades, the disease is even now in yet another period of activity). When I was first diagnosed there was no one to whom I could talk openly and freely about my feelings. I realized that there must be others in the same situation and so, for me, began the long work of changing this.

Patients with inflammatory bowel disease (known as ibd) have often been considered psychologically as well as physically flawed. Initially the disease was held to be an external, physical expression of an internal, psychological turmoil which, due to their inhibited, immature nature, these patients refused to vent in a healthy manner as anger, frustration or grief (Almay 1980). (If this were true, then the research evidence that getting patients to recognize and express emotions openly **cured** ibd, seems notable by its absence.) Thus until relatively recently many patients with inflammatory bowel disease were condemned not only to suffer a distressing and embarrassing disease, but also to be labelled as psychologically inadequate – a view which, despite research findings to the contrary (North *et al.* 1990) is still extant amongst some psychological therapists (Magni *et al.* 1991; Smith *et al.* 1995).

This notwithstanding, more enlightened approaches have generally prevailed and organizations such as the National Association for Colitis and Crohn's disease (NACC) have also radically altered the standing of people with ibd. With the support of NACC I undertook a major research study into the place of counselling in the care of people affected by inflammatory bowel disease. That study took an overview of the experiences and counselling needs of patients, but in this chapter I want to focus on a very particular group of clients – those who had ulcerative colitis severe enough to warrant a major surgical intervention and who chose the option of an internal pouch rather than an external stoma.

It is important to state that most people (around 80%) with ulcerative colitis will not require surgery for their disease. I am amongst that 80 per cent at present, but working with those for whom surgery is necessary, particularly when my own disease is active, means careful attention to both my professional and personal needs. An informed, supportive supervisor and a strong, empathetic counsellor are absolute requirements at this time. For an increasing number of the 20 per cent of ulcerative colitis patients who do require surgery, there will be a choice of procedures.

In this chapter I have amalgamated the experiences of four clients who chose and were able to have a pouch. With such a small number it cannot be claimed that their experiences are typical or representative. But they spoke openly and honestly about their feelings during one of the most traumatic periods of their lives and for that reason, if no other, what they had to say is of importance to those of us who work with people in the struggle to 'make able again' a life that has changed for ever.

For the past 12 years I have worked as a specialist counsellor within a large gastroenterology unit in a hospital in the south of England. The people I see are mainly referred by members of the gastroenterology team, although a few come from other gastroenterology units in hospitals further afield. The number of people in the UK affected by ibd is rising and although research into new treatments, both medical and surgical, is ongoing, the cause of (and therefore the cure for) the disease is currently unknown. Ibd is at best an extremely unpleasant disease to live with and can, at worst, be devastating. Counselling people with ibd requires a degree of courage, resolve and endurance – qualities which the patients themselves display in abundance.

What is inflammatory bowel disease?

Inflammatory bowel disease (ibd), is the collective term for two ongoing diseases of the intestines – ulcerative colitis and Crohn's disease. **The initials ibd are often confused with ibs or irritable bowel syndrome, but the conditions are entirely separate.** Ibd affects approximately 120,000 men and women in Britain, about 1 in 600 of the population. People of all ages can contract the disease but the 8000 new cases every year are predominantly amongst a younger age group, usually between 15 and 35 years of age.

The symptoms of ibd are distressing on account of both their nature and the system of the body they affect. People with ibd can experience severe and sometimes uncontrollable diarrhoea, pain, fever, lethargy and blood loss, as well as other extra-intestinal symptoms such as skin, joint or eye problems. The symptoms, which fluctuate unpredictably, can give rise to much anguish, embarrassment and shame. Although medical treatment, often including the use of steroids to dampen inflammation can help to alleviate the condition, sometimes surgery is required.

Surgery

In severe cases of ibd the entire colon from the ileum (where it joins the small intestine) to the anus may have to be removed. The cut end of the small intestine is then brought out onto the abdominal wall via a spout-like opening called a stoma through which waste products from the small intestine are discharged. The patient has no control over the evacuation of waste and thus there is the necessity of having to wear a bag over the stoma. This operation, which has been well tried and tested over 50 years, is known as a permanent ileostomy and may bring great relief of symptoms for patients with both ulcerative colitis and Crohn's disease, but at an obvious price. However, in the last 20 years or so it has been possible to offer patients with ulcerative colitis an alternative option – the ileal reservoir or internal pouch. In this procedure the colon (or large intestine) and the rectum are removed and the end of the small bowel is cut open and folded and stitched together to form an internal pouch-like receptacle. This is then joined to the sphincter muscles just above the anus. This procedure is usually performed in two or three separate operations to allow time for adequate healing before the next stage is attempted. The aim is that the pouch thus created will store waste products inside the body until voluntary evacuation takes place.

Since ulcerative colitis affects only the colon, its removal and the formation of a pouch using the unaffected small intestine is a logical and viable procedure. Because Crohn's disease can affect any site in the alimentary tract, including the small intestine, forming a pouch from this tissue is not a viable option and therefore this operation cannot usually be offered to those with Crohn's disease.

The pouch

The pouch has two immediate advantages over an ileostomy. It does not require the wearing of an external bag and, since the anal sphincter muscles are retained, it offers continence and control over evacuation of the bowel. On the basis of body image and perceived preservation of sexual appeal, ulcerative colitis patients may consider the pouch to be a much more attractive proposition than an ileostomy (Nicholls 1983).

If there are no surgical reasons precluding the formation of a pouch, the decision whether to have an ileostomy or a pouch will lie with the patient. If the patient has been extremely ill with ulcerative colitis – perhaps feeling tired and unwell, needing to use the lavatory dozens of times a day and losing bowel continence – the prospect of relief from these symptoms and a better quality of health is so welcome that the form it takes may be immaterial. Because ulcerative colitis occurs only in the colon, its removal means that the disease is effaced from the body and if the ileostomy brings no problems of its own normal health will be resumed. Indeed, because of its proven track record and because only one operation is required, some patients will choose an ileostomy even when a pouch is possible. But for many patients the thought of having to wear 'the bag' can be profoundly unacceptable. Even people whose health has so relentlessly (albeit gradually) deteriorated that they have had to normalize a grossly abnormal quality of life may nevertheless state that this is preferable to having an ileostomy. Often recently diagnosed patients will say that they 'would rather die than have that done to me'. For many, the thought of sexual contact with another person whilst wearing a bag is extraordinarily daunting (Burnham 1977), especially where a stable relationship has not yet been formed.

Information

The pouch procedure can be much more onerous than the formation of an ileostomy and there are a number of possible complications, particularly immediately post-operatively. It is recognized that patients must have full information about the possible disadvantages as well as the advantages of the pouch since they need to be fully committed to the procedure. Thus material in many different formulations is available: written, audio, video and electronic. Pouch patients' groups also offer information and experiences from pouch owners, as well as the opportunity for putative pouch patients to speak personally to those who already have had the procedure.

Counselling issues around ileostomies and pouches

As a counsellor for people with ibd, the question or actuality of ileostomy and pouch surgery will arise for a significant minority of clients. Some are referred to counselling when surgery is first mooted while some are pre-existing clients whose condition gradually or suddenly reaches the point where surgery becomes inevitable. The counsellor's role, which is well understood by the gastroenterology team, is not to gain the client's compliance but to allow and encourage clients to explore all the thoughts and emotions around their situation. Because of the level of illness most clients will have experienced or currently be experiencing as a result of their ibd, most seem able to accept that they need some form of additional intervention. They may well wish to explore possibilities other than surgery, such as a change in drug therapy, an increase in current medication or alternative therapies, although many will have had a long enough relationship with their medical consultant to recognize that surgery has not been mentioned lightly.

Many clients will arrive at an awareness that surgery may be the only option if there is to be a chance of achieving a worthwhile quality of life. Giving people sufficient time and space fully to express all their fears and doubts about surgery can allow them to make a decision they had hoped never to face. The people affected by ulcerative colitis whom I have counselled have been rigorous in their investigation of the choice before them and I have been impressed by their thorough consideration of the merits and pitfalls of each procedure. In every case of clients who chose the pouch, their actual experiences contained elements for which the information available had in no way prepared them. It was striking how many of these issues affected all the clients and how much of what was said by any one individual resonated with what was said by the others.

Pre-operative concerns

What follows are observations based on the four clients mentioned earlier in this chapter. Acceptance that surgery is necessary is hard. Clients spoke of the realization that not only could they not 'get well' without it, but that 'getting well' would have to be redefined. It was no longer about getting back to the way things were before the disease. The surgery would bring a new version of what constituted 'well'. The clients in question were still young, but they felt they had lost so much of their youth to the illness. At this moment of reflection, clients also felt that they could afford to admit to themselves how much they had had to integrate illness into their lives. One client observed that her middle-aged parents had more energy than she had. When a surgeon spoke to a client who had to have an emergency temporary ileostomy three months previously about the possibility of conversion to a pouch, she spoke of the chaos of her feelings about even more changes being made to her body. Her initial experience in hospital had been traumatic and she felt that the pouch procedure was one more thing going to be 'done to' her. She was also managing quite well with the temporary ileostomy and wondered if she should 'go looking for problems'.

All the clients articulated concerns of a spiritual as well as physical and emotional nature. This was particularly well illustrated by one client who spoke of the forthcoming removal of his colon as 'evisceration'. Having ulcerative colitis had always made him feel different and the prospect of this operation strengthened the feeling. This client spoke of immanent 'unwholeness' and possible 'spiritual unacceptability' if part of him was removed. He wondered what manner of being he would be post-operatively. He felt he would be rendered 'a mutation', something unacceptable to that which had created him. These feelings were not related to any overt religious belief on the client's part, but seemed to come from a deep spiritual sense of what constituted 'a human being'. Indeed the somewhat biblical connotations of the language commonly used about the pouch reinforced this sense of the profundity of what was about to be undertaken. The pouch is often spoken of as being 'created' or 'fashioned' and, witnessing this client articulating his distress about his spiritual acceptability, I was reminded of Job's cry of hope and belief 'And though … worms destroy this body, yet in my flesh shall I see God'. In what form would this client be 'reincarnated', as he had originally been created or as he had been refashioned? There was no response possible to such revelations except the preservation of a deeply respectful, open silence.

In order to explore the physical implications of such a vast change, we conjured another, much more mundane image of an identity parade in which the client was taking part. He could not be distinguished from the others until an X-ray machine was used and then his alien status would be revealed. The word 'alien' occurred many times with clients. Clients with ileostomies frequently spoke of their stomas as 'alien' in the early stages, but the fact that the pouch was hidden did not seem to alleviate this feeling. Indeed it almost seemed to make the alien-ness even greater. A client (echoing Goffman 1963) talked of her ability to '"pass" as someone ordinary' whereas inside her body (and her head) she was so different.

Eventually clients committed themselves to the surgery, whatever it would bring. In most cases this decision was supported by their families who had seen the effects of the illness upon them. However, not everyone close to the clients was necessarily of the same opinion. One client spoke of his contemporaries urging him not to accept such a radical option and advocating the investigation of alternative approaches. The client, despite his own fears and uncertainties, felt that their suggestions were unrealistic and betrayed their profound lack of understanding of his situation. In fact he felt their stance was cruel 'the tyranny of the alternative approach,' as he put it. Watching clients go through the pre-operative stage, knowing some of what **might** await them, knowing nothing of what **would** await them, was painful. The clients longed to know if they were making the right decision. I could only hope to support them in making the best decision they could.

As the time for the operation drew nearer clients experienced great anxiety over this issue of choice. Those who had chosen the pouch were aware they needed to have hope and belief that the pouch would work for them. The fact that a permanent ileostomy would still be available should the pouch fail was known to them, but certainly not one they wished even remotely to contemplate at this stage. A client who had been very unwell for a long time before the operation was worried that he might still be unwell even after undergoing surgery. There seemed to be no certainties. Although families could be supportive, sometimes their intense desire for a successful outcome for their loved one could be experienced as oppressive. One client spoke of the necessity to keep optimistic for the family's sake, whereas the reality was fear, uncertainty and indecision right up to the day of surgery.

Post-operative concerns

Some clients would ask me to visit them after surgery whilst they were inpatients. At these visits, whilst there was relief that the operation was over, there was shock at the reality of the magnitude of the surgery. Understanding the theory of what had been done, and why, was different from experiencing it. This shift from knowledge to actual personal experience seemed to have the effect of distancing clients from those looking after them. This was true even if the surgery had gone as expected, but was even more marked if there had been complications. At a later stage clients talked about this time as one of great fear and loneliness. They felt that few people were able or willing to try to understand how they felt and believed that this was because their distress was too powerful and thus too painful for others to bear. One client who had had severe complications said that she felt the staff 'concentrated on the problem, the mechanics, the situation'. Whilst she appreciated that this was necessary, she was devastated that 'they never seem to focus on me'. She described herself as 'merely the pouch carrier' and felt that if she did not cope she would be 'failing the pouch'. She believed that her complications were such that no one knew quite what to do with her and therefore everyone needed her to be brave and stoical – a situation she found quite terrifying. She felt that in order to cope with the multiple problems she was having, the health professionals had had to put aside their own natural human feelings, but the result for her was that she was left feeling inhuman. It was a relief for this client to let all this be known to someone not directly involved, who could therefore allow her to express feelings that, having been deemed unacceptable and dangerous, had had to be suffered alone.

Another client spoke of the fact that although the medical and surgical care were excellent, his feelings were simply not understood by his attendants. He had been unprepared for the amount of pain, which he described as 'like a tidal wave'. He felt that the shock this had been to him was not appreciated by most of his carers. His experience had been overwhelming – 'those first few days are burnt into my memory' – but he felt that the gap between what he had felt and the way in which he had been treated had been an unbridgeable abyss.

Living with the pouch

After leaving hospital and a period of recovery, if all goes well, the temporary ileostomy can be closed and the pouch fully rejoined to the small intestine. This is a smaller operation than the formation of the pouch, but it is at this point the pouch is commissioned and the new system is put to the test for the first time. It was usually some weeks after this that clients returned to counselling again. Not all of them chose to do so. For some people it seemed that the counselling was firmly associated with the pre-operative period, a time in their lives which they wished to leave behind. I had noticed the same phenomenon previously with some clients who had had ileostomies. I appeared to represent the 'bad old days' and their natural desire was to get on with their lives. Perhaps the same was true with some pouch patients.

However those who did wish to resume counselling usually kept up some contact in the interim via telephone or letter. Actually seeing clients again was a moving occasion. The physical changes that had been wrought in them were hidden but because I was privileged to be their witness I saw the effects of those changes in their eyes. I knew that some of them had been through dreadful experiences that they were attempting to understand and that all of them had been through a major event, which to the outside world simply did not show.

The counselling period following the final operation can include intense and powerful work. For one client, it was not the first time she had had her pouch rejoined. She had had numerous severe problems with both the pouch and the temporary ileostomy. She had had to live with the ileostomy for a considerable length of time and thus its eventual removal felt very strange. She described the sensation as 'like having a phantom limb. I wake up and for a moment I think it is still there' (see Salter 1992, p.846). She knew that she wanted to begin to integrate the experience into her life (which seemed to correspond with integrating the pouch into her body), but felt that her medical experience had in no way prepared her for the task. She spoke of hospitals 'processing' patients and 'shooting them out the other end with no idea of how we are to live and become whole'.

Another client who resumed counselling about three months after her operation was experiencing anaemia and a degree of pouchitis (inflammation of the pouch) – not uncommon problems post-operatively – and was having to get up several times at night to empty the pouch (which is frequently the case while it is settling down). She was also getting used to the new bodily sensations that told her when she needed to empty the pouch and whether the pouch was properly empty. She was physically exhausted. She was aware that she needed time and peace to 'rethink' herself and to refashion her body image which had been 'totally smashed'. This all came at a time when both health professionals and those close to her were urging her to 'be well again' and to 'put it all behind her'. She felt that because the results of the surgery were hidden 'people feel it is all the same as it was – getting back to "normal", but it is not "normal"'. She knew that she had to create a new body map, but others seemed unaware of this requirement. There seemed to be no recognition of the huge shock to both her physical and emotional systems and she felt very lonely.

Making emotional adjustments

As time passed and clients grew stronger they began to speak more freely about the most frightening and painful episodes they had endured. For one client this was triggered by a problem with the pouch which made her afraid to return to hospital. She spoke of a previous examination which she described as 'excruciating. The worst pain I've ever experienced. Like passing broken glass, crushed and rebroken'. At this time she was also experiencing flashbacks to her stay in hospital when, shortly after surgery, she had been through a procedure that had left her 'terrified and humiliated'.

Another client said that what had happened to her was so horrendous that the health professionals attending her seemed to wish her to erase it from her memory, something that was of course impossible. She wondered how on earth then could 'everyday people' grasp what had happened to her. How could they believe what she had been through? She went on to say that since she had first had ulcerative colitis as a young girl she had been told she should 'not dwell upon it, not have feelings about it, just "get on with it"'. She strongly believed that this was recommended solely for the benefit of other people.

Clients seemed to need time and space in which to begin to grasp the enormous changes they had sustained. Three months after the pouch operation, one client spoke of the profound change to her anatomy and allied it to the profound change in what constituted 'herself'. Together we imagined her drawing an outline round her body to include all that was 'her'. When she had the temporary ileostomy, the line had initially excluded the bag which was 'not her', or 'alien'. Gradually, as time went on, the bag began to merge into the line becoming, as she put it, 'quasi me'. (She expressed the view that had it been permanent it might later have become 'fully me'.) But with a pouch, because it was internal, how could such a definitive line ever be drawn? It is true to say that, unlike an organ transplant, the tissue involved is 'me' but it has been reassigned and put to another use. Her body image had been 'exploded'. Whilst this client was grappling with these immense issues, an old school friend of hers, who happened to be a health professional in another field, offered the opinion that she was 'too fixated on her bum'.

This client's workplace was very supportive and she returned to work at a local branch of the organization. A few months later she was offered a much desired training place at an office on the other side of the country. She was concerned about whether she could cope with what would be required of her and was having dreams filled with anxiety and dread. In particular she dreamed that everyone on the course had been allocated a room in which to live. The room she had been allocated contained her hospital bed. Although still experiencing some problems with the pouch, she felt her body was in the process of healing. Her mind too was hard at work healing itself of wounds as unseen as those of the pouch.

It seemed that the emotional repair work needing to be done could only take place once the physical healing was well under way. One client found that she needed to go back over the trauma of the whole of the past three years starting with the sudden onset of the disease and her first hospitalization. At this time she'd been unable to process any emotional material and had handled the situation by 'living it in the third person'. She now needed to integrate that experience, but was having to battle with both those who desperately wanted her to be 'well' and those who, whilst actually having no idea of the enormity of what she had been through, encouraged her 'to leave it behind her now'. She said that their rationale was that because she now **looked** all right, she must **be** all right. She was aware of a judgemental, internalized voice that agreed with this reasoning, telling her that she **should** now be well, but she also understood that this did not allow her time for emotional healing. Another client took the time to tell and retell the entire desperate story of her illness and the horrors that she had endured over many years as a result. She was at this time not yet 30 years of age. We likened this work to the recounting of heroic sagas, which in order to be heard and honoured were accorded a special time and a sacred place for their telling.

Living with a refashioned self

Trying to 'refashion' the self after pouch surgery was an ongoing task. A client whose pouch was still in the 'settling down' phase (pouch owners report that this can take around two years) commented that she could not 'get a fix on myself. Who, what, how am I? Well or ill?' She was experiencing some pouch problems which led her to say of her pouch, 'Is this the illness or the cure?' This was further exacerbated in this client's case due to the fact that since her ulcerative colitis was of sudden and devastating onset she did not have any real experience of living with its attrition. She had been 'well' and then suddenly 'ill'. It was difficult for her to say, as so many clients could, that 'this may be hard to deal with but it is so much better than living with ibd'. She also revealed that she made a point of eating something not recommended for a pouch owner every day. In that way she would have something to blame if the pouch did not function properly. She was scared to eat a totally recommended diet because if the pouch did not function well after that she might have to accept that things could not be made any better.

For many people the pouch settles down well and their quality of life improves radically. Others have problems that mean they are having actively to 'cope' with their pouch years after the original operation. This situation seems to mean that the emotional coping has to go on too. One such client was in a dilemma regarding accepting a new job. She was ready to move on from the job she was in, but afraid of what might lie ahead. Her current workplace had been extremely accommodating with her operation and the subsequent problems. Would the new people be as understanding? In filling in the health form she could honestly state that she did not have any ongoing illness, but she certainly had ongoing needs related to her health. Would stressing or even mentioning these needs jeopardize her chances?

We also thought about what she would say to her pouch if she could. She immediately said that if she could have one wish, it would be that her pouch could talk to her. She would ask, What bothered it, what it liked, what it did not like. She explained her wish by saying that a stoma was an external entity so its state could be observed and appropriate remedial action taken when required. With a pouch there were no obvious signs. 'You don't know what's happening and whether it's happy or unhappy.' She was still having to plan her life around the suitability, accessibility and privacy of loos, in a way similar to before she'd had the operation. 'And I'm supposed to be cured!' This led her to reflect upon what was meant or what she meant by 'cured'. Just what was acceptable? Did she have an acceptable quality of life? And acceptable to whom? She added that although she did not even wish to think it, she also wanted to be able to voice what she felt she could not voice elsewhere – that maybe the pouch was not working for her.

When the pouch does work well for a client, especially after a difficult start, all the pain, both physical and emotional, can be seen as meaningful and ultimately valuable. Clients spoke of a new start to their lives, new confidence in their bodies and a new pleasure in living.

I make no claim that the clients I have seen are representative of the majority of pouch patients. It could be argued that, since they were referred to a counsellor, they constituted a group in which psychological difficulties were more to the fore. But it could also be argued that what singled out these clients was that they were presented with the opportunity to talk about what they were feeling and, insofar as what each one said had echoes with the concerns of the others, possibly these feelings are more common than is realized. I am sure at least that the emotional impact on the patient of having a pouch procedure is not generally fully appreciated, perhaps because the pouch is internal rather than external. The necessary surgical work is so genuinely brilliant and sophisticated that the concomitant necessary emotional work can be unrecognized by health professionals. Clients spoke of feeling totally unprepared for this 'emotional aftershock' which they did not feel was explained or discussed adequately, if at all, beforehand. One client reflected that it would have been of immense help to her if the doctor had even briefly mentioned that there were emotional ramifications to having a pouch procedure. It would have prepared her and allowed her to be more comfortable and at ease with the idea of emotional as well as physical healing time.

That fundamental issues of a philosophical nature should figure so strongly in the work to be done was surprising at the time, but in retrospect, given the nature of the surgery, seems entirely appropriate. Work done with pouch clients has been some of the most rewarding of my career. Seeing a client through from the first suggestions of surgery to an outcome more successful than either of us could have dreamed is heady stuff. Even when things are less than perfect, this work seems to create a depth of relationship that makes a particular bond between client and counsellor. A client said that she felt proud at having survived all that she had. Perhaps a counsellor who has witnessed a journey of that magnitude cannot help but feel the reflection of such an accomplishment.

Reflections

Although there is a dearth of research material on the psychological experiences and needs of pouch patients (Beitz 1999), there are phenomenological studies by specialist nurses and accounts by patients themselves describing the lived experience of having a pouch (Beitz 1999; Salter 1992; Walls 2001). What I have read tends to reinforce my tentative view that what the clients I have seen felt was not unique to them (although the individual experience that encompassed the feeling was). There seemed to be broad areas which the clients shared, perhaps the most telling of which was their utter unpreparedness for the psychological and emotional shock of having a pouch.

The literature available for patients is largely technical in nature, describing what to eat, how to manage the function of the pouch, care of the anal skin, possible pouch problems, etc. Whilst knowing about these things is undoubtedly valuable to patients, there is seldom mention of psychological matters. The clients felt that the message given therefore was that normal people had no psychological issues to deal with and that having them was a sign of weakness. This was unfortunately reinforced by certain of the patient accounts of living with a pouch that were relentlessly cheerful and upbeat in tone. Humour is such an individual matter that what may be funny to one person can be horrifying to another. The noises and smells that can accompany pouch emptying may have to be accommodated by all pouch patients and humour can have its place, but these things can also be a cause of great distress which 'toilet humour' then exacerbates rather than ameliorates. One client was appalled by the 'forced cuteness' of this approach and felt that it demeaned and diminished her experience. When patients do reveal their true feelings (Walls 2001) the results can be extraordinarily moving and undoubtedly affirming to others.

Both the literature and the clients also agreed upon the need for pouch patients to have time and space to discuss their feelings, without the pressure of health professionals deciding how long this should be (Salter 1992). This is not something that can easily be accomplished on a busy ward. Perhaps this is where counselling from someone informed on the subject but outside the immediate situation can play its part.

Life with a pouch can be very good for many patients, but it is not as good as life with a healthy colon. In order to arrive at a newly fashioned self, a self 'made able' again that can accept and accommodate this truth, a long and arduous journey negotiated with the most delicate manoeuvring is required. Many health professionals will have their part to play along the way, but if at a very human level a companion is required for part of the journey, perhaps it is the counsellor who can best provide that special and privileged service.

References

Almay, T.P. (1980) 'Psychosocial aspects of chronic ulcerative colitis and Crohn's disease.' In J.B. Kirsner and R.G. Shorter (eds) *Inflammatory Bowel Disease* 2nd. Edn. Philadelphia: Lea and Febinger, pp.44–54.

Beitz, J. M. (1999) 'The lived experience of having an ileoanal reservoir: a phenomenologic study.' *Journal of Wound, Ostomy and Continence Nursing 26*, 4, 185–200.

Burnham, W. et al. (1997) 'Sexual problems amongst married ileostomists.' *GUT 18*, 673–677.

Goffman, E. (1963) *Stigma. Notes on the Management of Spoiled Identity.* Harmondsworth: Penguin.

Magni, G., Mauro, P., D'odorico, A., Sturnido, G.C., Canton G., Martin, A. (1991) 'Psychiatric diagnosis in ulcerative colitis. A controlled study.' *British Journal of Psychiatry. Mar. 1991, 158,* 413–415.

Nicholls, R. (1983) 'Proctocolectomy: avoiding an ileostomy.' *Nursing Mirror 156*, 7, 46–47.

North, C.S., Clouse, R.E., Spitznagel, E.L. And Alpers, D.H. (1990) 'The relation of ulcerative colitis to psychiatric factors: a review of findings and methods.' *American Journal of Psychiatry 147*, 8, 974–981.

Salter, M.J. (1992) 'What are the differences in body image between patients with a conventional stoma compared with those who have had a conventional stoma followed by a continent pouch?' *Journal of Advanced Nursing 17*, 841–848.

Smith, G.J.W. Van de Meer, G., Ursing, B., Prytz, H. And Benoni, C.(1995) 'Psychological profile of patients suffering from Crohn's disease and ulcerative colitis.' *Acta Psychiatrica Scandinavica 92*, 3, 187–192.

Walls, S. (2001) 'Gusty to gutless in 24 hours.' *Roar!* Newsletter of the Red Lion Group St Mark's Hospital Watford Road Harrow Middlesex HA1 UJ, 19, 1–2, 15.

Chapter 8

Counselling in Mental Health Rehabilitation

Kevin Brenton

Introduction

The shift of philosophy in the last decade from the purely functionalist biomedical model of mental health care to a more holistic standpoint has added credibility to the use of psychosocial and psychological interventions alongside traditional psychiatry.

I currently work as a team leader for an assertive outreach team within the setting of mental health rehabilitation in an NHS trust in West Sussex. I achieved registration as a mental health nurse some 15 years ago and I quickly felt constricted by the medicalization of mental health with its emphasis on the treatment of the 'diseased' body that apparently took little account of preventative health care or the social aspects of health and illness. Having worked for the last 12 years solely in the area of mental health rehabilitation, the emphasis in the late 1980s on psychoeducational and psychosocial interventions for people with severe mental illness and their families had a big impact on my professional growth. The increasing acceptance of these types of interventions brought to the fore an array of effective and well-researched alternative approaches, which in turn created an arena that allowed me to work with my patients in a more holistic and humanistic way. I undertook a variety of workshops and short courses in counselling skills in the early 1990s, particularly within a client-centred model. However, it was my undertaking an MSc, to train as a rehabilitation counsellor, that afforded me my greatest personal growth and professional development. In this chapter I will explore how my own growth and the insights I have been afforded with regard to the counselling process have impacted on my work in the mental health field.

I believe it is important to state at this point, however, that I do not dismiss any previous way of being. I merely accept that the position from which I experience my environment changes as part of an ongoing process of movement and that any previous position of experiencing and relating to others was necessary for me at that moment. To disregard or criticize previous facets of myself is surely to disregard growth. Mearns and Thorne (1988 p.37) argued that 'the work on the self can never be complete and the counsellor is confronted by a lifetime's task if she is to remain faithful to her commitment'. If this sounds unduly demanding it needs to be remembered that counselling is about change and development and I believe that an unchanging counsellor is well on the way to becoming a professional charlatan.

Rehabilitation in mental health

The field of mental health rehabilitation can encompass a huge range of disabling conditions, from severe and enduring psychotic or bipolar disorders to more transient affective disorders. In order to reflect on the concept of rehabilitation it is useful to reflect on the concept of disability. There is lack of definition of the term 'disability' in that it has been defined in many ways throughout history depending on the structure and value systems of each society. Albrecht and Levy (1981) argued 'the fact that definitions of disability are relative, rather than absolute, has led to some sociologists in particular to conclude that disability can only be properly understood as a social construction' (cited in Swain *et al.* 1993, p.49). With this in mind it is important to distinguish the term 'disability' from individual impairment, be it physical or mental. Finkelstein (1980) defines impairment as lacking part or all of a limb or having a defective organ or mechanism of the body, and disability as a disadvantage of restriction of activity, caused by contemporary social organisation which takes no or little account of people who have physical impairments' (cited in Borsay 1986, p.183) The proposition that many psychiatric conditions are no more than social constructions has also been put forward. This school of theory became known as 'anti-psychiatry'. Szasz (1961) stated:

> Debate has raged over the past twenty years as to whether or not 'mental illness' exists in the way that physical illness does, or whether its treatment represents a clear example of a take-over of behavioral problems, and

problems of living, by psychiatrists. (Szasz 1961, cited Patrick and Scambler 1986, p.179).

Szasz argued that mental illness was a myth and that 'the notion of mental illness exists as a mechanism for social control, for medicalising, medicating, even incarcerating those regarded as social misfits' (cited in Kennedy 1981, p.100).

Therefore we can see that people experiencing disabling conditions are regarded as 'deviating' from the normal level of accepted functioning. Disability lies, not in their impairment, but the socially constructed values and expectations placed upon them by society. Wolfensburger (1983) defined the disabling of 'individuals by society' as 'social devaluation'. He described the need for society to adopt a new set of attitudes in order to revalue 'individuals at risk of devaluation', which became known as the principle of normalization. The fundamental principles of normalization are that disabled people have the same rights as anyone else, that disabled people have a right and a need to live like others in the community and that services must recognize the individuality of disabled people. The mission of psychiatric rehabilitation is to help individuals with psychiatric disabilities to 'increase their functioning so that they are successful and satisfied in the environments of their choice with the least amount of professional intervention' (Anthony, Cohen and Farkas 1990, p.151). This process is no different for people with mental health problems than for those with other major disabilities. It is a subjective experience of recovering a new sense of self and purpose within and beyond the limits of the disability (Deegan 1988).

If the concept of mental illness is viewed as a mechanism for social control, then it could be argued that one of the most potent aspects of the medicalization of the individual is the application by physicians of diagnostic labels. When an individual is labelled with a psychiatric diagnosis it usually has the unfortunate consequence of 'formally' setting them apart from 'normal' people. As Scambler (1997, p.173) argued, 'people's stigma can come to dominate the perceptions others have of them and how they treat them'. At this point their deviant status dominates all other aspects of their individual identity and they can be viewed in terms of their label, that is, 'mental' or 'schizophrenic' along with society's stereotype of that condition. This can often see people with mental illness shunned or socially isolated, and interactions can often be dismissive or belittling. This is over and above the individual's own impairment and the often disruptive symptoms they may be experiencing.

The counselling relationship

There has been significant research into and development of psychoeducational and psychosocial interventions with patients suffering from severe and enduring mental health problems and their families (Brenton 1997; Falloon *et al.* 1984; Gamble and Midence 1994; Huddleston 1992; Mueser, Gingerich and Rosenthal 1994). As previously stated, many clients have had difficult life events that go well beyond their illness and benefit from therapeutic interventions to move them past these experiences. Others may require ongoing psychosocial interventions to assist them not only to come to terms with the losses associated with having a chronic illness, but also to manage relapses in their condition. This can often involve enabling a greater understanding of their own idiosyncratic early warning signs that can indicate a change in their condition.

I use an integrated model of working with my clients that encompasses a variety of interventions. However, the empowering emphasis of the rehabilitation process means it is important to work from a person-centred perspective. Unlike more directive models of treatment or therapy, person-centred counselling is a facilitating process, where the emphasis is on the counsellor providing a milieu that empowers the client and is conducive to his reaching insights and growing by his own exploration of himself. In order for this to happen, the counsellor as well as the client must be open to change and growth. Rogers (1967, p.27) stated: 'Life, at its best, is a flowing, changing process in which nothing is fixed.'

As already stated, the counsellor needs to provide a climate that empowers the client. In this context, one area that warrants study must be the relationship that occurs between counsellor and client. Rogers (1967, p.33) argued that if he could provide a particular set of circumstances within the relationship, 'the other person will discover within himself the capacity to use that relationship for growth, and change, and personal development will occur'. However, the relationship also remains one of the most difficult concepts to study. Clarkson (1992) stated:

> It is difficult for a fish to study and discuss water since it is the very medium of its life. It is also difficult for psychotherapists and counsellors to study the relationship since it is the very 'water' in which we and our clients live and breathe and find our meaning. (Clarkson 1992, cited in Dryden 1992, p.2)

When considering the concept of the relationship, Carl Rogers stated:

> In my early professional years I was asking the question, how can I treat, or cure, or change this person? Now I would phrase the question this way: how can I provide a relationship, which this person may use, for his own personal growth? (Rogers 1967, p.32)

This statement holds considerable significance for me when reflecting on my earlier motivations for moving into a helping profession and, further still, the wish to study counselling. My background was in the very medicalized milieu of mental health nursing, with all the structured practicality and emphasis on control that remains the backbone of the clinical sciences. It ingrained in me a need to 'make better', to 'cure', to be responsible for creating change in my patients, always through a logical process of clinical interventions and procedures. It also led me on many occasions to feel a lack of contentment and doubt in my abilities to achieve the very demanding goals that I expected of myself.

Accepting the patient as a human being with rights and responsibilities has challenged the traditional conception of the 'patient' role and added credence to the concept of the 'therapeutic alliance'. The patient is given back a sense of control and empowered to become an active participant in the care package, central to which is a positive relationship with the therapist in which information is readily exchanged both ways and mutual expectations, responsibilities and goals are negotiated. I believe this creates challenges for the rehabilitation counsellor working in this field. In order truly to empower the clients it is important to deliver interventions on their terms as well as maintaining a professional credibility within current health-care systems. Rather than working in what is often viewed as 'elitist' isolation from other mental health disciplines such as CPNs or social workers, it is important that practitioners delivering psychosocial or other counselling interventions are fully integrated into multidisciplinary teams.

This can be seen quite clearly in the assertive community treatment (ACT) model. Originating in Canada and the USA, it has been widely evaluated and shown to be successful in using the community as the treatment arena (Kirkpatrick and Landeen 1999). A modernized version of this model, referred to as assertive outreach teams (AOT), is now being implemented across the UK as part of the national service frameworks for mental health. Key elements of the AOT model include working 'in vivo' in the client's own environment, low client-to-staff ratio, higher frequency and length of contact, and a multidisciplinary team case management approach. The team approach allows a blurring of the boundaries between disciplines in order to deliver a wide range of psychosocial interventions on the client's own terms. Whilst maintaining a recognition and respect for the professional philosophies and specialized skills that each discipline contributes, the model also takes account of the generic core business of the team that is undertaken by all disciplines.

Personal counselling

It is important that the counsellor is able effectively to create an environment which the client may safely use to explore areas of the self that may be painful. I believe that counsellors have a responsibility to explore themselves in sufficient depth to maintain self-awareness of what they bring to the relationship. Personal counselling has been a valuable and enriching part of my growth, both as a practitioner and a person, particularly in highlighting my own areas of resistance. Having been enthused by the prospect of entering a counselling relationship, I recall how I used the time in the early sessions very superficially, carefully avoiding issues that felt uncomfortable. On later reflection this was a very necessary part of the process for me initially. It allowed the relationship to develop until it no longer seemed threatening and I felt myself to be in a safe place. Only then did I become less inclined to intellectualize and allow myself to experience feelings. Even at this time, however, as I started to explore parts of myself I had previously chosen not to acknowledge, making sense of my feelings and accepting the insights I gained was still difficult. As Mearns and Thorne (1988, p.24) state: 'Listening to the self is one thing. Coming to terms with what one hears is an altogether different matter.' It was only when I started to implement changes based on my understanding that I realized how much my own counselling had acted as a catalyst that allowed me to bring together as a whole many other parts of my life experience.

Experiencing the relationship from the perspective of being a client allowed me to appreciate more fully how important it is for the counsellor to create the conditions that will encourage the client's self-development. Even though I had absorbed what I had learned theoretically about these conditions from the work of Carl Rogers, my personal experience added a sense of realism to his hypothesis about the necessary core conditions of congruence, empathic understanding and unconditional positive regard. Initially, probably due to my biomedical background which sets great store in the clinician remaining professionally distanced, I had great difficulty feeling comfortable with the concept of 'congruence', or 'genuineness' as it is sometimes described, and with the ability to create this within my working practice. Mearns and Thorne (1988, p.14) argue:

> The more the counsellor is able to be herself in the relationship without putting up a professional front or personal façade the greater will be the chance of the client changing and developing in a positive and constructive manner.

The counsellor who is congruent conveys the message that it is not only permissible but also desirable to be oneself. I believe, now, that congruence is achieved through a counsellor's overall way of being. I have learnt that the counsellor must be true to his own feelings in order to promote the same in the client. Rogers reinforced this point when he argued:

> It has been found that personal change has been facilitated when the therapist is what he *is*, when in the relationship with his client he is genuine and without 'front' or façade, openly being the feelings and attitudes which at that moment are flowing *in* him. (Rogers 1967, p.61)

As with many areas of personal growth, movement occurs as a result of the insights gained from our experiences. I believe I am now more congruent within my working relationships, not because I better understand the concept, but because I have now experienced congruence and been able to recognize the value of my experience. My own counsellor's way of relating congruently within our relationship encouraged me to develop a higher degree of acceptance of myself. In turn I felt encouraged to try to be true to my feelings and experiences within all my relationships, particularly those with clients.

It was through my personal counselling that I became aware that I did not often allow myself to experience feelings in my everyday life; and that it was possible that I would not recognize them if I did. This insight made me feel very vulnerable and led me to question the validity of my work with clients. After all, how can the counsellor demonstrate empathic understanding if he is not in touch with his own experience? Having reached this position, my understanding of my relationship with others was then greatly enhanced by learning about the structural model used in transactional analysis.

Transactional analysis, founded by Canadian-born psychiatrist Eric Berne, 'provides a language and set of concepts for understanding human behaviour and interactions' (Nelson-Jones 1984, p.19). Berne theorized that there are three ego states between which each of us switches throughout our lives. He named them Parent, Adult and Child ego states (Berne 1964). Klein describes these ego states as follows:

> The Child ego contains our feelings. When in our Child we cry when we are miserable, laugh when we are happy. We are all the things a baby is, demanding, self-centred, loving, spontaneous, honest, uninhibited and lovable. [The Adult ego state] is our storehouse of facts and skills gained from the objective environment. It is without feeling. [The Parent ego state] contains our taught concepts of life, the values and generalisations explicitly given us by our parents. When we are in our Parent we are usually behaving like one of our parents did or in accordance with precepts they taught us when young. (Klein 1980, p.11)

Over time I was able to learn through counselling how my motivating drives and ways of relating to others had been dominated by my Parent ego state. As a result of this I realized I had denied myself access to a necessary part of myself for a considerable period of time: that of my Child. I came to understand that I only allowed my Child to influence my experience in an adapted form. Berne (1964, p.26) stated: 'The adapted child is the one who modifies his behaviour under the parental influence, behaving as the father (or mother) wanted him to behave.'

This new understanding led me to reflect on a long-standing resistance to the benefits of 'creative' therapies, ways of working that required using imagination, or that could be interpreted (by my Parent) as play. It was in fact the power of imagery that altered my appreciation of creativity. In one session, my counsellor suggested that I often seemed to neglect or dominate my Child. This immediately sparked a very vivid and very powerful image of a neglected child, alone and unkempt. The strength of this image and the very powerful way it helped me to connect with my feelings has since enthused me to try to introduce imagery in my work with clients.

The anxiety I felt about working with the strong emotions experienced by clients has been reduced by my increased insight into my own feelings and motivations. Rather than directing clients into safer areas when I feel challenged, I can now encourage them to 'stay with the feeling'. Although the insights gained through my own counselling have allowed me to feel more comfortable working with my clients' strong emotions, it is nevertheless essential that I do not direct them to face feelings until they choose to. I have learnt that many mental health clients who come for counselling bring with them myriad defences. These defences, although often negative or dysfunctional, are likely to form an integral part of how they interact with the world around them. They have often been developed over a considerable period of time and as the counselling relationship develops they will continue to dictate the pace at which the client explores painful issues.

Clients who have been diagnosed with mental health problems sometimes feel stigmatized by the label of 'madness' and this may create additional barriers and a reluctance to engage in any form of therapeutic alliance. The following case study highlights the importance of creating a safe environment for the client and working at his or her pace, as well as the importance of 'containment' and 'staying with the feelings' for movement to take place.

Mark

The client, whom I will call Mark, was referred for counselling by a behaviour therapist who had been seeing him for approximately a year. Mark had suffered an injury at work. He had been receiving behavioural intervention because of his inability to work and more recently for a needle phobia, which he felt had developed out of his regular attendance at a pain clinic. It was suggested that counselling might help Mark's level of frustration and anger, which he acknowledged was often out of proportion to situations that provoked it. He described being in a permanent state of anger and bitterness, to the extent that any slight provocation caused him to explode.

Mark had two children from a previous relationship and was now married to Rachel, who also had two children from a previous relationship. He had four sisters, but with little apparent contact. Although Mark consistently indicated that he had suffered a traumatic childhood, he remained very resistant to relating any of his family history, other than to comment very flippantly that his mother was an alcoholic and his father a convicted paedophile.

Mark had suffered a back injury at work just over a year earlier, which he reported had left him disabled. He was able to walk only a short distance and spent most of his time in a wheelchair. He described every day as being the same, usually spent in front of the television, with occasional trips out in the car. At the time of referral Mark was in the process of making a compensation claim against his employers for negligence. He believed that any life problems he now faced were as a direct result of the injury to his back and the ongoing legal process reinforced this for him.

Following referral, Mark had to wait approximately six weeks before I was able to offer him an appointment and we met for an initial assessment interview.

> The first session is an opportunity for both the counsellor and client to make some kind of assessment of their ability to work together. On the part of the counsellor, this assessment includes whether the client is likely to make good use of the time offered, and whether insight will contribute to behavioural change. (Jacobs 1988, p.22).

The initial session was very uncomfortable. Mark's body language was hostile and I felt attacked by an extremely challenging verbal assault, in which he complained about his waiting time for therapy. He also questioned in minute detail my qualifications and background. He was particularly critical of the medical services overall and eager to point out that he had now seen about 30 'so-called professionals' and had not been helped by any of them to date.

Brown and Pedder stated:

> Seeking help from a stranger is bound to arouse anxieties and provoke conflicts additional to any already underlying a patient's symptoms. What is this person like? Will he be able to help? Will he want to help me? Will he think I'm wasting his time? Will he judge me harshly as too bad or too mad to be helped? The patient's wish to protect himself from the dangers implicit in questions such as these can conflict with his intention to be honest. (Brown and Pedder 1979, p.73)

During the initial and subsequent few sessions, in order to generate a sufficient level of trust for therapeutic working, it was necessary for Mark to 'test' not only the environment he had now entered, but also my abilities to contain the issues he raised. He made frequent reference to his 'red mist anger', became extremely confrontational and would maintain that he usually frightened off most health professionals. It quickly emerged that Mark always reverted to this pattern of behaviour at times of anxiety. Initially somewhat threatened and 'battered' by Mark's engagement, I felt that I had completely lost control of what was happening in the sessions, which in turn made me feel both inadequate and vulnerable. Mark had ensured his own safety by projecting his initial anxieties onto me.

Much has been written about the importance of 'containment' in the counselling relationship (Bion 1962; Winnicott 1954, 1965). At this early stage I was able to identify through supervision the importance of being able to contain the feelings being projected by Mark and see them as a vital part of building a trust relationship. The importance of the trusting relationship is reiterated by Brown and Pedder who argued:

Reticence and mistrust at interview exist over and above unconscious defence mechanisms. How the therapist meets the patient and responds to his tentative approaches helps to determine whether the patient feels the necessary initial trust. (Brown and Pedder 1979, p.73)

It was important to reflect back to Mark early on that his initial aggression had appeared to be testing the environment and myself. Mark was able to recognize that this was the case and, having demonstrated I was able to contain his initial attack, the sessions started to feel safer. The early issues that Mark brought to the sessions centred on his accident and the changes in his life. He spoke at length about the numerous physicians he had seen as a result of his accident, emphasizing that many did not believe the extent of his injuries. Shortly after this he brought a report to the session detailing the results of a recent magnetic resonance imaging scan, which showed no evidence of injury to his back. In the sessions that followed Mark remained very anxious that I should not view him as 'mad' and told me about several very rigid fantasies regarding psychiatric care, usually centred around patients being 'hosed down' or in some other way cruelly treated. The source of these fantasies was not apparent at this time and only came later into our understanding.

During the course of the sessions there were several breaks. It was very important to recognize the significance of the missed sessions and what was being indicated with regard to the relationship as a whole. Mark missed many of the early sessions when the previous session had been particularly difficult or challenging. Whilst I reiterated the importance of informing me when he was unable to attend, there were still occasions when Mark did not show up and did not let me know, which often felt as if I was being punished.

The main themes that emerged in the early sessions centred on Mark's relationships. He recognized that he had very purposely ended many of his relationships following his accident, as he believed that since the event he was unable to have any sort of meaningful life. He demonstrated an overwhelming need to maintain control of those around him and quickly reverted to aggressive behaviour whenever this was threatened. The very passive-aggressive element of his nature could clearly be seen in his marriage to Rachel, previously his landlady, whom he married several months after his accident and who now cared for him on a full-time basis. He spoke of allowing his wife to go out occasionally and sleep with other men because he could no longer manage a sexual relationship, but made firm rules as to her time of return and that she should not discuss it with him.

His constant need aggressively to control relationships with both his wife and others around him was becoming increasingly overshadowed by the suggestion that there may have been no recognizable injury to his back. This led Mark to question whether he could be mad, which in turn led to fantasies that he would be detained under the Mental Health Act and incarcerated in an institution. At this point we attempted to reflect on pain as an issue and that his pain could have different sources. In one session he appeared to gain a fair degree of insight, when he recognized that his injury only formed a small part of the pain he felt inside. He commented at one point that 'there are other pains that mix in to make an overwhelming pain'. Mark quickly suppressed this experience and, although many issues appeared to surface for him, he stated that this was not something he wished to look at this time, choosing instead to look at issues which were safer and more superficial.

In my approach with Mark, I placed deliberate emphasis on the interpretation of transference within our relationship, as a way of understanding conflicts that Mark was experiencing in his everyday life. Cooper (1987) described transference as:

> an enactment of an earlier relationship and the task of transference interpretation is to gain insight into the ways that the early infantile relationships are distorting or disturbing the relationship to the therapist, a relationship which is, in turn, a model for the patient's life relationships. (Cooper 1987, cited in Sandler, Dare and Holder 1992, p.46)

Final formulation

After 31 sessions of counselling, Mark's therapeutic movement had been considerable and his position was very different from at the start of therapy. Initially the central issue felt as if it was about Mark's need to maintain a controlling position in all his relationships, including the counselling relationship. He has since been able to reflect with greater insight into the pain he felt. He was able to recognize that his back injury, albeit the catalyst which brought him into counselling, was responsible for only a small part of his pain, and that much of it was related to earlier life experiences which he had very successfully repressed prior to his accident.

The more traditional views of mental health might argue that bodily disability predisposes the patient to hysterical illness. In the past this has been referred to as 'somatic compliance' (Breuer and Freud, 1893–5, p.40) or 'pathoneurosis' (Ferenci 1916–17, pp.78–79). The anti-psychiatry view would be that bodily illness teaches the person how to be ill. Szasz argued:

> One's own sickness and the responses of others to it – with which it is inextricably intermingled – becomes a model, or a rule, which one may later choose to follow or not follow. This is then one of the ways that a person learns to follow rules that foster dependency, by exhibiting signs of helplessness. (Szasz 1972, p.215)

Mark's 'illness behavior' (Mechanic 1972, cited in Mayou, Bass and Sharpe 1995, p.9) can also be seen as a social communication that endeavours to gain legitimacy for the sick role that may or may not encompass the altered expression of emotional distress, which he was unable to express more directly.

In a later session when he was once again reflecting on his anxieties regarding psychiatry, Mark touched on childhood experiences when his mother was close to being admitted to hospital for alcoholism on several occasions. He recounted how she beat him and his sisters and he re-experienced much of the anger and abandonment he felt at that time. Although he still believed that the trauma he endured as a child was his fault, he had gained insight as to how it might have affected his current relationships. It became less important for him to have a firm diagnosis of his injury and, although he remained in a wheelchair, he had become much more active and positive in his outlook. Having gained insight into the earlier issues that he had repressed, Mark described his life as a 'cone', with the accident at the pinnacle and widening out below to many more issues that had yet to be resolved.

There were many aspects of my work with Mark that materialized into valuable learning experiences. Maintaining an awareness of the transference of feelings and emotions allowed me to appreciate the importance of being aware of my own experience within each session. Much can be learnt about the client's experience by maintaining an awareness of the dynamics of the overall relationship, as well as the client's or counsellor's individual experiences within it. I have also learnt to appreciate that many theories contribute to the understanding of the therapeutic relationship between counsellor and client and that several of the principles outlined by different theorists may be integrated into the counsellor's work. Whilst my work with Mark had been rooted in a person-centred, existentialist framework, I believe it possible and desirable to maintain a knowledge of other theories of intervention which may be integrated into my overall approach. This can only serve to provide a richer understanding of the relationship as it matures. Rogers (1967, p.63) identified as one of his core conditions the concept of 'unconditional positive regard'. Jacobs (1988, p.13) highlighted that 'viewed psychodynamically, this quality in the counsellor represents for the client the transferring onto the counselling relationship all that is good in the parent–child relationship'. The psychodynamic counsellor would therefore expect such unconditional regard to encourage a positive transference relationship between counsellor and client.

Supervision

Having already highlighted the importance of the counsellor's ongoing development as an integral part of the counselling process, I feel it is important to mention supervision and the crucial part it has played in developing my understanding of my work with clients. Supervision is aptly described by the BAC (1996, p.1):

> A formal and mutually agreed arrangement for counsellors to discuss their work regularly with someone who is normally an experienced and competent counsellor and familiar with the process of counselling supervision. The task is to work together to ensure and develop the efficacy of the supervisee's counselling practice.

The very individual nature of each counsellor's position and the bringing together and sharing of experience cultivate further reflection and bring fresh insight into working practice.

Whilst this supervisory process has been recognized as an integral part of good practice within the counselling field for many years, it is only recently being advocated by professional bodies within the biomedical field of mental health service delivery. The recent emphasis in mental health nursing upon experiential learning and reflective practice (Sainsbury Centre 2001) has further highlighted the need for effective clinical supervision as an integral part of every practitioner's development. Although the term 'clinical supervision' has existed within the health service professions for several years, it has often been confused with performance management or managerial appraisal and, as a result, was viewed by many as a punitive rather than facilitating process. Whilst it is important to acknowledge that within most health service systems practitioners are required to work towards specific objectives, both organizationally and personally, evaluation of performance should not be equated to the supervisory process which serves a different purpose.

As with any facilitating process, an important part of supervision for me has been that it is 'supervisee led'. It has remained consistently important for me to retain the freedom to take responsibility for my own supervision as part of my overall reflective process. This involves seeking out a supervisor who I believe has sufficient skill, at any particular moment, to provide an enabling environment in which I feel safe to reflect on my practice. As with all helping relationships, I believe it is equally important, within the supervisory relationship, to ensure that roles and responsibilities are clarified and that a working contract is agreed. It is equally important that this contract is subject to regular review and evaluation to ensure that the time is used most effectively and both supervisor and supervisee are able to acknowledge that the relationship continues to remain productive. This also helps to ensure that the relationship maintains a degree of congruity and focus.

In the early stages of working with a client I found that I finished the sessions feeling exhausted and often frustrated at having little clear idea of the theme. It was through supervision that I was able to examine my own motivations and come to realize that my desire to 'fix things' had affected my interventions. The themes of the sessions were not always evident because I was the one doing all the work. My current supervisor is a qualified psychodynamic art therapist whom I actively sought out as a result of fresh insight that I gained from individual counselling and my work with clients concerning imagery and creative therapies.

Conclusion

In conclusion, I believe that over time my way of understanding the counselling process has altered dramatically. My previous need to maintain control through a strict set of boundaries and a façade of professionalism always led me to believe I would discover a set of therapeutic techniques that, when used properly, would produce the desired result in the patient. This way of working, desirable as it then seemed, avoided taking stock of my own part in the process. I now try to recognize feelings and experience each moment. I have learnt that the role of the counsellor is not static. Counselling is an ongoing process in which the counsellor moves along with the client as the relationship changes and develops. I believe that this is beautifully summed up by Rogers (1967, p.21): 'The more I am open to the realities in me and in the other person, the less do I find myself wishing to rush in to "fix things".' I am now more able to appreciate the value of my own experiences and the contribution they make to the therapeutic process. My increased sense of self-worth has reduced my need for control and heightened my belief in my value as a person. 'For the person centred counsellor the ability to love themselves is, in fact, the cornerstone for their therapeutic practice, and in its absence the usefulness of the helping relationship will be grossly impaired' (Mearns and Thorne 1988, p.23).

References

Albrecht, G. and Levy, J. (1981) 'Constructing disabilities as social problems.' In G. Albrecht (ed) *Cross National Rehabilitation Policies: A Sociological Perspective.* London: Sage.

Anthony, W., Cohen, M. and Farkas, M. (1990) *Psychiatric Rehabilitation Centre for Psychiatric Rehabilitation.* Boston: Boston University Press.

BAC (1996) *Code of Ethics & Practice for Supervisors of Counsellors.* Rugby: BAC.

Berne, E. (1964) *Games People Play: The Psychology of Human Relationships.* London: Penguin.

Bion, W.R. (1962) *Learning From Experience.* London: Heinemann.

Borsay, A. (1986) 'Personal trouble or private issue? Towards a model policy for people with physical and mental disabilities.' *Disability, Handicap & Society 1,* 2, 179–195.

Brenton, K.J. (1997) 'The Chichester Project: effects of group psychoeducational intervention in schizophrenia care.' Unpublished dissertation, Brunel University College.

Breuer, J. and Freud, S. (1983–5) 'Studies on hysteria'. In *The Complete Psychological Works of Sigmund Freud,* vol. II (1955). London: Hogarth Press.

Brown, D. and Pedder, J. (1979) *Introduction to Psychotherapy: An Outline of Dynamic Principles and Practice.* New York: Routledge.

Cooper, A.M. (1987) 'Changes in psychoanalytic ideas: Transeference interpretation.' *Journal of American Psychoanalytic Association 35,* 77–98.

Deegan, P.E. (1988) 'Recovery: the lived experience of rehabilitation.' *Psychosocial Rehabilitation Journal 11,* 4, 11–19.

Dryden, W. (1984) *Individual Therapy in Britain.* London: Harper Row.

Dryden, W. (1992) *Hard Earned Lessons from Counselling in Action.* London: Sage.

Falloon, I., Boyd, R.H., Jeffrey L. and McGill, C.W. (1984) *Family Care of Schizophrenia: A Problem Solving Approach to the Treatment of Mental Illness.* New York: Guildford Press.

Ferenci, S. (1916–17) 'Disease or path-neurosis.' In S. Ferenci (1950) *Further Contributions to the Theory and Technique of Psychoanalysis.* London: Hogarth Press.

Finkelstein, V. (1980) *Attitudes and Disabled People.* New York: World Rehabilitation Fund.

Gamble, C. and Midence, K. (1994) 'Schizophrenia family work: mental health nurses delivering an innovative service.' *Journal of Psychosocial Nursing 32,* 10, 13–16.

Huddleston, J. (1992) 'Family and group psychoeducational approaches in the management of schizophrenia.' *Clinical Nurse Specialist 6,* 2, 118–121.

Jacobs, M. (1988) *Psychodynamic Counselling in Action.* London: Sage.

Kennedy, I. (1981) *The Unmasking of Medicine.* London: George Allen & Unwin.

Kirkpatrick, H. and Ladeen, J. (1999) 'Rehabilitation for people with enduring psychotic illness.' In M. Clinton and S. Nelson *Advanced Practice in Mental Health Nursing.* Oxford: Blackwell.

Klein, M. (1980) *Lives People Live: A Textbook Of Transactional Analysis.* Chichester: Wiley.

Mayou, R., Bass, C. and Sharpe, M. (1995) *Treatment of Functional Somatic Symptoms.* Oxford: Oxford University Press.

Mearns, D. and Thorne, B. (1988) *Person Centred Counselling in Action.* London: Sage.

Mechanic, D. (1972) 'Social Psychological factors affecting the presentation of bodily complaints.' *New England Journal of Medicine, 286,* 1132–1139.

Mueser, K.T., Gingerich, S.L. and Rosenthal, C.K. (1994) 'Educational family therapy for schizophrenia: A new treatment model for clinical service and research.' *Schizophrenia Research 13,* 99–108.

Nelson-Jones, R. (1984) *Personal Responsibility Counselling and Therapy: An Integrative Approach.* London: Harper & Row.

Patrick, G. and Scambler, D.L. (1986) *Sociology as Applied to Medicine.* London: Bailliere Tindall.

Rogers, C. (1967) *On Becoming A Person: A Therapist's View of Psychotherapy.* London: Constable.

Sainsbury Centre for Mental Health (2001) *The Capable Practitioner: Report to the National Service Framework Workforce Action Team.* London: Sainsbury Centre.

Sandler, J., Dare, C. and Holder, A. (1992) *The Patient and The Analyst.* London: Karnac.

Scambler, G. (1997) *Sociology as Applied to Medicine.* London: Saunders.

Swain, J., Finkelstein, V., French, S. and Oliver, M. (eds) (1993) *Disabling Barriers – Enabling Environments.* London: Sage.

Szasz, S. (1972) *The Myth of Mental Illness.* London: Paladin.

Winnicott, D.W. (1954) *Collected Papers: Through Pediatrics to Psychoanalysis.* London: Tavistock.

Winnicott, D.W. (1965) *The Maturational Processes and the Facilitating Environment.* London: Hogarth Press.

Wolfensburger, W. (1983) 'Social role valorization: A proposed new term for the principle of normalization.' *Mental Retardation 21,* 6, 234–239.

Chapter 9

Rehabilitating the Problematic Drinker in the Community

Richard Bryant-Jefferies

Introduction and background

Since 1995 I have been working for the Acorn Community Drug and Alcohol Service in Surrey, offering a person-centred alcohol counselling service in primary health care settings. The location provides an opportunity for close liaison to develop with other primary health care team members, including the general practitioners (GPs). Whilst many people can resolve alcohol problems through counselling support, others do need medication to treat associated symptoms, assessment for detoxification and mental health input as part of the rehabilitation process.

I did not choose this area of work through any specific motivation, but I have been enormously grateful for the experience that it has given me. I have not had an alcohol problem myself and have been pretty much teetotal now for the last ten years, not as a result of my work, but because I no longer enjoy the experience. Does this make it more difficult for me to help people with this problem? My experience is no; in fact most clients say that I have an empathy with their inner world and an appreciation of their experiences. They feel I am very much 'with' them.

My first experience of a person with an alcohol problem was a manager early in my working life. Like many people, I did not see it as something that needed addressing. I did not try to help. In fact, I don't think I saw it as a serious problem until he died, when his locker was found to be full of empty sherry bottles. Even then, I had no concept of what it meant to have an 'alcohol problem'.

The painful truth is that alcohol does damage to the human body, when taken in sufficient quantities. Medically recommended safe drinking in the UK is 14 units a week for women and 21 units a week for men.[1] The more that is drunk above these figures, the greater the risk of damage to health including: liver damage, gastric ulcers, pancreatitis, oesophageal varices, various cancers, peripheral neuritis and a range of brain problems including blackouts, memory loss, mood swings, depression.

Alcohol can also disrupt self-awareness and open the person to feelings and thoughts otherwise suppressed which are not part of that person's normal waking self, for instance, anger, belligerence, irritation, violence, overwhelming sadness. One client told me: 'I just become so angry, I seem to provoke arguments, and the smallest things wind me up. I'm usually really quiet, but alcohol does my head in.' I am no longer surprised by the degree of personality change that alcohol can induce.

Value of a person-centred approach

I have sometimes asked what it is I offer that clients value. Some of the responses have been: 'You didn't judge me, or push me to change, but let me have time to make my own sense of everything. This helped me begin to realize for myself what I was really doing, and why I wanted to change.' I try to offer the client sensitive companionship, seeking to travel with them on their psychological journey at their own pace, whilst being a supportive presence where that is needed. I truly believe that empathy, genuineness or congruence and unconditional positive regard must be present in order to create a climate of relationship that is growth promoting (Rogers 1980, p.115). Problematic drinking often has its roots in relationship difficulties and I find that my clients appreciate a counselling approach that is fundamentally relational. Being in a genuinely warm and accepting therapeutic relationship challenges assumptions and self-beliefs which may often have been generated in cold, rejecting or chaotic relational environments.

Little has been written about offering a person-centred perspective on counselling people with alcohol problems. Generally, the approach does

---

1   A unit is a single measure of spirits, a small schooner of sherry, half a pint of normal strength beer, lager or cider, a standard glass of wine. Some of the higher strength cans of lager are 4.5 units. Volume in litres x % alcohol content = number of units.

not advocate the use of different responses to specific conditions. Farrell (1996) has described his experience of working with addictions among homeless people from a person-centred perspective. Miller and Rollnick (1991) have described a 'motivational interview' approach. People often know they need to change, but find it hard to break out of habits and patterns of thought that have been established over time and which sustain problematic alcohol use. A person-centred approach enables the client to experience and contrast the 'inadequacies in old ways of perceiving' with 'new and more accurate and adequate perceptions', along with 'the recognition of significant relationships' (Rogers 1951, pp.223–4). In my work I enable clients to experience tensions that arise within themselves as the urge to change becomes more persistent whilst facilitating a relational environment which stimulates a person's potential towards greater self-awareness, self-efficacy and self-reliance.

Clients can be extremely needy and demanding. They may be exhibiting challenging and sometimes desperate behaviour and attitudes previously used to get attention or to survive that leave me feeling quite disorientated. I have learned to respect the use of alcohol as a coping mechanism and to appreciate just why it can seem such a good friend in times of trouble. On hearing a client's story I am often left with a sense that their choice of coping may have been quite reasonable in their situation. Given a similar set of experiences I may have made the same choice. My ability to accept people for who they are and to be open and sensitive to the person who is often masked by alcohol use has certainly increased, and I am grateful for this. This helps me feel more whole and more in touch with the strengths and vulnerabilities of being human.

Challenges of the work

Alcohol use is rarely the whole issue. Drinking can be self-medication to alleviate symptoms stemming from a mental health condition and/or strong emotional factors that are the result of past or current trauma. No two people with alcohol problems are the same. This challenge holds part of the attraction of this work for me. I have to be able to respond to many possibilities. At times I can feel as if I am riding on an out-of-control roller coaster. It is invariably worse for the client.

Working as an alcohol counsellor within the NHS means that I have an agenda: to help clients resolve problematic alcohol use. Some counsellors may not feel at ease with having a predetermined goal. In many respects I may adjust the pure counselling role to become more of an alcohol support worker at times, or an advocate when liaison with other health and social care professionals is called for. Whilst there are times when I would love to have a straightforward counselling role, this is simply not always possible. Supervision plays a key role in ensuring I keep my own clarity and boundaries in the work I am doing.

There may be challenging questions that can arise within a counsellor who has little experience of working in this area. Will I be able to work with this client group? Can I hope to understand someone affected by alcohol use? Will I be safe? Can anything be achieved? These were certainly some of my own thoughts when I began this work. I was on a steep learning curve, but I had good trainers – the many clients I have seen over the years. 'Once an alcoholic, always an alcoholic' is a stereotypical phrase that undermines the belief that someone can overcome an alcohol problem. I am firmly convinced that working with this client group is worthwhile. Change may not come quickly and may not take the form I expect, but it can and does happen. I have seen people regaining control, discovering capacity for self-reliance, and I have heard children declaring that it is 'great to get my mum back'. These are the spurs that encourage me to carry on.

Some people say that they cannot work with clients unless they stop or control their drinking. In the community, the luxury of abstinence or control may not be available. I work with the person with all his or her complexity and sometimes do need other professionals involved, partly for their own speciality, sometimes simply to spread the load.

The intoxicated client

Sometimes clients arrive for counselling having had a drink to steady their nerves, particularly for a first session or after a relapse. I can still offer them warmth and acceptance and work at developing the counselling relationship. There are also clients who arrive drunk. While little counselling seems possible, I can give them care and concern, along with an appointment for another day, highlighting in a supportive way that it might be helpful if they had not drunk, or had drunk less, prior to the session. For some clients, turning up severely affected by alcohol can be their way of showing just how desperate their situation is, or how much alcohol has a hold on them. I have frequently been surprised by how much people can gain from sessions in which, at the time, there appears to be little therapeutic contact. Turning people away because they have had that drink, or maybe a few, may for them be yet another in a long line of rejections.

When does rehabilitation begin?

From the moment contact is established with the client – an initial telephone call, a letter or a face-to-face meeting – the rehabilitation process begins. Receiving a warm and courteous response from whomever they see in an agency helps to put the client at ease, and at the same time begin the process of challenging long-held beliefs: 'I am not worthy of being helped'; 'there are others worse than me, it's all hopeless anyway'; 'I don't respect myself, why should anyone else?'

People turn for help with many assumptions and expectations about services: 'Will I be treated with respect?' 'Will they listen to me and hear my problems, my hopes, my fears?' 'Will I be told to stop drinking, that there is no other option.' In my experience it is important to be sensitive to these concerns that are often deeply felt by the client.

Controlled drinking or abstinence

Community services frequently provide a controlled drinking or 'social drinking' alternative to residential, abstinence-based programmes. Cantopher (1996) suggests some factors which point to a 'better than one in ten chance of controlled drinking: female, young, in employment, in supportive relationship, no history of addiction to alcohol, a short history of problem drinking'. However, with all these factors present he suggests the chance of success remains less than 50/50.

In my experience controlled drinking can be a realistic option, particularly when an alcohol habit is not ingrained or excessive and the drinker is able to make significant changes to a life style or self-concept that contributed major drinking triggers. Some, however, find it impossible to maintain control after the first drink, unable to resist the craving for the next, and the next: 'One never seems enough, I just get the taste and it becomes a fast track to oblivion.' Often the alcohol generates powerful mood changes, affecting the client's motivation to stop. An abstinent life style is likely to be the only realistic and sustainable goal. People say to me, 'Unless I have a certain amount it seems pointless having any, but when I do drink I become like another person, an angry me breaks through and it usually ends in trouble.' I hear the desperation as people struggle to break free of their alcohol use, knowing that so much is at stake if they fail. I am left respecting the awesome nature of what they face.

A question commonly heard is, 'Can I try controlled drinking? I really can't see me never drinking again.' I will offer counselling to support clients who want to attempt to control their alcohol intake rather than abstain. If it does not work, the client may then be able to recognize his or her need for abstinence and have greater motivation to achieve this, leading to a greater likelihood of success.

The world of the problematic drinker

'I try to drink secretly. I don't want people to know. I don't feel good about what I do, but if others at home knew I'd be in trouble.' Whilst many people have this experience, not everyone with a drink problem is devious. Hiding bottles can be a sign of discomfort about what they are doing. Two factors that frequently present among people with alcohol problems are high levels of emotional sensitivity and a history of losses or a particularly significant loss. When I mention this to clients and enquire about their experiences of loss they are frequently surprised. I explain that loss often lies behind the use of alcohol and offer to listen to their unique story, helping them to understand how alcohol may have been used to dull emotional pain or to cope with feelings of emptiness or loneliness.

Range of issues linked to alcohol use

'I yearn for peace, for some other normality. But I can't get the hurt, the memories, and the feelings out of my body, out of my head. Alcohol helps me forget, but it is a temporary respite.' Alcohol problems can have a messy and painful foundation that will require addressing if sustainable change is to be achieved. Issues that I have encountered working with problematic drinkers include:

1. In childhood: sexual and physical abuse, rape, emotional and physical neglect, violence within the family dynamic, exposure to constant arguing by parents, parental problematic drinking, bereavement, parental divorce and/or relationship break-up, frequent and unsettling house moves, constant criticism from significant others, bullying, emotional neglect.

2. In adulthood: victim of violence, sexual assault, rape, divorce and relationship break-up, loss of job, bereavement, physical pain, work and family stress, financial problems, lack of access to their children.

As a result, clients present a whole range of difficult symptoms, for instance, depression, anxiety or panic attacks, low self-esteem, lack of confidence, unresolved or uncontrolled anger, frustration, phobias, sleep problems, bad dreams, obsessive-compulsive disorders, suicidal thoughts, self-harm. The alcohol can provide a welcome though temporary anaesthetic, or it can take the person more deeply into a nightmare world.

Defining problematic drinking

I would define problematic drinking as a style of drinking that generates a problematic effect, either for the drinker or for others. This perspective embraces health, social, economic and criminal factors. Alcohol becomes a problem when it begins to be the central focus of an individual's life. Whilst it does not always have to be the amount drunk that is indicative of a problem, often it is, with the risk that alcohol use itself becomes less of a habit of choice and increasingly a drug of dependence. It is distressing to watch this occurring and can leave me feeling sadness and regret for the client; anger towards the availability of this mood-altering, addictive substance; and a determination to offer an opportunity to explore the possibility of change.

Dependence

'I have to drink, first thing in the morning, and then through the day. It's the only way to stop the shakes, sweating, anxiety attacks.' These are typical signs of physical dependence, yet dependence does not always mean drinking throughout the day. People can consume enough in an evening on a regular basis to maintain levels of alcohol within the body to get them through to the next evening. However, withdrawal from alcohol is dangerous. When a person is dependent, unmedicated withdrawal can lead to fits, hallucinations and risk of death.

'I have to drink to steady my nerves, to get out of the house, to face people, really to do anything. I feel so desperate, I hide myself away sometimes, avoiding people, I don't want them to know I drink.' Clients may not always see this psychological dependence as a problem. It might have been that way for a long time, but the alcohol-dependent person who has realized he or she needs to change their drinking is frequently in a very desperate position. They have to keep drinking, yet they are beginning to hate it. I have seen people waiting months for in-patient detoxification where there is inadequate service provision, feeling helpless to bring to an end the cycle of dependence that has them in its grip. It is difficult to watch, knowing that a human life is being put at risk.

Detoxification and rehabilitation in the community

Gradual alcohol reduction

'I found slowly reducing really helped me make sense of what I was doing. And it felt good to be actually doing something about it for myself.' The experience of increasing control and autonomy is powerfully therapeutic. Whilst people reduce their consumption at different rates, there is often a point at which they need to stabilize and deal with other issues before further reduction. Strong feelings that had previously been suppressed by the alcohol begin to break through, or memories of traumatic incidents surface.

A serious drinking habit can take up many hours and I frequently hear people commenting: 'It's all the time I'm getting back. What do I do with it? It's leaving me feeling more and more that I should fill it up with drinking again.' Creative brainstorming can play a vital role in helping the client come up with ideas. Sustainable rehabilitation has to include strategies not only directed to changing the alcohol use but also towards altering life style. I normally feel optimistic about people's chances of reducing, having positive expectations, whilst remaining realistic and in touch with the client's experience of the process.

Community detoxification

Community detoxification involves the use of medication to help stave off withdrawal symptoms. This could take place at home, with professionals, friends and relatives offering support and monitoring, or a mixture of being at home and travelling to a community alcohol team or a GP surgery. Where there is a high risk of problematic withdrawal symptoms, physical and/or mental health complications, or lack of a supportive environment, in-patient detoxification is recommended. Being able to offer encouragement during this difficult process and watching the person change is a reward in itself, even though I know that whilst giving up is one part of the process, maintaining change brings its own set of challenges and difficulties.

One-to-one support

Many of the clients I see with alcohol problems are in danger of an 'emotional overload'. Feelings may have built up to the point where alcohol can no longer suppress them and be ready to spill out. The client needs a safe and supportive environment where this can occur. 'My counsellor was there, a consistent presence in my life. I needed somewhere to unload my fears and to risk sharing my hopes.' One-to-one counselling offers time and a confidential space for clients to tell their story and feel heard, to make sense of themselves, of the factors that have contributed to their drinking, and to plan their next steps realistically. Approaches vary. What seems important is the development of an increasingly open and trustworthy relationship between client and counsellor. Frequency and length of contact can vary. I may see clients weekly for an hour if there is a need for in-depth work or frequent support because of major problems in their lives. At the other end of the spectrum are monthly check-ins, contact with the service being a safety net for the client; this may be a full hour, but can be 15 to 20 minutes.

Group work

One of the comments I hear frequently in groups is: 'I feel accepted in this group; I do not have to explain myself because I am with people who understand.' This is a powerful experience, often in marked contrast to how they frequently feel in other settings, for instance, at home, at work or with medical services. Groups also offer a place where there is great scope for people to be themselves in the company of others. It can be their first experience of not being alone with the thoughts, feelings and behaviours that they previously believed marked them out as different. In the group, what may have been a lonely experience becomes a shared one. 'It was such a relief to hear someone else describe what I feel; maybe I'm not going mad after all.'

Groups are also valuable places for people to offer and receive help. Someone shares an idea for coping with a situation and others take that idea away to add to their own list of resources. I also find that group members are normally good at challenging each other. They are not easily fooled; they have been there, made the same excuses themselves. Some groups are open and unstructured offering an opportunity for person-to-person encounter and for a focus to develop naturally from the needs of group members. I prefer to work this way. I also recognize the value of group work with a predetermined and structured focus, exploring particular issues linked to alcohol use, for instance, anger or stress management, drinking triggers, cognitive features of alcohol use and relapse prevention.

My experience has been in facilitating groups with a 'no drinking prior to the group' policy. A group member who smells of alcohol and whose behaviour is affected by alcohol can disrupt the group for others who may be seeking abstinence or controlled drinking. The dependent drinker, however, may be left without a service. For this reason there is also a need for 'wet groups', though with the proviso that attendees seek to limit alcohol intake simply to what will enable them to be there.

Working in a group, I enjoy being part of an unfolding process. I enjoy observing people challenge and support each other; the sense that 'we are all in this together'; the shared despair; the attentive listening by clients and counsellors; the wonderful humour that can generate smiles on faces that have not known a sober smile for many a year. It can be draining and sometimes, in discussion after the group with my co-facilitator, we have to spend time making our own sense of what went on. Alcohol is usually a focus in the group, but not always. I think this is healthy. Why not offer a space for people to talk about other things that are significant to them? Most people like to have time to just 'chat'. In groups which I have facilitated members have sometimes initiated coffee mornings, gradually building social confidence together.

Life style and social skills support

'I never go out much, no friends, and I'm not really confident with people anyway. I prefer my own company. I used to use alcohol to get confidence, never really had any of my own.' Social isolation can be a big problem, whilst for others there is a need to break free of social networks that are alcohol centred, realizing that to return to them after detoxification or achieving a controlled drinking pattern will simply put them at too much risk. 'All my friends drink, they don't understand. Most of them have a problem, but can't see it.' It is sad when someone realizes that the people they thought were friends are actually drinking companions.

Alcohol-free social events or outings can be extremely helpful, as can any social experience that is carefully organized and responsive to the sensitivities of the clients. Very practical needs may be addressed: managing money, looking for work, taking a responsible parental role within the family. In addition workshops, classes and opportunities for creative expression can usefully be offered.

Handling high-risk drinking situations can be dealt with in groups. Scenarios can be played out, ways of handling them tried and tested and then discussed. Perhaps someone needs to explore ways of dealing with the pressure of 'go on, just the one, you'll be OK', or 'what do you mean you won't drink with me, what's wrong with my drink?' or the persistent questions when they return to work after time off to sort out their alcohol use 'so what was wrong with you, then?'

Day programmes

Day programmes provide structure and a safe place to be. Clients may receive one-to-one counselling, group work and/or social skills development and support. This is an ideal situation, for it offers a more holistic response to a client's needs and provides greater opportunity for a more integrated process of rehabilitation. Day programmes may also provide an environment that can minimize temptation where professionals are on hand to talk something through. A range of non-alcoholic drinks will generally be available, the client being given autonomy to spend time maybe reading the paper, chatting with other clients, reading a book, watching videos and generally being treated as a trustworthy human being.

Working with the problem drinker

Why change is so difficult – power of habit

Change does not come easily unless one has a reason to want to change, and even then it can be hard to break out of familiar habits. When we know a particular experience makes us feel 'good' or 'better' or 'normal', it is difficult not to repeat it. I find it hard to walk past a cake shop sometimes, or stop before eating the whole packet of chocolate biscuits. Being told we have to stop or cut back on what we like, or what has become so much part of our life, can provoke many diverse feelings: anger, resentment, panic, determination to carry on, relief that it is in the open. Seeing a client for the first time, I am never too sure what their feelings are going to be; often there are very mixed feelings.

Clients motivated to resolve an alcohol problem can experience powerful conflicts between their thoughts and behaviour. One client described a journey to the off-licence: 'All the way I had this conversation going on in my head. Part of me was saying "you need that drink, you deserve it", the other saying, "don't be stupid, it'll only mean trouble". My body kept walking. I bought my drink, I drank half a can and realized I simply didn't want any more. I threw the rest away.' At least this client was in touch with both sides of the internal debate. For others the response is instinctive: 'One minute those feelings of emptiness were not there, then they were. I just went for that drink. I don't remember thinking about it.

One minute I was OK, the next I was out with a bottle in my hand. It all happened so fast.'

After such experiences I encourage clients to be with their feelings and thoughts about what happened, then help them break the process down. They can usually highlight the points at which they might have made different choices. The whole process is put into context. What had triggered the urge to drink? Often habits are hard to break because the person is acting out of a conditioned instinct, with little sense of being able to make a choice. Reclaiming the power to choose is a key factor in rehabilitation. This is probably the most rewarding part of the work for me: helping clients regain their ability to make free choices and to act on them to provide themselves with a satisfying experience. 'I felt confident enough to invite an old friend around for a meal. It was great, and no alcohol. I couldn't really believe I could enjoy myself without a drink.' Often the looks of disbelief from clients who have recaptured a sense of non-alcohol-induced enjoyment bring a smile to my face.

A model of change

Change is a process. In the 1980s, a model was devised to explain the stages that people pass through when seeking to overcome a smoking habit (Prochaska and DiClemente 1982). It is widely used in addiction services and a model I find helpful in providing a framework for helping people to change and for defining interventions that are most likely to be helpful to the client. The stages of change in the original model (in a recent version it includes a 'preparation' stage between contemplation and action) are:

- *pre-contemplation*, where a person is not seeking change
- *contemplation*, the idea of change is now on the agenda
- *action*, a planned change is being put into effect
- *maintenance*, the change is being maintained as envisaged
- *lapse or relapse*, the person has been unable to maintain their change in drinking behaviour.

PRE-CONTEMPLATION

Clients whom I see in the pre-contemplation stage have usually been referred by someone else: a doctor, psychiatric team, social worker or family member. I listen to what they have to say. I accept their experiences and perceptions whilst seeking to help them link their drinking to problematic effects, generating within them a clearer awareness of realistic discomfort about their drinking. The intention is to achieve some authenticity concerning what is happening. I offer an information leaflet, genuine concern for their well-being and time for them to reflect on what has been said prior to a follow-up appointment.

CONTEMPLATION

Working with clients in contemplation means I am often entering into a deeper process of exploring and understanding the nature of the drinking problem, the patterns, the associations, the causes and the effects. Drinking diaries can be helpful in this. Some people do not realize how much they drink, the cost or the time spent. 'I got through £80 last week, and it was an average drinking week' is not an uncommon response for a regular, heavy drinker. People say they have not brought their diary back because 'I was too ashamed, I never realized I drank so much'. We explore their reactions and this generally leads to them connecting with their motivation to change. As part of this process I find it helpful for clients to contrast the advantages and disadvantages of changing their drinking pattern. Advantages are motivational factors; disadvantages are threats to sustainable change.

Some people will choose not to address their drinking because of fear of change, concern over the discomfort it will bring them, inability to conceive of living with less or no alcohol, lack of belief in themselves. They may tell me about this, or they may simply stop attending. There can be a lot of sudden endings and I often take this to supervision, wondering what may have happened. I will then explore the relationship I had developed with the client, how it felt for me and how I am left feeling after the ending. Was there anything that I may have said or done that contributed to the client breaking contact which might have been offered differently? Sometimes I strongly sense that an opportunity has been lost and that tremendous problems are around the corner. Whilst I know it is said that people have to reach 'rock-bottom' to change, I am of the opinion that people can change before this, given the right encouragement and opportunity to tell their story and feel heard. Yet I also know that people change when the time is right for them. Where contact is broken my hope is that seeds have been sown which may contribute to acceptance of the need to change at a later date.

ACTION

People may take a long time before they reach the point of taking action. Decisions can take time – whether to go on a diet, what colour to decorate the front room, should I change my job, is this relationship still right for me, should I do something about my alcohol intake. Others move very quickly towards this point. Planned changes need to be realistic, owned by the client, set within a time frame, have some degree of monitoring or measurability, recognize and cater for potential relapse and include appropriate levels of support.

Relapse prevention plays an important part in contributing to a successful outcome, and devising how to handle a lapse or relapse should it occur. A lapse is a short return to drinking above what has been planned; a relapse is a return to the old drinking pattern. Successful and sustainable change of a drinking habit often requires more than one attempt. Depressive or negative thinking is a common drinking trigger. Something goes wrong and the thought process runs: 'Typical, always happens to me. Nothing is ever likely to get better. What's the point in trying? I'll have a drink to feel better.' Empathic responses given with warmth and openness often lead to a lot of hurt being experienced, then a process of unravelling that reaction, and finally the client realizing the possibility of choosing a more positive self-affirming response.

MAINTENANCE

Following the action phase comes the longer period of maintenance. How long does someone maintain a change before it becomes established? For one person six months of abstinence or controlled drinking will indicate sustainable change, others will remain with alcohol on their mind for a lot longer. Effective support systems are important, particularly early on, along with ongoing therapeutic support enabling the person to continue to develop greater self-awareness and control over the choices he or she makes, whilst freeing him or herself from habitual drink-related thoughts and reactions.

Some people choose to use Alcoholics Anonymous (AA) as a way of obtaining support and being part of what for many is like an extended family. They may choose to work the AA 12-step programme as a method of developing a more self-aware and self-controlling life style. I adjust my way of working in order to complement what they are achieving through AA. It is not for everyone, but it helps vast numbers of people and I respect that.

LAPSE OR RELAPSE

'I really did not want to come today. I didn't want to have to admit to you, and remind myself, that I messed up. I felt awful; I'd let everyone down. But I'm glad I came. I was really worried you might tell me off,' a client said to me after relapsing. It can seem the hardest thing in the world to ask for help when a lapse or a relapse is occurring; in fact, often people break contact with me at this time. Well thought out plans for change and support often go awry because something was missed, or the unexpected happened: sudden bad news, a person they had not expected to meet coming back into their lives, a drinking dream leaving them with symptoms of a heavy drinking episode, or memories of traumatic experiences resurfacing and overwhelming the person.

It is emotionally demanding to provide counselling to the client who has relapsed. Clients may frequently experience powerful, desperate feelings of hopelessness and helplessness. As a counsellor I am affected as well. I seek to enter into their world, to be touched by it, to be a companion in what may be a desolate and lonely place. Whilst communicating empathy, I also see my role as holding on to a vision of life beyond the relapse. Often the client has lost sight of this. The client's view can be anywhere on a continuum extending from 'what's the point, I may as well give up' to 'that's it, I have to stop, I've got to get it right this time'. Clients affected by alcohol may not always see things clearly, the alcohol driving down their mood and motivation to change. I am so thankful for being part of a supportive team at these times.

Growth of the client

I find that successful community rehabilitation requires significant personal growth within the client. A person who has attained greater self-insight and developed new responses that are integrated into their way of being is more likely to achieved the goal of not drinking in certain settings, or in response to particular feelings or situations Behavioural changes need to be underpinned by psychological growth.

A crucial aspect of rehabilitation is the client gaining clarity about his or her situation and developing less distorted ways of thinking, feeling and acting. The client becomes less dominated by negative or unrealistic thoughts about himself, the product of psychological adaptations to survive traumatic situations. 'The sights and sounds of violence are all I knew as a child, fear, uncertainty were normal for me. Now as an adult, I just seem to struggle with handling any kind of conflict, yet I keep provoking anger in others and myself.' As adults they seek to create or provoke situations in which similar feelings and behaviour can be present in order to satisfy this sense of 'normality' and the particular 'configurations of self' that are associated with it.

Resolving drinking configurations

Person-centred theory refers to configurations of self (Mearns, 1999) developing within the self-concept in response to experiences. These might be thought of as discrete identities within the self that an individual lives out of in reaction to circumstances. When alcohol use is associated, some of these become 'drinking configurations' (Bryant-Jefferies, 2001).

Counsellor: It seems your drinking is a kind of reaction to circumstances.

Client: Yes, I get the strongest urges to drink when I feel powerless.

Counsellor: Powerless to...

Client: Any kind of powerlessness. When I feel weak as a person, unable to cope, when things are too much for me, I simply drink.

Counsellor: When you feel weak, can't cope...

Client: But it makes me feel powerful, even though it messes things up. There's a 'weak me' that drinks, and a 'powerful me' that is the effect of the drinking. I need to find my power other than through alcohol.

Counsellor: The 'weak me' and the 'strong me', both aspects of you. And you want to access 'strong me' without alcohol.

Enabling clients to appreciate, at their own pace, associated thoughts and feelings and their connection with alcohol use is an important feature of sustainable rehabilitation. Clients who feels all aspects of themselves are equally valued and accepted by the counsellor can enter a process of self-discovery and self-questioning, creating fresh thoughts and feelings about circumstances and their own identity. They free themselves from being driven by alcohol-associated patterns from the past. To begin with this can be very painful as the client opens up to a fuller range of experience of himself. Yet from this comes the experience of greater wholeness, which becomes a powerful motivation to work the process through. It always touches me deeply to see this process unfolding as I find myself part of an increasingly full and fulfilling relationship with my client.

Recreating the family

Whilst families can be crucial in offering the support and encouragement that enables someone to resolve an alcohol problem, they can also provide a major block. I frequently hear clients comment:

> I drink because it is my way of rebelling against the constant criticism I get at home. If they want to moan at me, I'll give them something to moan about.

> We always drink together; usually my partner suggests we might open a bottle, but that is never enough for me once I get started.

> No one understands why I drink. I know it causes problems for everyone, but it helps me forget. Nobody seems to want to appreciate the benefit it has for me. No one listens.

For many people within families who are working to resolve an alcohol problem there can be a place for couple counselling or family therapy to address drinking problems within a family. Problematic alcohol use by an individual can be a symptom of a dysfunctional relationship or set of relationships. For the alcohol problem to be resolved, the whole relational process might need to be addressed. Many problematic drinkers carry a scapegoat role within a family dynamic. They are easy to blame. Sometimes it is appropriate, but not always.

Sometimes the family expectation is that the problematic drinker, after undergoing rehabilitation, is now 'cured' and can take on everything that had actually led them to drinking in the first place. This puts them at risk of feeling overwhelmed, trapped and powerless, and of returning to their previous coping mechanism – the alcohol. Yet it can be equally unhelpful to wrap them up in cottonwool: 'I just wanted to be treated normally, like everyone else.'

Family and couple counselling can also be helpful in building trust. Once lost or damaged, trust is not easily regained; lapse or relapse is always a possibility. A place where honest communication can be encouraged helps to keep everything open and visible. Constant accusations of 'you've been drinking' (particularly when they haven't, or it has been planned and controlled) may be well meaning and a product of genuine concern, but can undermine the fragile confidence that the reformed problematic drinker is developing. I have witnessed many power struggles in relationships in which a drinker may use alcohol as a weapon of control, or a return to drinking is provoked in order to render an individual powerless.

Conclusions

Alcohol problems can be resolved and sustainable change achieved through counselling in the community. It requires motivation and dedication from both client and helping professional. Changing a drinking habit invariably involves changes in life style, with the client gaining a sense of feeling freed up and able to 'move on'. The involvement of families and close friends can be pivotal in ensuring sustainable change in alcohol use.

Many alcohol problems are rooted in relational problems, in losses and high levels of emotional sensitivity. The willingness and ability to accept and work with the whole person, not just the drinking behaviour, is a vital part of helping individuals tackle an alcohol habit and the changes of thought, action and self-perception that are required. From my perspective, I encounter daily not only human fragility but also powerful forces of determination. I have learned so much and am so indebted to the many clients who have allowed me access to their inner worlds and to be a companion on their path to recovery from an alcohol problem.

References

Bryant-Jefferies, R. (2001) Counselling the Person Beyond the Alcohol Problem. London: Jessica Kingsley Publishers.

Cantopher, T. (1996) Dying for a Drink: A No-nonsense Guide for Heavy Drinkers. Lewes: Book Guild.

Farrell, M. (1996) 'A person centred approach? – Working with addictions.' Person Centred Practice 4, 1, 7–13.

Miller, W.R. and Rollnick, S. (1991) Motivational Interviewing: Preparing People to Change Addictive Behaviour. New York: Guilford Press.

Prochaska, J.O. and DiClemente, C.C. (1982) 'Transtheoretical therapy: Towards a more integrative model of change.' Psychotherapy: Theory, Research and Practice 19, 276–288.

Rogers, C.R. (1951) Client-centred Therapy. London: Constable.

Rogers, C.R. (1980) A Way of Being. Boston: Houghton Mifflin.

Further reading

Alcohol Services Directory: Services for Problem Drinkers in England and Wales. Dolomite Publishing, 107 Kings Road, Godalming, Surrey GU7 3EU.

Association of Nurses in Substance Abuse (ANSA) (1997) *Substance Use: Guidance and Good Practice for Specialist Nurses working with Alcohol and Drug Users.* London: ANSA.

Bryant-Jefferies, R. (2001) *Counselling the Person beyond the Alcohol Problem.* London: Jessica Kingsley Publishers.

Eurocare (1998) *Alcohol Problems in the Family: A Report to the European Union.* St. Ives, Cambridgeshire: Eurocare.

Plant, M. (1997) *Women and Alcohol: Contemporary and Historical Perspectives.* London: Free Association Books.

Velleman, R. (1992) *Counselling for Alcohol Problems.* London: Sage.

Velleman, R. (1993) *Alcohol and the Family.* Occasional Paper. London: Institute of Alcohol Studies.

Ward, M. and Goodman, C. (1995) *Alcohol Problems in Old Age.* Ware: Wynne Howard Publishing.

Useful contact addresses

Alcohol Concern
Waterbridge House
32–36 Loman Street
London SE1 0EE
Tel: 020 7928 7377
http://www.alcoholconcern.org.uk

Institute of Alcohol Studies
1 The Quay
St Ives
Cambridgeshire PE27 5AR
Tel: 01480 466766
www.ias.org.uk

Chapter 10

Counselling People Recovering from Drug Addiction

Cindi Bedor

Introduction

> Long soft fingers of early summer sun push through the blind at the surgery window and touch the opposite wall. I've rushed to get here from the office, eating my lunch in the car on the way, and now, sinking into a chair, I'm relieved to have a minute or two to relax before my client, Catherine, is due to arrive. Sitting here now, I begin to slow down, catch my breath, and savour these brief moments of warmth and sun. Several minutes pass, then several more and still I'm waiting for Catherine. I sense her presence and I feel her absence, though we've never met and it looks like she won't show up for today's appointment. In this sun-filled room I close my eyes and think about her.

Catherine has been referred to us five times over the past year by her GP who, in her most recent letter, says that Catherine is sorry she missed all the appointments she was offered and she promises to attend if we would send her another one, adding, 'Catherine is desperate to see someone.' I work for a busy drugs service and our counsellors are working to full capacity. How tempting it was to yield to the pressure of demand on us, to avoid another 'wasted' hour by referring her back to the counsellor employed by the surgery – who has also offered Catherine numerous appointments, all unattended.

The referral letters described Catherine as a 38-year-old woman who has a long history of amphetamine, heroin, alcohol and prescribed drug use. She was sexually abused between the ages of 5 and 11, has been hospitalized twice for 'breakdowns' and is currently unable to leave her house because she is agoraphobic. She is a single mother with two children, aged 7 and 12. The GP attributes Catherine's drug use to her sexual abuse and her pattern of relationships with violent men.

Wondering about her agoraphobia, that she may not have been able to manage the six-mile journey to our office, I decided to offer her an appointment at her GP's surgery, which is close to her home. So far, the process of meeting Catherine has been an active one for those of us who have become involved with her: the numerous letters written by her GP; the counsellors who have waited for her to arrive for appointments; the choices I faced in terms of our agency's resources; the work put aside (possibly another client) so I could travel to the surgery to see her.

Counselling

Counselling people with problematic drug use can be many things: challenging, stimulating and enormously rewarding; and it can be demanding, exhausting, confusing and disempowering. It is often considered a specialist area of work, despite varying and sometimes conflicting theoretical models practised within the field. The very phrase 'drug users' evokes a response wherever it is applied, reflecting the strength and diversity of thoughts, feelings and beliefs about drug use within our culture. Most people I meet are able to describe clearly an image they hold of a drug user, and I am guessing that you may already have an image of Catherine in your mind: dishevelled, dirty, lazy, selfish, manipulative, pathetic, lying, abusive, violent, weak, immoral, sick, in denial – the list of descriptive words within the collective vocabulary of our culture is long and the images are strong. Illegal and problematic drug use, or any chemical dependency, is a cultural taboo partly, I believe, because it is unresponsive to rational positivist approaches and interventions. It defies our cultural expectations that one is independent, always in control of oneself and one's life, responsible for one's decisions and actions and, above all, not needy or demanding. It seems we want to keep it 'out there', we do not want to be touched by 'it' or 'them'; or we act as though it is someone else's problem and pretend it does not exist. Each new version of the 'war on drugs' is a fresh attack on an 'enemy' that just won't go away.

The perspective I am presenting is my own, gathered over years of searching for effectiveness and meaning in my work with drug users. In my quest to understand addiction and to make a difference to the lives of others, my practice has changed many times. I adopted or combined different approaches and techniques, I made mistakes, adapted to new policies and learned from clients, supervisors and colleagues. I believe there is something human, *essentially human*, about addiction, which teaches us all that we are dependent and sometimes we are out of control, irresponsible, empty, 'hungry' and in need.

In the moment I meet Catherine for the first time, she will probably be seeing herself through the eyes of the world around her and may assume that I will look at her and see that image too. She may, at some level, be hoping that I have the answers she needs, that there is hope for her after all. And I will probably be carrying feelings of frustration and irritation about her absences, wondering about her motivation and ability to engage in counselling.

The initial stages of work

Our first meetings

Today Catherine does arrive, and I see before me a petite, immaculately dressed, beautiful – and terrified – woman.

She is apologetic and embarrassed about missing all the appointments. She looks down at her lap, where she plays with the rings on her fingers to stop her hands from shaking. I wonder if her shaking is due to nervousness or if she is withdrawing from alcohol, and I'm about to start my assessment of her drug use.

But Catherine begins the session first by quickly telling me that her name is Kit, not Catherine. Her father changed her name when she was very young, 'because it rhymed with shit, and I've always been little, and when no one was around he called me "a little piece of shit". He said I should have been flushed down the loo when I was born but 'round other people he called me Little Kit and the name just stuck.' She insisted that she wanted me to call her Kit.

Kit is painfully thin, and painstakingly beautiful. Her round child-like eyes search my face now for signs that what she has just told me is OK, then move quickly back down to her hands. She talks rapidly, moving from one subject to the next, never looking at me.

She tells me in meticulous detail about her daughters and how well she looks after them, how happy they are. She tells me that she has recently had a 'bad patch', which resulted in her GP's letters, but that she is much better now and in control of things again. She is not drinking or using any drugs other than the 'tablets' prescribed by her GP to calm her down during the day and help her to sleep at night. A quick glance at me.

'Everything is OK now, I'm fine really.' Her talking fills the space between us, it fills the entire room, and her story is absolutely watertight. She won't let me in.

Suddenly, Kit is out of her chair, ending our session twenty minutes early, 'I have to go now.' At the door she pauses, turns to face me, 'Oh, by the way, are you an addict?'

Shame

Two powerful feelings, shame and fear, are often present in the initial stages of counselling a drug user. Shame is the belief that one's self, the very core of one's being, is unwanted, unlovable, diseased or contaminating. It is not one's actions that are unacceptable, but the belief that one's very self is wrong. Shame is often experienced early in childhood: in Kit's case through the experience of emotional and sexual abuse. Several years ago I became alerted to the high incidence of childhood sexual abuse in my clients and began to keep informal statistics, merely noting if it arose in our sessions. I was surprised by the results. Taking a snapshot of my caseload at any given time I found that an average of 89 per cent of my clients have experienced some form of abuse (physical, sexual and/or emotional), including neglect, in childhood.

Our cultural expectations, and therefore our expectations of ourselves, to be able to cope with life and to be in control of ourselves, to manage our feelings and needs, can elicit enormous feelings of shame when this becomes impossible. There are times when, in the first counselling session, I can hear the voice of shame even when the words remain unspoken. 'I shouldn't need to be here. I should be able to deal with this myself. I don't know what's wrong with me, why I can't control myself.' For Kit, as for most of my clients, it was important that she somehow manage her feelings of shame at needing to see a drugs counsellor, and her fear that in my voice she will hear the judgement that confirms her embarrassment; that my eyes will 'see' and expose her in her shame. She may also feel acutely sensitive to my perception of her as a mother, as poor parenting – particularly mothering – is another source of shame. My clients manage these feelings in different ways. Some are angry, cynical, challenging, dismissive of me and counselling; some arrive very distressed; others, like Kit, fill the space by reassuring me (and of course themselves) that they really are coping.

Fear and control

The roller-coaster ride, feeling as though their world is *almost* out of control, that the pieces of their life are *only just* held together, brings panic, anxiety and stress to clients with problematic drug use. When I am asked if I am an addict, I believe I am being asked if I will understand this fear and, in the words of many clients, the 'madness'. They want to know if I will be able to understand what this craziness is like; if I will have the answers they need or be able to give them something to hold on to. The question is an important and challenging one. On one level it asks if we will have some common ground in terms of language, of understanding the mechanics of finding money, scoring and using drugs, and a shared understanding of the benefits, the enjoyment of using. Beneath the surface, the reverberations of Kit's question touch the places we hide away: the anguish of needs that have never been met; the things we do that we know are destructive in some way but that we still somehow need to do – that we cannot stop ourselves from doing – in order to avoid the painful places within ourselves or simply to have a few moments of relief and pleasure: eating, drinking, smoking, spending, working too much. This question catches counsellors off guard. Its directness can make us feel uncomfortable and it may be more frequently asked by substance users because of the philosophy that only an addict can help another addict, which is a cornerstone belief of Narcotics Anonymous (NA).

Relationships

Issues of relating and relationship loom large in my work with drug users. Dysfunctional early relationships will form the patterns for later attachments, as well as the relationship with one's self. Drug users often have a poor relationship with their body and at times seem disembodied. They will have a physical dependency and an emotional attachment to the drugs they use. It is no wonder, then, that our relationship will be a key issue in counselling. Many clients will have anxieties about what they imagine I will expect from them in terms of attendance, goal setting and achievement. I may be seen as someone with personal, professional and economic power who holds a position of authority and this may cause a degree of conflict for those whose identity is aligned with an illicit culture that directly challenges authority. Other fears relating to relationship have to do with being 'consumed' or abandoned by me, invaded or used. Clients may be very sensitive to power, trust and exclusion issues between us, due to early experiences when power was used against them, trust was broken and the feeling of belonging never known.

The themes of attachment and separation are likely to be present in all phases of work with drug users, and my experience is that relationship building and containment are the two crucial skills required of counsellors in the early stages. The core conditions of person-centred counselling (Rogers 1961, pp.61–2) are essential to hold the level of shame and fear drug-using clients bring to counselling. Reflecting and paraphrasing skills and establishment of clear boundaries build understanding between us and begin to ground and contain some of the chaos they bring. It has become increasingly accepted within the field of counselling, and it has been my experience in counselling drug users, that the single most influencing factor in treatment success, across a range of interventions, is the quality of relationship between worker and client.

Assessment

Kit's story

Kit has attended each of our contracted six sessions. She has either arrived late or left early and our sessions averaged 40 minutes. My goals have been to engage with her and to complete an assessment of her drug use. Kit gives me little opportunity to speak during our sessions. She clearly does not like the questions I ask about her drug use and is quick to move my attention to other crises in her life. Often she repeats stories she has already told me. The way in which she expresses herself and describes her world is in concrete terms, it seems she cannot explore her inner world and she struggles to think abstractly, visualize or to use her imagination. Occasionally the round-eyed child I met in our first session returns and she suddenly becomes embarrassed, looks down at her hands for a second, then is off again on another flight of words.

I have learned that Kit was given gin and orange juice from the age of 5 by her father, who sexually abused her while she was drunk. When she was 12, her mother asked her GP to prescribe tranquillizers to Kit because she was not sleeping at night, had nightmares, was pulling out her hair and was at times aggressive toward peers and teachers at school. That year her father left home and she never saw him again. She had her first panic attack at age 13, her diazepam was increased yet she was unable to leave her house to attend school.

But Kit did ultimately leave home: 'I was so desperate to get out so I got more valium for the confidence to do it.' She moved away, and found a bedsit and a job in a small office. At the age of 18 Kit was introduced to amphetamine and cocaine by her colleagues, 'to cheer me up'. Her daily routine for the next seven years was using amphetamine or cocaine and working during the day, taking some of her diazepam before going out drinking with friends and saving the rest to take just before bed. Towards the latter part of this time she began injecting amphetamine and buying temazepam on the street. She described herself during this period of her life as 'wild and fun', sometimes 'over-the-top' (violent) in clubs.

Kit was 25 when she collapsed at work, having had panic attacks for several weeks and 'getting really paranoid'. When she was released from hospital several weeks later, she had stopped using amphetamine and cocaine but had an increased prescription for diazepam and temazepam. She met Alan, the father of her daughters, who was a heavy drinker and she began drinking. This was a turbulent relationship. Kit was often beaten by him and after the birth of their second daughter he left them. Kit began injecting amphetamine again, saying she needed the energy to look after the girls. Five years ago she began using heroin when her new partner, a heroin user, moved in.

She had another breakdown at age 34 and her daughters were placed on the At Risk Register. Once again in hospital she stopped using amphetamine and heroin and says she has not used them since. For the past four years Kit has been taking her prescribed medication: diazepam, lorazepam and temazepam.

Although my assessment is far from complete and I suspect that she has omitted much about her drug use, I feel I am beginning to understand Kit's drug use. I suspect it is connected with her experience of childhood sexual abuse. It seems that her choice of drug is influenced by others and my hypothesis is that the function of her drug use is to help her manage internal conflict and emotional pain, to alleviate depression, and to provide her with the energy and confidence she needs to cope with life on a day-to-day basis. I have a strong feeling that just being alive is a struggle for Kit. Over the past five weeks I have also had a hunch that she is either using or drinking, though each week she replies that she is not. And each week I have sensed a desperate fiery energy about her, consuming the space and the very air of the room, and I have felt exhausted by her. I wondered about the driving force behind this 'forest fire' and the crises that just seem to 'happen'. What was the meaning of all this energy? Something was missing from Kit's story.

> Today, I follow my hunch from a different angle and ask, 'Kit, what about depression?' She looks at her hands, seems slightly stunned by my question. 'Oh…well…I usually feel worst at night, so tired of it all, when the girls are in bed, so I play a little game with myself. I take my bottles of tablets and take the tops off and then I drop the bottles on the floor. However many tablets come out is what I take before bed. If only one or two come out, I think, great, somebody wants me to live. If lots come out I think OK, it doesn't matter, so I take 'em and go to bed.'

Counsellors' dilemmas

Assessing a client's drug use can feel uncomfortable and in conflict with the values of counselling, particularly for counsellors who are in training or new to the field of chemical dependency. They often feel they are being directive or invasive and certainly there is a risk that an assessment or other form of data collection can reinforce the shame and mistrust that clients bring into counselling.

I have come to view assessment as two things: a counsellor's responsibility to their client and to themselves, and an investment in work that has the potential to become very complex. The purpose of an assessment is to determine whether counselling is appropriate for this person at this time and to gain some idea of just what we are working with, and working towards. Someone who is frequently and regularly using a mood altering substance, or who is engaged in chaotic drug use and life style, will not in my experience be emotionally available enough to participate in counselling. Other interventions, such as very focused cognitive work to help them reduce or stop their drug use, or primary health care, harm minimization, support or advocacy, may be more beneficial to them at this time. The assessment process is a time for my client and me to identify their priorities, which may be, for example, finding or improving their accommodation or registering with a GP.

It is also important for both counsellor and client to have a clear idea of what is appropriate and might realistically be achieved in counselling. Kit, at this point, seemed unable to relate to another person, to interact with me, and her thinking was so concrete that she could not reflect or explore within herself, or visualize herself being different. Other clients may be only weeks away from a court appearance at which they expect to be sentenced and, although we might touch on the connections between their drug use, its consequences and how it relates to life events, my aim would be to support them and help them plan for the decision of the court.

Risk assessment

When assessing drug use I am also assessing risk. I gather detailed information about what drugs are used, in what quantity, how they are taken, how often and how the drug use is funded. I ask clients for a description, in detail, of their using over the past month, then over the past three days. I ask how they have been feeling physically and emotionally and how they feel at this moment. I am trying to imagine their life: how they might be feeling emotionally and physically, what their days are like, where their anxiety and stress lie. It can be easy for counsellors to home in on the psychological mechanisms of their clients, to be eager to get to work on the underlying issues, and to overlook the person who is malnourished, run down and possibly too exhausted or ill to sustain a commitment to attend counselling sessions.

There is always an element of risk or unpredictability with illicit drug use in that users do not know the composition of the drug they are buying. Some, like Kit, increase this risk at times by 'tempting fate', using more of their drug or a cocktail of different drugs. I will then be looking for signs of self-harm or indications that other people might be placed at risk by their using, such as children, other family members or members of the public. In my first session with Kit I was alerted to the possibility that there may be some child protection issues because of her efforts to assure me that her daughters were well cared for. With this in mind, I talked about her children and explored the impact of Kit's drug use on them whenever possible, in all of our sessions. When Kit revealed that she sometimes took large amounts of tranquillizers before bed, I needed to respond to her in a way that would meet her needs as well as bearing in mind the needs of her two children, who may wake to find that their mother has overdosed or died. I have a responsibility to use my assessment of risk with my client wherever possible, to be clear with them about any risks involved, and to do this with care and sensitivity.

During our second session, Kit agreed that I may speak to her GP and that this would, wherever possible, be done with her knowledge and agreement. She said she had a good relationship with her daughters' social worker and preferred to speak with her directly, without my involvement. When she spoke about the way in which she was taking her tranquillizers, we agreed that we would both, separately, speak with her GP and that she would in future use her tranquillizers only as prescribed.

A good assessment enables me to introduce to my client the idea of a confidentiality agreement that will include other professionals if necessary, such as a probation officer, social worker or GP. If this is agreed early in the counselling process, I will be able to respond quickly to initiate crisis intervention or to increase levels of support if necessary.

The value of knowing my client's history

I attempt to note, in chronological order, the entire history of my clients' drug use, and here I am looking for connections between life events and their using. What patterns and themes emerge? I look especially for any times they have stopped, reduced or stabilized their drug use, as that offers them affirmation that they have been able to stop in the past and some indication of what the motivating factors may be for them. Clients often find this very useful. Possibly for the first time they are able to make some connections, to understand the meaning and purpose of their drug use, and to make sense of the 'madness'. It also challenges any denial that there is a problem.

Kit did not easily allow my assessment process and I often moved precariously between enquiring into her drug use, containing her energy and trying to build a relationship of trust between us. Many people working with drug users feel frustrated because they do not know for certain if their client is or has been using, and it can at times be difficult or impossible to know without conducting a drugs test. In my experience, a hunch or a feeling that something isn't quite right with them – or their story – can be as valuable. My hunch with Kit came from my sense of her desperation. Trusting this, and exploring her response to it, opened the way for us to truly connect for the first time. At last I began to feel and understand her pain.

Chaos

Kit asked to continue counselling, stating that she would come to our office for her appointments. She attended the next two sessions, cancelled the following three, did not show up for the next one and did not respond to my letter to her. Over the next eight months I heard different stories about Kit. Her GP was worried about Kit's increasingly chaotic lifestyle and declining health; other clients told me that she said I was her 'drug counsellor' and she wanted them to say hello to me for her. I heard that she was in a new relationship with a well-known dealer. Another client was using the needle exchange on her behalf.

Twice she rang our office asking for an appointment with me – 'It's urgent' – but she didn't attend. Another time she showed up at our office angry, wanting to see me, bruised from a fight she'd been in, looking pale and even thinner. She didn't attend the appointment offered her and later her boyfriend came in to our office to tell me that Kit was 'acting paranoid', wandering around the streets, afraid to come home. The children were placed in a foster home.

Counsellors' experience of the clients' chaos

Chaotic users can present the greatest personal and professional challenges to counsellors. The care and effort of building a relationship with them suddenly feels worthless in the face of missed appointments. Just when he or she was doing so well, just as we were about to start the 'real' work, they disappear. They start using again, sometimes they even get worse as their physical and mental health declines. They reappear in crisis and our attention is drawn to the acute symptoms they present. Some just cannot stop using, despite genuine displays of motivation, saying all the 'right' things and knowing exactly what they need to do. Sometimes they are arrested again and held on remand. They leave us standing, empty-handed, frustrated, disappointed and possibly doubting our skills and competence. They leave us facing our own version of chaos.

These are the times when no one wants to work with a drug user. Over the years, the challenges to my assumptions and expectations have been enormous: that the safe and nurturing environment I created would be 'good enough' and strong enough to hold them; that the insights they were gaining would open new doors of possibility to them; that they would be proud of the changes they were beginning to make and would want to do more; that there is always hope; that I can help. I never wanted to believe that some people decide, despite the pain, fear and stress in their lives and reaching their 'rock-bottom', that they don't want to change after all. Or that it is just too painful to change; maybe now is not the time, maybe never, maybe they just cannot change. With some clients I have felt deep sadness as I realized that they cannot accept affirmation, cannot even hear it, because not enough was given to them at a time when they could have received it, and by the people who mattered most to them. I have felt immobilized by all of this and by the emptiness I am left with when they go. I guess that, wherever they are, they too may be feeling a loss, perhaps of hope.

Containment of clients in chaos may be the best we can do, paying attention to their crisis whilst not becoming chaotic ourselves, and using our supervision to 'hold' us. In supervision I am able to regain perspective and make sense of what has happened. I have needed the reminders of my supervisors that I was working well with my clients and that I probably could not have done any more than I did with them. Above all, I needed to express my feelings of anger, sadness and grief; to have these understood and accepted.

Detoxification

Several months have gone by and a letter of referral is in my tray. It comes from a unit of the local psychiatric hospital requesting an assessment for Catherine, who sought admission to the unit last week.

We meet and Kit fills the space once more, words rushing from one topic to another, crisis after crisis to be dealt with. I stop her, and begin a long process of small-scale cognitive work with her. She has been using amphetamine, as well as prescribed and non-prescribed tranquillizers, for over a year, is restless and cannot concentrate. I start by focusing on her priorities and those of the unit. I introduce problem-solving skills, we identify her feelings and ways of expressing them and we write much of this down so she can remember and refer to them.

For the first four weeks in the unit, Kit rebels against everything: the food, the medication ('never enough'), the groups that drive her mad, the staff whom she mistrusts ('they're fucking analysing me all the time'), and so on. My aim now is to complement and reinforce the work of the mental health team and I focus on slowing her down. I ask her to sit without talking, to close her eyes and breathe deeply into her belly, exhaling slowly. After 30 seconds I ask her to speak, from her belly. This was impossible for her at first, but by our fourth session she was able to extend the time to one minute breathing deeply, and then speaking from within her body rather than from her racing mind.

Kit began to write, to make lists compartmentalizing her worries and goals, and to draw. She ate and slept regularly and attended the groups. She began to observe the people around her and talked about what she was learning. She often had violent nightmares. She would mention this to me but was unable to sustain an exploration of them. She was bereft without her daughters.

One day, Kit announced to me that she wanted a detox within the unit. She has not had a drug-free day for the past 27 years: 'I've just had enough.' We talked about the realities of the detox and her fears. We also agreed that our counselling would end when she began her detox, but that I would continue to meet with her once a week to support her during this time.

Detoxification, or detox, is the process of eliminating drugs from the body. Most drug users have made several attempts to detox themselves at home before they approach a drug service. Some are successful and may seek counselling to help them remain drug free, or they may contact us if they lapse into using again. Detox is a physical and, at times, a medical process, often funded and supervised by the medical professions. Depending upon the drug they are using and their individual circumstances, their detoxification process may take place at home or it may be supervised in a hospital or detox unit. Clients will probably be very uncomfortable whilst withdrawing and for several weeks following their detox. In Kit's case, her history of breakdowns and her ongoing contact with the mental health services led her into a psychiatric unit, where she would remain until she had stabilized physically and emotionally. Ultimately the staff team agreed to supervise her detox. There is currently no detox regime for amphetamine use, whereas detoxification from long-term tranquillizer use does require medical supervision.

It is a couple of weeks later and I have come to see Kit. One of the nurses leads me to her room. Opening the door, I find her sitting in an armchair in the middle of the room, which is in complete darkness. The sudden light startles her and she jumps. Slowly and gently I close the door, then pull up a chair next to hers. I can barely see her in the darkness, and she looks so tiny and fragile. Her eyes are closed and, though she is trying to move one of her hands, I can see that she just can't manage it. She tries to speak, tries again, and finally whispers words that I can only just make out. 'Sorry…sorry… can't talk.' She tries to raise the hand closest to me again. I touch it with my own and her tiny fingers wrap around mine, holding them tightly. For one hour we sit in the silence and the darkness. I hear her tears dropping into her lap.

A week later and Kit looks exhausted but is more herself. She is apologizing for being 'so useless and pathetic last week' and I'm surprised that she remembers so much of that hour. The profound effect it has had on her also surprises me. She's talking quickly again and I slow her down. 'So many things I wanted to say to you but I was in so much pain I couldn't talk and I was so afraid you would get up and go because I was being so useless and there was no way I could 'ave stopped you.'

Much later, when Kit was reflecting on that moment in her detox, she told me that she reached a point in her fear when she realized that there was nothing she could do but be what she was in that moment. When she realized that and accepted that I may just go because she was sitting in the darkness unable to talk to me, her fear dissolved, 'And it was like a big door opening to me and whatever it was that I've been looking for all these years just came in that door and filled me up, and all I could do was cry and I knew that you didn't know why.'

Rehabilitation

It is tempting to say that this is where my 'real' work with Kit began, except that every encounter with her and every phase we have been through has been real. But our work did change significantly from this point and the counselling process began. Kit soon returned home and our weekly sessions resumed at her GP's surgery and continued for just over two years. Without tranquillizers and amphetamine Kit's agoraphobia returned and she was unable to travel to our office.

Initially we focused on identifying ways in which she could cope with her daily tasks and manage her fears, including not only agoraphobia but also her nightmares, worries about losing her daughters, fear that she won't be able to cope without drugs and generalized non-specific panic. Depression overwhelmed her several times in the first year and each time I found myself admiring the tenacity with which she attempted to balance her application of new cognitive skills with 'riding out the storm'. Our every session was a container for Kit's bereavement and grief for the loss of her 'crutch and best friend' (alcohol and drugs), the loss of her childhood and much of her life, for her daughters who were still in care, and for the parents, partners, friends, achievements and happiness she never had.

Dealing with anger and grief

There were times when her anger erupted as she felt her grief and faced the difficulties of trying to put her life into order: bills and loans to pay; meetings with her daughters' foster parents and social worker; frustration at her fear of going out; rage and blame for her parents and teachers who violated and abandoned her. She felt she would never catch up on life, never be in control of it, never have friends who weren't drug users, never have a job and never have a place in the world.

Very slowly Kit began to see and know herself for the first time and was shocked sometimes by how much she was learning. Her thinking was less concrete, no longer set in stone, and she became insightful and imaginative. She learned from her feelings of depression, anger and panic; what events and thoughts they were connected to, how they moved in her body, how to contain them and when to let them move on. She no longer filled the space between us with rushing words, and when she did she would sometimes catch herself and laugh, knowing that this was just the time she needed to stop and listen to her internal voice. Her daughters were returned to her and she was proud of this achievement whilst daunted by the challenges it brought.

The process of change

Many people, including drug users themselves, assume that when they have stopped using drugs the worst is over. They expect their life to become different, suddenly easier and happier. Instead, they are entering the most difficult and challenging time, as they begin a process of internal change, come to terms with their losses and their current circumstances, and face unyielding, sometimes hostile, demands of the external world – all of this at a time when they are emotionally and physically fragile. It is a time of rebuilding and balancing. Within existing significant relationships, trust that may have been broken many times over many years needs to be repaired, relationships with other users need to change. A support system, so vital for encouragement and affirmation, may not be available to them, often because they have not been able to develop nurturing relationships with others. The level of need for affirmation, encouragement and a listening ear can exhaust those family members and friends who try to support someone at this time. It can be tempting for clients to engage in other behaviours that bring immediate gratification or self-esteem, such as shoplifting, gambling, over- or under-eating or entering into a new sexual relationship. For the majority of my clients, days that were once filled with acquiring money to buy drugs, then scoring and using them, and socializing with other users, are now empty of activity, meaning and contact with others.

Stress management

Stress management is a crucial skill at this time. Drug users are accustomed to relieving stress by using drugs and many return to using when stress and anxiety feel unbearable. They are then more sensitive to stress and just do not know how to manage it constructively. Increased emotional awareness and learning new life skills are key to stress management: expressing feelings and needs, communicating with others, affirming oneself, assertiveness, problem solving and managing money are but a few. Counselling can introduce the concept of balance to clients: balancing long-term goals with immediate needs, cognitive skills with in-depth therapeutic work; meeting the needs of others whilst looking after oneself. The mismatch of physical and psychological development can be frustrating for them. They are adults living in an adult world, wanting to step into adult roles, yet they may still have the needs, social skills and education of children or adolescents. Many times I find that I am feeling as impatient with them as they are with themselves, wishing they would 'grow up and get on with it' – to make their changes more quickly than they are able.

Collaborative working

My work with Kit involved other professionals at various stages. As I was formulating our counselling contract during my assessment of her, I gained her permission to include her GP in our confidentiality contract. Kit had a very good relationship with her daughters' social worker and we did not at that time identify a need to extend the confidentiality to her, but later, when Kit was admitted to the psychiatric unit, she asked that we include the social worker. At the same time, we agreed to contract with the mental health team of the unit. This enabled all of us to co-ordinate our work with Kit, to better support each other's work and Kit's, and to improve communication and trust amongst all of us.

Confidentiality agreements with other professionals involved with a drug-using client were initiated by government policy, which acknowledged the complexity of clients' needs and the need of the wider community for effective treatment for drug users. It is very difficult to include others in the counselling contract when the philosophy and training counsellors receive instil the strong message that counselling can only be effective when the boundaries are exclusive and protected. My initial scepticism and reluctance to part from my training changed as I began fully to appreciate the responsibilities inherent in working with drug users. I also saw evidence that careful contracting, good relationships with the other professionals and responsible management of the confidentiality agreement actually worked for the benefit of my clients and supported all of us working with them. Working with others in this way required of me a level of accountability I had never accepted before, as I attempted clearly to articulate what I do in my work and why.

Focusing our work

Our counselling training and experience equip us to identify, often very quickly, some of the issues that underlie a client's drug use. In Kit's case this was her experience of childhood sexual abuse and an abusive family system. The dilemma arises whether we treat the person or the drug use. There can be an assumption that if we work with clients on underlying problems, their drug use will become controllable or even stop. Counsellors may feel that if they focus only on the drug use they are working superficially, leaving out the person. Gaining a good understanding of how much and how often a client is taking a mood altering substance can help with this. If someone is using drugs on a daily basis, they probably will not be able to participate in counselling. If they are using much less frequently or bingeing, they may be able to look at some of their deeper issues. In my experience, finding a balance between the two seems to work most effectively: keeping their drug use in focus as much as possible whilst acknowledging their experiences and their pain. Kit and I never addressed her experience of sexual abuse. We often referred to it in our sessions, acknowledged its impact on her and its connection with her drug use, but she always stepped quickly back from the subject. Kit required all of her own resources and an enormous amount of affirmation and support from others just to remain drug free, to cope with a new drug-free lifestyle and to assimilate all that she was learning. I believe she needed to build a stronger sense of identity before embarking on the work concerning her sexual abuse. Some clients do choose to face underlying issues at some point in their rehabilitation; others never do and rebuild their lives in a different way.

Conclusion

Kit came into contact with workers from several professions over the many years of her problematic drug use and she may have encountered professionals using counselling skills anywhere along the way: with a member of the mental health teams, with a nurse in A&E, on one of the wards, or with a social worker. This is very different from counselling, which consists of a mutual agreement between client and counsellor to undertake the work and clear contracting of where, when and how the counselling process will take place. However, the value of those sometimes brief contacts when counselling skills are used can be precious for drug users who, despite the behaviour they present, long for contact that is human, non-judging, accepting, welcoming and honest. I have been very fortunate to work with Kit and many like her, who may come and go or have phases of chaos and using, but who somehow find a way of reclaiming their lives. They have shown me how to heal and be healed over and over again. Sometimes the solutions to chemical dependency seem so clear; other times the answers disappear and I am left with a great mystery.

> Today Kit and I finish our work. It's our last session and we haven't met for a month. Looking at Kit I notice for the first time that she seems bigger – not physically bigger, but I'm sure her presence has grown. Tears gather in my throat and suddenly I realize how much I'll miss her. As our session comes to an end I make the observation that she seems to have a larger presence today. Her eyes well up, 'I know, it's so amazing, I feel stronger, like I've really grown up. And there's something else.' She looks down, then her eyes, soft, quiet, tear-filled, are looking directly into mine. 'I wanted to tell you that my name is Catherine now.'

References

Rogers, C.R. (1961) *On Becoming a Person: A Therapist's View of Psychotherapy*. London: Constable.

Further reading

Listed below are a few sources that have inspired and influenced me, and widened my understanding of problematic drug use.

Mair, M. (1989) *Between Psychology and Psychotherapy: A Poetics of Experience*. London: Routledge.

Ram Dass and Gorman, P. (1986) *How Can I Help? Emotional Support and Spiritual Inspiration for Those Who Care for Others*. London: Rider. See pages 167–171 for a brief and beautiful account of a very human 'meeting' within the context of social action.

Rogers, C.R. (1951) *Client-Centred Therapy*. London: Constable.

Tyler, A. (1995) *Street Drugs: The Facts Explained, The Myths Exploded*. London: Hodder & Stoughton. Fascinating, readable and comprehensive, this is an excellent resource for anyone working with drug users. It contains detailed information about the drugs and how they are used. It also places drug use within an historical and cultural setting.

Woodman, M. (1982) *Addiction to Perfection: The Still Unravished Bride.* Toronto: Inner City Books.

Woodman, M. (1993) *Conscious Femininity: Interviews with Marion Woodman.* Toronto: Inner City Books. Not just for women! Both books by Marion Woodman offer a Jungian perspective of addiction and I have found them creative, compassionate and inspiring.

Useful contact addresses

ADFAM National
Waterbridge House
32–36 Loman Street
London SE1 0EH
Tel: 020 7928 8898

For families and friends of drug users.

DrugScope
32 Loman Street
London SE1 0EE
Tel: 020 7928 1211
www.drugscope.org.uk

One of the UK's leading sources of information and expertise on drugs.

Chapter 11

Counselling for Recovery from Addiction

A Personal Account

Frances Taylor

Dedicated to my dear husband.

Introduction

I was born in 1950, the younger of two children. By 1986 I had been using heroin for all of my adult life. My life had become a quest to acquire heroin; nothing was allowed to come between my habit and me. I had to have it. The fear of being drug sick and my desire to get stoned completely took me over. When I went into withdrawal, making money to score was desperate and sordid and so I made sure that I was stoned enough to make enough money to get stoned enough to make money to get stoned enough to … I did what it took. I sold drugs, possessions and my body. I was an opportunist thief and stole to support my habit and to feed and clothe my children. The police frequently raided my home so we lived behind barricades, often without gas or electricity. My life was squalid and sordid and I didn't know how to get out.

Drugs were no longer pleasurable. Sure, there was the odd batch of good quality smack that gave me the oblivion I craved, but mostly I was left wanting. I had destroyed my veins; getting a hit was a painful and lengthy ordeal which frequently resulted in abscesses. I injected into any vein that I could see and some that I couldn't see. I used my jugular and femoral veins to the point of their collapse. I was underweight and prone to severe chest infection due to self-neglect. Worse than my physical health and appearance though was my emotional distress. I protected myself from seeing the effects of my addiction with an effective, unconscious denial system. For a long time my defences were largely impenetrable, although sometimes I surfaced, stupefied by my life and its happenings and wanted to change it. I had no concept that, in order to do this, I needed to change.

From the age of 14, through until I was 19, I was using so-called 'soft' drugs. The way I used, even then, was as if I was on a mission. During these years I was also promiscuous. I was searching for a way to escape how I felt about myself. I had no desire to conform. It was the 1960s and cool to take drugs and free love was the order. My mother was permissive. Her mother had been very strict and she wanted to be more giving. She set few limits and rarely said no. I loved her and craved her approval, but I did not respect her. She was ineffective and I got what I wanted, having found ways to wear her down. My father, in contrast, was a gambler and not averse to being on the wrong side of the law. They met and married in three days at the end of the war. My mum, at 38, wanted children and her body clock was ticking away. My dad was at a loose end having spent most of the war years behind bars. My parents weren't happy together and lived separate and different lives. Mum was a hard-working woman with her own business, which left her little time to be with my brother and me. She was a gentle woman who hated arguments. My father was a charmer with a great sense of humour and an equally great temper. He had been a boxer and he let me stay up late, sitting with him to watch boxing on the television. We would cheer on the fighters together and I felt close to him and that I had got one up on my mum at the same time. She professed to hate violence of any sort, yet she married a man who had a genuine gift for tyranny. His moods depended on the outcome of the latest horse race. Sometimes I was his little princess; at other times he ranted and raved at my mum and my brother, frightening and bewildering me. He didn't pick on me until I became a teenager, when I started to speak up for myself and stand up for my mum and brother.

When we were very small we were looked after by a live-in nanny. My father was in prison for the first few years of my life and my mother had a hairdressing business at that time. I first stole when I was five years old. My mother told me I was bad and that I would end up just like my dad. I believed her, but had no idea what she meant. Later, I decided that I preferred to be bad than saintly and sanctimonious.

Although my school reports stated that I was intelligent, they reflected my lack of focus and application to schoolwork. I baffled my teachers. My mum appeared to be supportive and there was 'nothing wrong at home', so the problem had to be me. At the age of 13 I was expelled from school for an act of violence. I had been caught shoplifting several times and was shamed at assembly for it. No one noticed that I was angry, scared, hurting, miserable and confused, but they all agreed that I was bad and heading for serious problems. I always felt guilty and frequently tried to get back on track. I can remember having to check through the last few days every so often to find out if I had done anything to feel guilty about. I made peace with my mum every now and again by telling her what she wanted to hear. Yes, I was a bad girl, I was very sorry and I'd never do it again. I had to. She kept threatening to have a nervous breakdown. No one knew me. I tried so hard to be who she wanted me to be, but it wasn't possible. No one knew how I felt and no one demonstrated any belief in me. I grew up lonely. I needed an adult to care, to help me make sense of myself as I grew up. I was given criticism and a forecast of damnation. I needed someone to be strong and supportive. With ever-present feelings of shame for who I was, and guilt for upsetting everyone, I was ripe for addiction.

Beginnings of addiction

My first addiction was to food, then stealing, lying and sex. I was 14 when my GP prescribed amphetamines for weight control and the pill for birth control. I look back at myself as a teenager trying to create a make-believe family and trying to make it true through pretending. I would fantasize that my real parents would rescue me, pronouncing my mum and dad as impostors. Later on I stole clothes and make-up as I tried to find an identity, playing a more sophisticated version. I had no sense that who I really was was OK, so I needed to be who I wasn't. I learned that if I did what the boys wanted I got their attention and so I became promiscuous. I was out of control. I'm sure my mother didn't know what to do with me and she only knew a little of what I was doing. My father was not home much. When he was at home, there would be a major row, usually around the supper table, when he would find fault with someone or some thing. He would sometimes throw his dinner at the wall and I remember the spittle coming out of his mouth as he raged, terrifying us. When I was 15 I'd had enough of his tyranny and told him exactly what I thought of him. He tried to get hold of me and I stabbed him in the back of his hand with the carving knife. I had pinned him to the table, which gave me time to get away. My mother told me later that he was stunned by what I'd done and left the house never to return. I sought him out only once after that. I needed his permission to get married. It came to light later that he'd fathered our cleaning lady's child and had many affairs. He had a fiancée and had been living a double life for years. He married her and settled down with his new wife and a golden labrador until his death in 1972.

The era threw drugs my way and I caught them with both hands. I had relationships with men who were in the drug scene and I earned my street credibility. Drugs and violent men were my life. I found that they were stronger than I was. In the early years I felt safe and at last I felt as if I belonged somewhere. It was after I had children, when the violence increased and the drugs got out of control, that I became frightened. Using heroin was like coming home. It put me into a warm cocoon where I could not be hurt. It removed me from my feelings. It distanced me from my family's hypocritical values and morals. Heroin set me free to be someone of my own and gave me a strong identity. I had at last found something substantial through which I could define myself. It embraced me and made me feel complete, free at last from the constraints of my mother's imposed expectations. I didn't know about friendship and supportive, loving relationships, so I connected with others like me. I learned the drug culture from within it and my sense of right and wrong became eroded. My addiction to heroin required a commitment from me that I had never before given. I quickly learned how to do what it took to keep myself supplied. My love affair with smack was so important that I sold my soul to ensure my supply. I did many things I had sworn I'd never do to keep it close to me. My relationship with heroin was my priority. Over time I became my addiction.

Searching for a cure

The medical model route

My search for a 'cure' began when I was 25, which was six years after my first fix. There weren't many drug users in those days and the few services available were linked to psychiatry. I was admitted to a psychiatric hospital on numerous occasions and placed on an acute ward where patients were very disturbed. I was always very serious in my attempts to get clean. I didn't want the life I had for my children or myself. I always stayed for the duration and was discharged after completion of detoxification (detox). Detoxification meant ingesting a cocktail of drugs which usually included methadone, barbiturates, chlorpromazine and benzodiazipines. The ward staff were wary of me and I felt judged by them. It was the same old thing: I was a malingerer, taking up valuable bed space which would be better occupied by someone who hadn't induced their illness. The impression I formed was that they believed I had brought my problems upon myself and if I had more willpower I would be cured. I understood myself in the same way and so I made no progress and usually scored smack on the way home from hospital. I celebrated my cure with the substance I was dependent on. The years rolled by and I became more enmeshed in my addiction. I was unable to extricate myself and my hope eroded.

By 1986 seeing a drugs worker had become a compulsory component at inner city health centres for those, like me, who wanted help for heroin addiction. Services were beginning to consolidate. It was hard to find a sympathetic GP who would provide substitute medication without drug agency back-up. Gone were the days when I could register with a GP who would prescribe, unconditionally, the opiates which allowed me to exist. To addicts in my position the GPs, like the dealers, were like God. They held the power to give or deny me a few days' respite. I remember the agony of the occasions when the chemist queried the script and refused to fill it and how panic-stricken I was when I returned to the doctor to have a new script made out. I first had to get past the receptionists and then persuade the doctor that I wasn't conning him, before returning to the chemist with a new script in my hand. The time it took to get the formalities straightened out felt like an eternity. Anxiety seemed to exacerbate withdrawal symptoms and substantially increase my need for opiate.

Looking behind the addiction for the first time

There were now controls and rules hitherto unheard of. I found it much more difficult to con doctors. Professionals were becoming proactive in learning about addiction. There was a movement away from the standard medical approach of substitute medication and gradual weaning off to an exploration of the psychological underpinning of addiction. There was a long way to go, however, and to this day it is my experience that drug workers are undertrained in the complex dynamics of addiction and its underlying causation. From my position all this felt obstructive. I had no trust in anyone I perceived to have authority. I had no reason to believe this new approach would be any more helpful than the methods which had failed me numerous times before.

I was at yet another bleak place in my addiction. My mother had died three years before. I'd eventually got round to selling her house in which I had been living with my children and made my family homeless into the bargain. The idea was that we should move abroad, buy a bar and live happily ever after. I so much wanted a better life. The children were growing up and were unhappy. I had no idea how to go about setting up a business and so we went abroad on holiday until the money ran out. It took me just five months to spend it: drugs were easily available in Europe. We arrived back in Bristol with little more than the clothes we stood up in.

I couldn't go on any more and asked my husband to enter a suicide pact with me. I knew I was no good to anyone any more. He refused and was deeply distressed. My family had always seen me as strong, almost invincible; now they were confronted with my vulnerability. My husband and sons carried me through this period. I never regained my denial. I became frightened in situations in which previously I had no fear. My world had closed in on me. Using heroin, and all that it entailed to sustain my addiction, had become too hard and I was worn out. I could not verbalize or recognize this. My world was either black or white. I only knew extremes. I wouldn't say I wanted to stop using: I simply didn't think I could. I just wanted someone to help me and I knew that my husband and children couldn't. So in the winter of 1987 I signed on with a GP who had prescribed for me previously. I was told that if I wanted methadone, the only substitute offered, I needed to see the drug worker each time my prescription was due.

Counselling begins

Finding someone who believed in me

The worker attached to the surgery made little impression on me. Nevertheless for the first time in my life I attempted compliance. I was frequently thrown off the programme because I altered my prescription (script); lied to obtain more drugs; was frequently abusive to the health centre staff; and harassed other drug users to hand over their scripts to me.

At that time I had no idea that Bob, my drug worker at the surgery, was a counsellor, let alone a psychotherapy trainee, or that we would work together for seven years. I hadn't a clue what counselling was, which was fortunate because I'm sure I would have bolted if I had known more. I bolted often enough without that. The interesting and awesome aspect was that Bob, unlike the other medics, social workers, probation officers and well-intentioned officials I had encountered along the way, managed to convey that he saw me as a person with qualities and resources which could be made use of constructively. Despite my best attempts to prove that I was beyond redemption, he was persistent, wise, calm and humorous. He somehow managed to locate and trust the little bit of me hidden amongst the mayhem that held my inherent desire to get well. He recognized me as a human being who was stuck in a life style which was painful and chaotic. He helped me to face myself through acknowledging my pain in a deep and meaningful way. He helped me get well by enabling me to identify my inner resources and extend my capabilities. As I grew to trust him I was able to share with him the part of myself that I had always denied. I told him of the part of myself that I had learned to hide during my childhood. The essence of who I was slowly, slowly, slowly came together. All the fragments of me that had been pushed aside, sneered at, began to surface with this lovely man. He helped me to start to set myself free by honouring all that I shared with him. I'm not sure if it was intentional or simply my good fortune that I was never allocated another drugs worker.

In the early part of the process Bob saw my husband and me together most of the time. Johnny and I had clung on for years and it was wise of Bob to work with us as a couple. It would have been too much for us to cope with if we had seen the cracks in our relationship at this fragile stage. Initially we met at the health centre, right after we got our scripts from the GP. Our prime concern was to cash the scripts, so we were distracted and did not make any use of the session. Later we moved to a council estate on the outskirts of Bristol and Bob came to our home. I sometimes saw him alone and, although I would never have admitted it then, I enjoyed the time we spent together. We were more relaxed at home and after the statutory urine test (which I frequently rigged) we drank tea whilst we talked. Bob never seemed in a hurry and I began to see that he was committed to working with us and gradually learned to accept his support. He always turned up – many a time I hoped he wouldn't. He spoke with me about my life and initially I told him whatever came into my head. I lied a lot and, where other professionals were prepared to swallow whatever story I came up with, it was not so easy to fool Bob. He noticed and remembered details. Despite my best efforts to keep him at arm's length, he did get to know me and he seemed to understand how I felt about my life and myself. When I was in crisis, which was frequently, he did not back off, nor did he try to rescue me, but I always knew he was on my side. I remember feeling rage and frustration that he simply kept coming when he said he would. I tried to push him away and was, at times, atrociously behaved. It was, for me, terrifying to allow someone to care about me. I tested his commitment to me over and over again. We would talk when he came; that's all it seemed to be, talking. It was of course much more. I was beginning to notice myself in my life and to think that it might be possible for me to change. It was a very slow awakening as I clung unsteadily to my beliefs about myself and the world around me.

A couple of years after I met Bob, I had come to rely on prescription drugs topped up with copious amounts of alcohol. I was using heroin less frequently but could not see any major change, even though I had been able to use legitimate drugs. I was a long way off being a 'regular' person. I was isolated in my addiction and felt terribly lonely. I recreated another layer of denial to protect myself. Looking back, I now believe that if I had fully experienced what I had become, all at once, suicide would have been my only option. I remember Bob being constant, encouraging and supportive and I felt liked by him. He seemed to hold a trust in me which I had abandoned long before. He helped me recognize how limited my ability to make and exercise choice had been and how I needed to match my behaviour with my feelings of shame and guilt. It took me a long time to trust him and understand this at all; I thought he was very weird. It had been a long time since anyone who wasn't a fellow addict thought that I was anything but rubbish.

The middle phase of counselling

Life nearly ends and begins at 40

One day it struck me like a bolt of lightning that I was trapped. I had just passed my fortieth birthday and, contrary to my fantasy, there was no knight in shining armour coming to rescue me. I couldn't understand, for the life of me, how I was still stuck in addiction. This had never been part of my plan. The years had simply rolled away and nothing had changed. That day I went completely out of my head. I remember the drugs I used: methadone, heroin, speed, diazepam and vodka. I was arrested for shoplifting and knew I was likely to go to prison. I contemplated suicide once again and had I not had the primordial instinct of love for my children to hold on to, I believe that I would have taken my life that day.

The next day, without telling anyone, I went to see Bob. I trusted him enough to believe that if I levelled with him he would help me. I also trusted that he would not take my children away from me: I had always feared that if I said I couldn't cope then I would lose my children. They were all I had and my feelings for them kept me alive. Losing them would have annihilated me. I told him I could no longer live my life as I was and that I needed to be sent somewhere where I could learn to live as I wanted to. He heard my desperation and within three days I was, once again, in the acute ward in the psychiatric hospital. The difference this time was that after detox I was going on to rehab. I was never more frightened.

I spent three weeks coming off the drugs and alcohol. I had a rough time. I expected this, as each time I went through detoxification it was significantly more painful. It is a traumatic process when the drugs that the body has become dependent on to function start to exit the body. It's a shock to the body as it battles to make adjustments so that it can perform naturally. I have never had any medication which treated each symptom fully: vomiting, diarrhoea, shivering, shaking, muscle spasms, sleeplessness, sneezing fits and worst of all the body's rawness and acute sensitivity in the nerves. In addition to this are the psychological symptoms: the resurrection of feelings which are magnified by the body's vulnerability; the constant confrontation of one's desire to use; and the anxiety of entering a system of recovery where there are no guarantees. I clearly remember the relief when withdrawal symptoms were allayed by the ingestion of heroin. It was so great to feel heroin coursing around my body, bringing it back from fragmentation to wholeness.

Rehabilitation

'I'll give this recovery lark a go'

I was not a model patient. The ward staff seemed to have little sympathy for me and, as always, I was the only addict on the ward. Bob was away, but had asked his colleague, Jenny, to visit me each day. I had put myself so completely in Bob's hands that, even though I was pissed off with him for taking a holiday, I felt safe with her. I had met Jenny before and liked her. It turned out that she had worked in a rehabilitation centre (rehab) and so I was able to find out what it would be like there and what would be expected of me. Jenny painted a picture of peaceful ambiance where I would have to work hard. She endorsed my sense of needing to prioritize caring for myself, resting and recovering. I was able to go to rehab once the court agreed to adjourn my case until I had finished treatment. I went straight to rehab from the hospital. Jenny drove me and I was so nervous I couldn't even manage to roll a cigarette.

I was in rehab for 13 weeks. I don't remember much about the first few weeks except that we were governed by a handbell which a fellow patient had the dubious privilege of ringing. The bell summoned us to rise, eat, attend lectures and go to group therapy. I thought it was all stupid, but I'd made a decision that I would give this recovery lark a go and if I wasn't happy by the time my youngest child was 16 then I could kill myself in the certain knowledge that life was crap. (At that time I thought when he was 16 he would be an adult and wouldn't need me.) In group therapy I was silent and withdrawn and in the community I was aggressive and defensive. I remember one of the women in my group said she thought that I was scared. Too right! I was expected to confess all the things I'd done to maintain my habit. I was full of guilt and shame and expected to be given a hard time. Instead I was cared for and respected, which was both baffling and excruciating. I was an excellent self-prosecutor and judged myself without compassion. I was unable to voice how I really felt. I needed time to learn the words to describe my feelings. I was numb for a long time. However, the rehab was a safe place. There were strict rules: if patients were suspected of drug use, they were tested and discharged if suspicions were confirmed; there were expectations for us to behave appropriately and if we did not comply we risked discharge. I needed enforced boundaries and structure to feel safe enough to come out of my shell and trust the people around me. It was many months before I could begin to trust myself. I stuck it out, built a recovery toolbox and left the rehab a 'success'.

Using group support to set boundaries and allowing others to help me

I saw Bob regularly, attended Narcotics Anonymous meetings every day and, when the court gave me a probation order instead of the custodial sentence I was expecting, the probation service paid for me to attend group therapy. I felt like an alien and I was terrified. My struggle had only just begun. In order for me to sustain my recovery I knew, intellectually, that I needed to set some boundaries with my family. I knew in my heart that if I stayed in my marriage I would return to substance misuse. I needed to be adult for the first time in my life. I set ultimatums and followed them through. I separated from my husband whilst he went into treatment and tried to rebuild his life. I was alone, except for Bob and the people I met in NA. I severed contact completely with my 'using' friends. Bob was there supporting me in my decisions, always allowing me to find my way through the debris left by my drug use. My family did not recognize me any more. I would not allow any drug use in the house, no matter how hard they tried to influence me otherwise. We all had problems and all I could do was try to sort out my own and support my youngest child to adjust to the new life. We were both very lonely and very, very angry.

Bob remained steadfast. I was overwhelmed with grief. The pain exhausted or stressed me. Bob continued to hear how much I hurt and encouraged me to keep letting it out. It was as though by telling him about my pain I was unburdening myself. His frequent response to me was to ask what it was that I needed. When I needed something that was impossible for me to get, for example, comfort from my mother, he helped me come to terms with my loss and explored ways that I could learn to comfort myself. When I felt that I couldn't cope, between sessions, I would sometimes have a pretend conversation with him and work out his likely responses. I found this reassuring and a useful way to identify what it was that I needed. Furthermore I became able to measure how urgent my need was and to respond accordingly. By doing this I could have his wisdom and love on tap whenever I needed it.

Much later, he told me that he had seen two strands of me: one which was fragile and one which was very strong, and that he had made a commitment to stay with me for as long as I needed him and for as long as his circumstances would allow. He was the only person I could really trust. Bob challenged my view of myself. He appeared to be able to see and value aspects of me which I had buried long ago. I think that because he was able to see more than I could, I was able to know that there was more to me than I believed and I began to accept the possibility that I was lovable. As I began to have compassion for myself, the dawning of self-understanding and forgiveness began. I began to view myself, not as a bad person, but as someone who had been disabled through addiction. I was able to know that, throughout my life, I had had limited choices and, given the power of the drug culture, I had been unable to behave differently. Quite simply, I hadn't had the resources to get out.

Rebuilding my identity

Week by week, month by month, year by year, we tackled my problems by discovering the roots of my problems. I gained a sense of what I needed in my life and how it was for me when I was growing up. I didn't have much of a chance to live well; no one showed me how. My mum and dad weren't equipped for that task. I was so angry with my family, my teachers and all those people who failed to help me recognize my needs.

Gradually I became stronger and started to rebuild my life and develop ambitions. I came to be able, not just to admit my difficulties, but to find solutions. I became able to decipher what I was capable of and what to accept and let go of. I could see that I could help myself and, through the process of my own recovery, my children became able to take responsibility for themselves and in turn ask for the help they needed. Tragically, Johnny, my husband, was unable to stabilize in his recovery and died as a result of heroin use.

Bob never flinched from my pain, which at times felt unbearable to me. I was able to grieve my many losses and celebrate my survival within this relationship. My feelings were paramount. I was cared for no matter what. He was the first human being who sustained interest in me. He gave me support and challenge. He confronted my behaviour without compounding my sense of shame. He encouraged me to trust myself and to learn through my mistakes.

The ending phase of counselling

The time came when I began to be able to live my life in peace and I remember the wonderful feeling of completeness the first time I experienced that all was well in my world. I was noticing beauty in life. I saw colour and vitality around me. I felt, at last, human. Bob worked with me for about six years into my recovery. Our ending came about because he moved to Yorkshire with his family. We took three months to end, which gave me time to deal with his departure. I was very, very angry that he was leaving me. It compounded my belief that everyone I loved left me. Now, he too was abandoning me. He created the space in the last months for me to express my anger towards him. He shared with me his difficulty in leaving me. He told me that his fantasy was that my sense of abandonment and subsequent anger would overwhelm me and that I would return to heroin use and die. As he told me this we both wept. I knew his fantasy was borne out of his concern and love for me and I absolutely knew that I wouldn't need to make it true. We both knew that I could adjust and that I would survive. It was never going to be OK for me that he was going away and nothing could ever make it completely all right.

As we said our long goodbye Bob helped me identify and acknowledge that I was the major player in my recovery. We went over how I struggled to make use of my strengths and that sometimes the steps I took were giant ones and sometimes tiny ones, and yet I had managed to dig deep enough to get what I needed from him and myself. He used to drive me barmy with his oft-asked questions, 'What is it that you need? How would that help?' I didn't have a clue most of the time, but I would have to find a realistic response and then he'd ask me, 'How might you get/have that?' I recall that very often I already had what I needed, but hadn't fully known it until then. As we reaffirmed my passage from drug addiction to recovery I really knew that I could keep him with me and let him go at the same time.

Learning from the process

I asked Bob many questions during this time. One thing I needed to know was why he had persevered with me? Why had he not washed his hands of me? What made him continue to work with me when I was so vile to him? How did he know that I was genuine when I asked for help? This is what he told me.

He said he wanted to listen to me, to hear me tell my story and through the telling he was able to see beyond what I said. He said he sometimes got a glimpse of an unhappy, broken, desperate woman who had spirit and beauty, who was both loving and lovable. He said he saw a woman who had intelligence, humour and guts. He said that he saw a woman who had imprisoned herself in addiction in order to exist. He said that he knew that woman held the key to her freedom. And he said that he wanted to share her delight when she was free to feel the wind in her hair and the sun on her face as she ran laughing on a beach with her beloved children. He told me he trusted that she could be so. He said that he knew all that about me and he wanted to help the woman I was and am to know all of that about myself. He said that my life was valuable and worthwhile. And now I know it is.

Conclusion

As I work towards my conclusion I want to say something about 'readiness'. My first requests for help to live without drugs stemmed from my recognition that I was out of my depth and I very much wanted to find a way to stop. I am convinced that, had I been regarded positively and supported through counselling to understand myself, I would not have spent so much of my life in the grip of addiction. I believe that when addicts ask for help it is because they can no longer cope with themselves and their lives. There is a model of working with addiction which emphasizes that timing is an essential component if one is to achieve recovery from addiction: pre-contemplation, contemplation and action. I have yet to meet any addict who does not contemplate stopping using. We just need people to help us find a way. I know that when I went for help I didn't get what I needed. I had no concept of what I needed then so I could not ask for it specifically. I relied on the people who professed to be able to help me. Their help failed me time and time again until I felt utterly defeated. I needed to find a way to live. I had children and I knew that my life wasn't right for them. I took them to places that weren't safe for adults, let alone children. I didn't give them what they needed emotionally or physically. Sometimes I was cruel and neglected them. Social services and the police featured in our lives. Why didn't they protect my children from my addiction and crazy behaviour? Over the years there were many opportunities for intervention.

Nobody, save Bob, cared enough to help me recognize my opportunities. I had no choice but to justify my addiction and I did so by finding a rationale for it. I told myself that no one really cared about me, which was probably true. I told myself that life was crap and it was best to be ruthless and take what I could because there were no free rides. I told myself that I was different from everyone else, flawed in some irredeemable way. To survive I needed to compound my belief that the only people who understood me were other junkies. I spent years constructing this belief and yet I know in my heart that if one person had shown me there was a way to make it all stop, I would have been first in line.

It wasn't until 1986–7 that I heard of people 'getting into recovery'. Until then all I knew was that people either kept using or died. I have lost many people I cared about. The world has lost many, many bright, intelligent people, for the want of a safe place and a skilled person to value them enough to commit, no matter what, to helping them move on in their lives. The greatest tragedy of all is that drug abuse continues to increase. Nowadays everyone knows someone who has been in trouble with drugs. Drug addiction is still widely misunderstood. Effective treatment is massively under-resourced and cost effectiveness remains the statutory and voluntary agencies' prime concern. The rationale for the breakdown of treatment is that the addict wasn't ready! If the addict is not ready, then why does he or she keep striving to find a solution? We do, you know. Many, many nights were spent trying to find a way out and the nights became years of squalor and sordidness. I am angry that I lost so many years. I am deeply saddened that my children lost their right to a happy childhood. I take responsibility for all that I did and someone needs to take responsibility for the prejudice and ignorance that I encountered in my search for a solution.

Chapter 12

Narrative ideas and stories of disability

Kim Etherington

Introduction

This book is full of stories – some told by people who have been through a process of rehabilitation themselves, such as Frances Taylor's story of rehabilitation from drug and alcohol misuse or that told by Diana Sheppard about her rehabilitation from stroke. There are also many other stories relating to disability and chronic illness embedded within the chapters written by professionals working in the field of counselling in rehabilitation, each one adding the rich dimension that personal experience brings with it. We all have stories to tell about our experiences of health and illness and disability – our own or that of others, because our lives are all touched by these matters, although we may not always recognize in what way.

My own stories

I wondered which of my own stories had been fundamental to my interest in the field of disability and rehabilitation and I looked back to my first conscious memory of impairment and remembered Mrs Bill who moved into our neighbourhood when I was 8 years old. Mrs Bill was 'deaf and dumb' (nowadays she would be referred to as a 'profoundly deaf signer', but in 1948 it was different), as was her husband Mr Bill who went off to work each day as a carpenter. They had a little girl of about three, and a few months after they moved in Mrs Bill gave birth to another little girl. I became very involved with the family, popping across the road to their house almost every day to push the baby out in the pram and generally help with the children. As one of a large family myself you might have thought I'd seen enough of babies to last a lifetime but what I had never seen was a baby girl. I had seven brothers and was pretty sick of the sight of boys, so having a baby girl to look after was something of a treat. Mrs Bill taught me to sign the alphabet on my hands and in this way we could converse. I felt very proud of this ability and have not lost it to this day.

But as I thought about all this I realized that my experience of disability was even closer to home than that. My father had been a young soldier in World War I and had been retired from the Army on a disability pension even before I was born when he was in his fifties. He was a semi-invalid throughout my childhood and now, with hindsight, I realize that what he was suffering from would today be diagnosed as post-traumatic stress disorder. However this condition was only listed in DSM III for the first time in 1980, many years after my father's death in 1956 when I was almost 16 years old. All I knew as a child was that his irritability, which sometimes spilled over into aggression, his dependence on alcohol and cigarettes and his depression, made us all miserable when he was around. As he grew older his drinking and smoking led to arteriosclerosis which created problems with walking, and he had cataracts on both eyes that made him increasingly blind. So my father's ill health and disability influenced our whole family, in economic, social, emotional and practical ways.

At the age of 18, two years after his death, I began training as an occupational therapist and my interest in rehabilitation became professional as well as personal. As a young woman I was firmly stuck in the 'helper' role. I had not looked inside myself to discover my own need for help (Etherington 2001). It was not until I began training as a counsellor that I recognized how my identity as a helper might be vicariously meeting my own needs for care and support that I been deprived of for far too long. I needed to 'habilitate' myself, to learn to live for and through myself, before I could meet the needs of others. The concept of the wounded healer is a familiar one to many of us who enter the caring professions. Some people reject the word 'healer' because of its associations with the 'expert role'. Nouwen (1994) offers an alternative view, suggesting that what we offer others is a form of hospitality, our ability to pay attention to the guest: 'It requires first of all that the host feels at home in his own house, and secondly that he creates a free and fearless place for the unexpected visitor' (p.89). He goes on to say:

> When we have found the anchor places for our lives in our own center, we can then be free to let others enter into the space created for them and allow them to dance their own dance, sing their own song and speak their own language without fear. (Nouwen 1994, p.91)

So as helpers we need first to know our own stories and to understand how they might influence our listening.

However, the very first story that came to mind when I thought about this chapter was about my experience of having a child with a disability, Michael, our firstborn. So I wrote 'The Mother's Story' and wondered how it could be useful in this book. I began to speculate how my husband would have written his version of these events and then asked myself, 'I wonder how Michael would write it?' Tentatively I approached them with the idea of writing their own stories about this period in our lives. I was unsure how they would respond, but to my surprise and pleasure they both agreed to write their accounts, neither of them having seen mine. So we each wrote our story in isolation from the others. I do not intend to analyse these stories but I will use them later in this chapter to draw out ways of thinking about narratives of disability and rehabilitation.

What do we mean by narrative?

The word 'narrative' comes from the Latin root 'narrare' which means 'to narrate or tell' and a narrative is an account or telling of a story. So narrative and story are often used interchangeably, although a story is often about a specific event or events which are linked together into an overarching narrative (McLeod 1997).

Narrative also refers to the structure of a discourse: a structure that depends on a remembered past, that leads to an anticipated future with events temporally connected. Stories are an interpretation of events and when we interpret we impose an order on the experiences we describe (Abma 1999). Each story within a narrative is in some ways like a mini-novel or play. There are actors and scenes that evoke emotions and require an audience; events are connected by a plot which brings specific events into a meaningful whole.

As soon as we begin to think about telling a story we imagine an audience, and that audience will shape the kind of story that is told: so storytelling is a social activity. In writing 'The Mother's Story' I became aware that I was influenced by the idea that my son and husband would probably read it, as well as readers of this book. I might be known in different ways to some readers; others would not know me at all. Some readers might be people with whom I have an ongoing relationship; some may have known me at other times in my life, in other roles. Some may be in tune with my thinking; others might reject my views. I would be leaving myself open to comment and criticism from all of the readers, whether positive or negative.

Michael's and his father's stories would similarly take these matters into account but they are perhaps less likely to be known to the readers and for that reason they may feel they risk less. They would however inevitably also take into account that I would read them and they would read each other's. So when we tell our stories, we are influenced by our expectations of our audience and the stories we tell about an event might be different in one setting from another.

As we listen to or read stories we fill in the gaps by making our own interpretations which are informed by our personal knowledge, experiences and questions. In this way we recognize a degree of uncertainty and ambiguity and that there are many possibilities. 'I wonder what they mean by that?' we might ask ourselves, or we may make our own interpretations without considering that there are other meanings that can be ascribed. None of us hears a story exactly as it is told. We fill in the gaps as we imagine they are intended and, in that way, we construct the story for ourselves about what we think the narrator tells.

Stories of counselling

Counselling grew up within the post-war culture of individualism and positivism which is often referred to as the 'modern' era. People looked for certainty and 'truth' as something that actually existed – if only it could be found. Alongside this, therapy encouraged people to look inside themselves in a search for the 'true self' or the 'inner core', which psychoanalysis construed as dangerous, dark, sexual and aggressive and the humanist tradition saw as full of potential for good which could be 'actualized', given the right conditions for growth (McLeod 1997).

These are some of the cultural contexts within which clients' stories have traditionally been heard and which encouraged counsellors to think about problems as located within the individual. Today this view is being challenged by postmodern therapies, notably narrative therapy, which is informed by social constructionist and post-structuralist ideas. These ideas propose new stories about identity and 'self' – ideas that we are many selves which are constructed and change over time in response to the social contexts of our lives and experiences. I will not expand to any great extent on these ideas here but would refer interested readers to the work of the growing number of writers in the field (Freedman and Combs 1996; Monk *et al.* 1997; Payne 2000; Speedy 2000; White and Epston 1990).

Narrative practices assist people who are marginalized by their cultures to reclaim their voices and to value their stories alongside the dominant discourses. People we read about in this book – whether disabled, chronically sick, mentally ill, drug or alcohol misusers – have been marginalized to a greater or lesser degree by societal and individual attitudes. In every chapter we have heard the voices of those whose lives have been affected by the imposition of dominant discourses on their experiences.

Counselling and therapy has fought to establish itself as a profession through training that has valued theoretical knowledge, technical skills and personal development, whilst also acknowledging the value of personal stories. However, because stories are so ordinary, so normal as part of our everyday world, we may underestimate their value as a therapeutic tool.

It's only a story

Historically, storytelling was valued as a means of basic communication; in the oral tradition learning was passed on from generation to generation. Cultural values and sense of identity were transmitted through legends and myths (McLeod 1997). In modern times, with the growth of scientific knowledge, stories were valued less. If 'it's only a story' we may not really take it seriously as a way of transmitting knowledge and in recognizing that 'narrative truth' can be different from 'scientific fact'. Bruner (1986, 1990), in developing his theme of 'cultural psychology', highlighted the distinction between paradigmatic and narrative knowing and thus provides us with a means to value both kinds of knowing. We each develop stories, both as teller and listener, from within a limited range of knowledge through which we create meaning and a sense of identity. Frank (1995) recognizes:

> The stories we tell about our lives are not necessarily those lives as they were lived, but these stories become our experience of those lives… Life moves on, stories change with that movement, and experience changes. Stories are true to the flux of experience, and the story affects the direction of the flux. (Frank 1995, p.22)

Storytelling has been part of my life from as long as I can remember. Both my parents were Irish, so 'the blarney' became part of my vocabulary at a very early age. 'Being full of the blarney' meant that the narrator was a gifted storyteller and also implied that stories were full of exaggeration in order to heighten their powers of persuasion. But I didn't know that then. As a child stories provided me with a sense of social identity through the legends and myths of history as seen from the Irish perspective. I was mesmerized by my father's stories and songs of how the English 'black and tans' (soldiers drawn from the ranks of prison inmates in the UK) came to Ireland and dragged young men out of their beds at midnight to hang them at the crossroads. But I was born in England and I listened to these stories whilst struggling to understand how I could possibly be 'the apple of my father's eye' whilst also being one of 'the enemy'.

My mother's stories were not told within the male-dominated centre of the family but were overheard by me as she gossiped to her female friends over cups of tea across the hearth. Sometimes she came and sat on my bed in the gathering dusk and told me stories about her life on a large country estate that overlooked Galway Bay where her stepfather was the estate manager and gamekeeper. She painted an idyllic picture of a very different life from that which she lived in England. Sometimes she sang mournful songs, her homesick eyes gazing into a distance I could not see and of which I had no part. From her stories and songs I learned that women had no control over their lives but gained their rightful place in the world by adapting to the needs of others, particularly men.

Whenever I tried to tell my own stories in my family of origin I had the distinct impression that, as a female, my stories were less privileged, in that they were 'neurotic' and 'irrational'. So it was with this mixed sense of the value of stories and an abiding desire to have my own story heard and validated, that I began my training as a counsellor. I was taught that stage one (of the Egan model) was to enable clients to tell their story. Back then, in 1987, I was not in a position to understand fully how valuable this process could be. I understood it was a necessary preliminary to the 'real work' of stage two: 'understanding', and stage 3: 'action'. Indeed we were cautioned not to spend too long in the first stage or to become 'bogged down' in the story (Egan 1986). This fitted with my earlier training in the family that valued 'thinking' over 'feeling' and was, of course, part of the grand narratives of the modern era.

Narrative practitioners, however, privilege stories and take up a stance of curiosity, of 'not knowing', and are receptive to learning from the storyteller as the expert on themselves, paying close attention to power dynamics and attempting to suspend notions of expertise in the therapeutic relationships. The practitioner maintains an awareness of the social and political context of the work, recognizing that the co-constructed conversations with clients will have wider implications.

Stories of disability and illness

In postmodern times we can value the richness and diversity of 'local' knowledge which can be set against 'grand narratives', most of which emanate from within modernist and positivist notions about the nature of self and the world in which we live.

The 'grand narratives' in which illness and disability have been embedded are usually identified as the 'medical model'. The medical model saw patients in terms of symptoms that need to be cured and was based on the assumptions of the superiority of scientific and medical knowledge as science developed and took over from religion in the eighteenth century. Later developments in the field of laboratory science firmly established the biomedical model, which was at its peak in the 1950s. The biomedical story sees the patient as a problem to be solved, a disease to be cured, and the solution lies in using a scientific approach. All of this is based on the dominant story of 'normality' as the baseline for living and locates the problem within the impaired individual.

However, a challenge to the biomedical view began to emerge from within the medical world as professions such as nursing and occupational therapy developed. With this challenge came a growing need for knowledge to put alongside the medical model, whilst simultaneously the medical model was increasingly incorporating psychological and sociological perspectives. In turn psychology and sociology were themselves changing and applying these changes to health and social care (Cooper, Stevenson and Hale 1996).

Further developments ensued with Engel's biopsychosocial model (1978) which was accepted by both academics and practitioners. It was seen as a model that could provide an holistic understanding of the individual's experience of health, impairment and disease. Later this model was located within a framework of general systems theory which recognized that biological, social and psychological perspectives exist complementarily, each one affecting and being changed by the other. A growing interest in the biopsychosocial model highlighted the increasing unease concerning the power of biomedicine and its associated 'individual' models of health, illness and disability (Etherington 2001).

Against this background people with disabilities themselves claimed their right to tell their own stories and to speak for themselves through grass-roots organizations run by disabled people that have been referred to as the 'disabled people's movement', and by influencing social policy and political campaigning (Barnes, Mercer and Shakespeare 1999, p.2). Disability, which had previously been defined against a background of modernism with its positivist assumptions, marginalized and excluded disabled people from 'mainstream' society. This definition is increasingly challenged and redefined within postmodern and social constructionist perspectives to take its place among a range of multiple realities that values difference and does not privilege the dominant stories of 'normality'.

The social model of disability, which emerged through the pioneering work of some disabled people (Oliver 1990, 1996), challenges the 'individual model' and the 'medicalization' of disability in which it was seen as a personal tragedy. The social model emphasizes instead the need to recognize that impairments which people sustain, whether from birth or occurring later in life, do not in themselves necessarily create disability. Disability occurs within a social context and within disabling environments that create barriers for people who have impairments (Swain *et al.* 1993). However, this model too has its critics from both outside and inside the ranks of disabled people who have argued that it does not resonate with some disabled people's experience of impairment, especially that of women and those who feel that the distress and disability they experience from their particular impairment would be little affected by changes in their environment or in society itself (Woolley 1993).

New stories are continually emerging and increasingly disability is understood in terms of the relationship between impairment and physical and social environments. Disability can be defined in these terms as:

- an individual problem
- a social construction
- a social creation (Oliver 1993).

So the stories people tell in rehabilitation counselling are often about some form of cultural, societal or personal conflict. They tell something about the social context and identity of the teller. In telling and retelling stories, new meanings are created, new identities formed and contexts changed.

Chaos stories

However there are some stories that do not develop over time and therefore do not move on. They have no sequence, no remembered past and no anticipated future, so they defy narrative form and have been referred to as 'pre-narrative stories' (Reissman 1993, p.23). These stories are hard to tell and may be even harder to listen to. These stories do not tell of how the person feels but are often expressions of the chaos the person experiences in his or her life. Frank (1995) refers to these as chaos stories 'because the present is not what the past is supposed to lead up to, and the future is scarcely thinkable' (p.55). These stories are sometimes told by individuals whose medical condition is sudden and unexpected, such as a stroke, or perhaps those who are newly diagnosed with a life-threatening condition, or one in which the future is uncertain such as multiple sclerosis or cancer.

The challenge we face is to hear these stories without pushing the tellers to connect with their feelings before they are ready, whilst at the same time not colluding with their avoidance of painful acceptance of present reality. If the story touches unrecognized painful parts of our own experience we may be tempted to move too quickly away from the client's experience; our own wounds may be threatened by exposure.

Frank (1995) eloquently describes such stories as 'told on the edges of speech…in the silence that speech cannot penetrate or illuminate' (p.101). So how can stories be told in silence? There are of course many forms of non-verbal communication such as drawing, clay work, performance, mime, etc., or simply paying attention to the client's body language which tells a story of its own. The body can bear witness to emotional and bodily distress through the development of symptoms. As counsellors we must not limit the client to our own ways of helping but have awareness of the multiple referral resources such as massage, bodywork, reflexology and creative therapies.

Sometimes people communicate chaos stories with a vividness that indicates they are not being experienced as past events but are still experienced as the present: unassimilated fragments that cannot take their rightful place as memories of past events until the story has been told and closure is attained. These might be presented in the form of flashbacks, nightmares, intrusive thoughts and images (Etherington 2000). The process of honouring and accepting these communications can begin the process of helping the story to be told and thus create the memory.

Chaos stories often remain as background to what then becomes a 'quest' story (Frank 1995). As the teller claims a voice new selves are formed; a self who has survived can become an agent of his or her own life and gain some control, a self whose body may be permanently or temporarily changed, a self who may have faced death or whose life has acquired new meaning. The narrative may then become that of a 'journey', the purpose of which is to understand the nature of the journey one has previously made. The stories told by both Di Sheppard and Frances Taylor in this book are examples of 'quest stories'. Both these women describe the 'boon' (Frank 1995) they have gained by undergoing their journey of recovery and rehabilitation, which they now pass on to others through the testimony they provide by publishing their stories.

As we listen to clients we may hear alternative stories of success and achievement that the teller has been unable to recognize in his or her own stories because they may have been submerged by life's problems or negative attitudes. In challenging the dominant story we may be able to create a loosening of rigid constructs and allow new meanings to emerge. So the client telling the story is not only reporting events but reconstructing his social identity (Gergen 1991, 1994; McLeod 1997).

Thinking with stories

The three stories I now present speak for themselves. I offer you, the reader, a chance to think with these stories rather than about them. Arthur Frank (1995) says:

> To think *about* a story is to reduce it to content and then analyze that content. Thinking *with* stories takes the story as already complete; there is no going beyond it. To think *with* a story is to experience it affecting one's own life and to find in that effect a certain truth of one's life. (p.23)

A mother's story

He was the kind of little boy who was into everything. Just three years and two weeks old and already an expert at filling up the lavatory with toothbrushes, flannels and towels – in fact anything he found lying around in the bathroom. He already knew how to empty cupboards in the blink of an eye, how to draw giants on the landing wall, how to strip the wallpaper next to his bed. We were no strangers to the local children's hospital where one week he had a piece of his sponge rubber mattress removed from high up inside his left nostril, and the next week a dried pea from his right nostril that had swelled up so much in the damp environment that the doctor couldn't easily remove it. He had been born 9lb 12oz and continued to be 'larger than life' so the shock was all the greater on the day he became disabled.

He had cried that morning when I lifted him out of bed and placed his feet on the ground but he soon recovered and rushed about in his usual way although still complaining of pain. 'He's been complaining of a pain in his knee,' I told the doctor later that morning, feeling sure I was being over-protective, especially since he had spent most of the time in the waiting room climbing on and off chairs, chasing a kitten. 'Take him for an X-ray just to be on the safe side,' the doctor said as he wiggled my little boy's legs in the air. 'Kids are always getting aches and pains; it's probably nothing.'

I fumed and fretted as I waited in the A& E department later that morning – by now convinced that I was wasting time, my own and everybody else's. I was four months pregnant, feeling queasy and knew I had to be at work that afternoon. The waiting room was bursting at the seams with screaming children and fraught mothers. There was the interminable delay of waiting to see the doctor, then waiting in the queue for the X-ray, then waiting again to be seen after the result of the X-ray was known.

I saw the X-ray up on the wall as the doctor faced me across the desk. It looked like a picture of a snowstorm, just a mass of white flakes where the ball at the top of the femur should have been. I knew this wasn't our X-ray, probably the one belonging to the child who had been seen before us.

'I think we should keep him in overnight for further tests,' the young female doctor murmured softly.

'Why?' I asked.

'There are some changes in his X-ray and we just need to check them. If you wait outside I'll get a porter to take you up to the ward.'

Numbly I walked out of the room and Michael ran ahead of me. I glanced back over my shoulder and saw the doctor watching him. Later she told me she couldn't understand how he could possibly have walked out of that room with both heads of femur completely destroyed. I sat in a daze back in the waiting room, then remembered to telephone his father who worked in a hospital across the city. 'I'll come straight over,' he said.

They dressed Michael in a little white shift and took him, screaming, out of my arms. My arms felt too empty. I walked away from the ward down the long corridor and met my husband walking towards me. 'What's wrong with him?' he asked.

'I don't know,' I said, still dazed. 'They said they want to do some more tests.' We went back to the ward together and the ward sister told us the doctor was with Michael and would talk to us if we waited.

'He's got Perthe's disease,' said the registrar perkily. 'He'll be in hospital for at least a year. See that little chap over there, he's got the same thing. We'll have to make a frame for Michael like that one.'

We peered into the ward and saw a very small boy lying flat on his back, tied across his chest with a metal band, his legs as far apart as they would go and each one bandaged down onto a metal frame. It was like a crucifixion. All I could hear ringing in my ears was, 'He'll be in hospital for at least a year.' At that moment I didn't think it could feel worse if he had said, 'Your child is dead.'

Later that day we wandered around the silent house, tripping over the go-kart we had given him for his birthday just two weeks before. His new shoes lay unused and never would be worn by him now. It had been hard to find the money for them when we bought them only the previous week. I looked into his bedroom and the ache in my chest felt unbearable.

All this happened over 35 years ago in 1965, and as I write this today the pain is still fresh. We were told we could visit for half an hour each day and a whole hour on Sundays. Bowlby's theories of separation and attachment, although by then published, had yet to influence how hospitals practised. He spent visiting time crying 'Don't leave me Mummy', so visiting was a torment for all of us. After three days of this I could bear it no longer and I went to see the consultant. 'Why can't we have him at home?'

'We've never done that,' he replied.

'Yes, well I'm an occupational therapist and I can manage him at home,' I said – never having seen or heard of Perthe's disease before. The consultant said that if we were really serious we could try it out once Michael had been fitted with his frame which had to be made to measure. He reassured us that we could bring him back as soon as it became too much. It was obvious that he thought that would be 'when' and not 'if'.

The Perky Registrar said, 'He wouldn't be going home if he was my child!'

'Do you have any children?' I asked.

'These are all my children,' he replied pompously. I felt like hitting him. The children on the ward lay looking at the same spot on the ceiling every day for a year and sometimes longer; I wondered if the 'cure' wasn't worse than the condition. These days children with Perthe's disease are not treated on frames but kept on bed rest instead.

Taking Michael home twelve days later was the best and most difficult thing we'd ever done. His father made a contraption from the wheels and brake of an old pram so that we could take him out because there was no wheeled vehicle provided. His legs being so far apart created lots of problems. He couldn't fit through a doorway unless lifted onto his side, which was increasingly difficult in my state of advancing pregnancy. There was no ready-made clothing to dress his lower body. We became inventive in ways we didn't know were possible before. My training as an OT was invaluable. I had been taught to think laterally about problems of disability, access and aids for daily living.

We were left to our own devices: no visits from a health visitor, district nurse, GP or anyone, except for the day when the young staff nurse from the hospital turned up on her scooter to see how we were doing. I have never forgotten that act of kindness.

Down each side of Michael's legs there were wide strips of adhesive tape to hold the traction tapes in place. From time to time these became loose and we had to return to the hospital to have them replaced. I still have vivid pictures of the day I was told to hold his head whilst a junior nurse slowly tore these plasters off his legs as he screamed in agony. I shouted at her to stop, to use some solvent, to find someone more senior to undertake this procedure. She told me to shut up or get out of the room if I could not contain myself. Michael's bright red little face, screwed up in pain, poured with perspiration. I thought of all those children on the ward who did not have their parents there to protect them, who were at the mercy of others as he now seemed to be. So I stood my ground and refused to allow her to continue until she finally had to leave the room and seek assistance. The senior nurse then applied solvent and stripped the plasters off without further ado.

So Michael lay on the frame for a year during which his little brother was born. He was at the stage when he should have been learning to kick a football, ride a tricycle, climb on a climbing frame, instead of which he lay on a frame of leather and iron that kept him immobile and under constant traction. At night he cried out as he tried and was unable to turn over in his sleep. During the day he threw toys around the room and at me, in frustration.

And when at last a year passed he came off the frame. Being able to put my arms around him and hold him on my lap that day was like filling a hole that had been left in my heart. He had to learn to walk again, having a Thomas splint on one leg to support the hip that was to take a full two years to heal, and a built-up shoe on the other foot to level him up for walking. His legs were wasted and for one month after coming off the frame he was not allowed to attempt to bear weight upon them whilst he waited for the splint to be made. His father made him a wooden platform on castors across which he lay on his stomach whilst paddling himself along with his arms. The local children envied him this mode of transport and took turns to roll him off and try it out for themselves on the hill outside our house.

Once the caliper was fitted he became again the little boy who jumped off the garage roof, who climbed over rather than walk around any obstacle in his way. He was back on form but starting a long way further back from where he wanted to be. He wore the caliper during his first six months at school and was called 'cripple legs' by the bullies and fussed over by the 'big' girls who mothered him. He still remembers the bullies' taunts.

I ask him if he remembers what it was like for those two important years of his young life and he says he doesn't remember much at all. Looking at him today, nobody would even guess that he had been through all that. He is a six-foot-two, well-built, very successful businessman and a supportive, loving husband and much loved daddy, and he is still 'larger than life'.

I still remember the fear, grief, rage that I felt at that time and for a long time afterwards, as well as the joy of the day he was released from the frame. And I know all our lives were changed by that experience.

The father's story

We were young, short of money and very naive when Michael was born and our apprenticeship into parenthood was a real struggle. By the time Michael reached two years of age I felt much more in tune with my role as father. He was becoming a real character as he discovered language and the means to express himself. Michael was quite a boisterous child, bold, adventurous and frequently into some sort of mischief.

Shortly before his third birthday we took him to Ireland for our first holiday. We had a great time playing on the beach or roaming through parkland. On our return we prepared for his birthday. I had bought him a go-cart, which proved to be a great success, but he did not enjoy it for more than a week or so.

We lived very close to Alder Hey hospital in Liverpool and several times we had to rush him there. Once he had a severe attack of croup, other times we visited A&E to have a piece of foam removed from his nose to be followed a little later for removal of a dried pea, always under noisy protest.

On the morning Michael cried with pains in his legs the GP suggested an X-ray. It was midday when Kim phoned me at the lab where I was studying. She was distraught and almost incoherent. I just about gathered that there was a serious problem and Michael had to stay in hospital. Kim was ashen faced and in floods of tears when I arrived.

As the news dawned on me that our very bouncy boy was an invalid and would need to stay in hospital for nine to twelve months, I felt completely helpless, bewildered and desolate. The X-rays of his hips were ghastly images of the head of each femur like a disintegrating prune. Why did this happen to our child? How could we cope? I was lost for a solution.

The time Michael spent in hospital was very painful for us. I was more submissive and compliant with the views of the medical experts than Kim, who became increasingly critical and challenging. Visiting was a terrible ordeal. The whole hour was spent with him pleading with us not to leave. As we left I would feel a terrible gnawing in my gut from the pain and anguish at seeing him so distraught. The hospital's attitude was to keep children as in-patients until they were recovered and only the medical solution counted in their approach to child health. Perhaps the final straw for us came when we learnt that Michael had been slapped by a nurse for shredding a comic she had given to him. Kim made up her mind then that we must care for Michael at home, no matter what the difficulties would be for us.

She was a trained occupational therapist with experience of dealing with disability. Initially I was doubtful that we could cope, especially as she was four months pregnant, but her commitment was unyielding. She knew about caring for the disabled and I could deal with practical problems. When we decided to take on the experts and remove our child we were opposed, ridiculed and denied any help or support by the hospital. Only an appointment in three months to see the consultant kept our link with Alder Hey. When Michael was strapped to a padded steel frame with his legs extended and feet wide apart, a friend took him home in his van.

The next few weeks challenged our inventiveness. First of all I took the pram base and fitted a platform over the springs with clips to secure the frame. We now had a means for visiting the shops. On a wet day an old plastic mac was draped over his body and legs and Michael would hold an umbrella over his face. I was initially embarrassed at the attention we received, but this soon passed and in fact the contacts his condition brought us were very heart warming and supportive. The next task was to remove the passenger seat from our car and build a platform on a level with the back seat. We could just about all squeeze in for a visit to the zoo and the Christmas grotto. Michael was now dealing much better with his infirmity. We had children come to play with him and to encourage this we often put him out on the driveway in the front of the house.

I would buy a small pack of Lego each week for him and we tried to provide lots of toys, but his frustrations frequently erupted when he broke or threw his toys across the room. I read Brer Rabbit to him at night, his favourite book and he always wanted more. One Sunday I left him briefly on his own only to find that he had ripped several pages from my book of British birds. In anger I smacked him and instantly regretted it. He was expressing his frustration in the only way he could.

Michael had returned to nocturnal wetting and this meant finding a solution to protect him at night. He also suffered from terrible constipation and rebelled vehemently at our attempts to insert a suppository, when he screamed in rage. It was a horrible experience for us. Occasionally we would let him sit up on the frame, although it was against the 'rules' of the hospital. This helped him use a potty, but for meals we would generally turn the frame over so that he lay on his stomach. Everything we did was directed to making his life easier, even if we sometimes did break the rules.

Peter was born five months after Michael came home. We frequently pondered on what it might have done to Michael if he had stayed in hospital and arrived home after many months to find a new baby in the home. We were relieved that we could involve him in the impending arrival and he accepted the new baby without difficulty, especially as Kim always took the trouble to keep him very much included in Peter's care.

Kim's mother came to live with us after the first three months of Michael's disease. Her help with Michael was invaluable and he was very fond of her. She also proved to a great help with the new baby. I was reaching the stage when I had to write up my PhD thesis and needed to work late each night. I went through periods of deep despair at that time, feeling I was being pulled in too many directions at once. There was a lengthy thesis to be written, a new baby and a disabled child to nurture, a wife to support and a mother-in-law to placate. I realize now that I have allowed so many memories of this bleak period to fade.

We visited Alder Hey for X-rays and check-ups every three months and each time we went with some trepidation. Was he healing? Had we been good parents? Had we taken too many liberties in allowing him to sit up? The healing process seemed painfully slow and it was a full 12 months before he was judged fit to go on to calipers. But there was a sting in the decision; we would need to wait 10 to 14 days until the calipers were made. The hospital now had to deal with informed, competent and determined parents. Against some opposition we took him out of the frame on the understanding that he would not bear weight on his legs. We took great care to protect him from this risk. I put casters on a square board so that he could shuffle around on his bottom.

Having Michael in calipers brought fresh problems. He had forgotten how to walk and there were frequent tears as he lost his balance and crashed to the floor. We moved to Somerset a few months later and in the new community he experienced ridicule from children at the village school at his clumsy movements on calipers. The aftermath of Perthe's disease on his social, emotional and physical development concerned us for many years.

What did we achieve by challenging the hospital? Certainly we remain convinced that we did the right thing. We were able to maintain a nurturing environment and Michael never appeared dissociated from the family. He is now a healthy, well-adjusted married man with a family of his own. Following our lead, other parents removed their children with Perthe's disease from Alder Hey and provided home care. In retrospect I like to think that we made some small contribution towards hospitals rethinking the issues on child care and in taking a more holistic approach to recovery from disability.

Michael's story

I sometimes wonder how much I actually remember of the early days of my Perthe's disease and how much I think I remember, based on hearing my parents' stories and seeing photos from those days. After all I was only three years old.

Somewhere in the back of my mind I do seem to recall a period of total frustration and anger. Anger with being strapped down to a steel and leather frame, anger with my parents, anger with my body and anger with myself.

I have memories of sitting in the front and back gardens of a little semi in Liverpool watching normal kids running around, screaming and playing with toys. My toys. That's about it. But the things I really remember, and the things that have helped shape the rest of my life, come later.

After coming off the frame I was put on to calipers. I must have been about four or five years old I suppose. I remember going to my new primary school when we moved house, on my calipers, of course. The first thing I discovered was three high stone steps into the classroom. If you really want to draw attention to yourself on your first day at a new school, not being able to get up the steps and having to get help from a teacher is the way to go. Everyone in the school seemed to know the cripple had arrived. Kids of course have a way of making sure you know you're a cripple, that you're different and that they don't really want you there. Funnily enough one of my best friends, even to this day, is one of those kids. He told his parent a robot had started at the school.

School was hard. I was picked on by the big kids and tormented with names and cruel jibes, the way kids do. It hurt. A lot. After coming off the frame I had to learn to walk again. An odd experience I suppose for a five- or six-year-old. Most of your friends can run around like mad things and you're taking it easy because your legs bend oddly and your feet stick out the wrong way. Easy pickings for the bullies and easy for the other kids to make fun of. And they did.

The first benefit of being different was the Doc Martens. DMs were cool. They were also banned at the secondary school I then attended, aged about 13. However I was given permission to wear them, 16-holers as well. Right up my ankles, polished lovingly with ox blood polish. And the excuse was that they helped my legs and feet point in the right direction. That was good.

The bad thing about the legs was that I had to do cross-country instead of rugby. That's about the time the bullying started again. I guess one develops a kind of 'victim' mentality at that age with the legs, the calipers, the cripple walk. You sort of ask to be picked on. Not on purpose of course, more like some sort of radar that goes out to the other kids saying 'come and pick on me – make my life shit – here I am guys'. I suppose being in a Catholic boys school made it all the easier. It was terrible, living in fear day by day that you were going to get beaten up, insulted, hit, kicked or even smacked around the head all the way through geography by the sharp end of a 12-inch ruler. I still want to kill that kid. He probably works in an office now and has forgotten we ever met. Bastard.

The first time I ever felt like 'me' was in the first term at university. The legs worked. I walked normally. I could even run without anyone noticing

I was different. I don't know when the change in my head happened. I suddenly decided enough was enough. I was going to be me. Nobody was going to ruin my life. I was going to be like everyone else. Better, even. I could be whoever I wanted to be and nobody was going to stop me.

I discovered a new confidence, a new attitude, a new awareness of myself as a person just like everyone else. From that point on, things changed. I guess the reason I don't remember much of the earlier details is that I don't want to. That was another person, another life. One I don't want to remember much.

I sometimes find myself acting badly, saying stupid things, upsetting people and wondering why I do it. I always come back to the early days and the problems I encountered as a kid. In a way I seem to over-compensate. I don't know why. I actually feel very lucky. Now I have my own two-year-old, I look at him and wonder how my parents ever managed me with that kind of energy, stifled and diverted into my angers and frustrations.

It's amazing to think that a disease of the hip in a three-year-old can forge and shape the mentality, behaviour and thinking of a thirty-something man. I'm convinced, though, that it has had a major part to play in the shaping of my personality, for better and for worse. I hope, in the long run, for the better!

Crystallization

Three stories like different facets of the same crystal. Each facet is valid and each one unique to the perspective of the narrator. 'What we see when we view a crystal, for example, depends on how we view it, how we hold it up to the light or not' (Janesick 2000, p.392). Through each of these facets we catch glimpses of the other stories that sometimes overlap. Richardson (1994) suggests that each view of the crystal is partial, complex and deep. The following questions are offered as tools for 'thickening' these stories.

1. What does disability mean in the context of these stories?

2. In what ways do each of the narrators' experience 'disability' within the social, cultural and economic context of their lives?

3. What similarities/differences do you perceive in these stories?

4. These stories are located in the 1960s in Liverpool. What historical factors might shape these tellings?

5.   What is the impact of bullying on the child's experience of himself?

6.   What is the impact of social conditioning on the father's view of himself?

7.   How does the environment disable each of these narrators?

8.   What are the enabling forces for the child?

9.   Are there other communications within the stories? What does the use of language communicate to you?

10. Having read other parts of the mother's story, what parts of her earlier life may have impacted on her experience at this time?

11. As the listener/reader of these stories how are you touched or changed?

12. What questions do you want to ask?

13. These stories could be seen as stories of 'personal tragedy': what are the alternative ways of viewing them?

14. How does the child re-author his life?

15. Where do these stories touch your own life?

16. How do these stories extend your own story?

If you would like to respond to any or all of these questions by email I would be interested to hear from you. It may be that I would use your emails for a future research project, so when you reply please bear this in mind. However, I would ask for your explicit permission if I were to do that. If you would like to respond anonymously that's fine – if you wish to have a reply then I will need your email address. If you wish to identify yourself in your response but would not want your identity to be attached to any further use of your response (e.g. for research) please indicate that in your message. My email address is: kim@effingpot.com

Looking forward to hearing from you!

References

Abma, T. A. (1999) 'Making meaning of narratives.' R. Josselson and A. Leiblich (eds) *The Narrative Study of Lives, vol. 6.* Thousand Oaks: Sage, pp.169–195.

Barnes, C., Mercer, G. and Shakespeare, T. (1999) *Exploring Disability: A Sociological Introduction.* Cambridge: Polity Press.

Bruner, J. (1986) *Actual Minds, Possible Worlds.* Cambridge, MA: Harvard University Press.

Bruner, J. (1990) *Acts of Meaning.* Cambridge, MA: Harvard University Press.

Cooper, N., Stevenson, C. and Hale, G. (eds) (1996) *Integrating Perspectives on Health.* Buckingham: Open University Press.

Egan, G. (1986) *The Skilled Helper.* 3rd edn. California: Brooks/Cole.

Engel, G.L. (1978) 'The biopsychosocial model and the education of health professionals.' *Annals of the New York Academy of Sciences, 310,* 169–181.

Etherington, K. (2000) *Narrative Approaches to Working with Adult Male Survivors of Child Sexual Abuse: The Clients', The Counsellor's and the Researcher's Story.* London: Jessica Kingsley Publishers.

Etherington, K. (2001) *Counsellors in Health Settings.* London: Jessica Kingsley Publishers.

Frank, A. (1995) *The Wounded Storyteller.* London: University of Chicago Press.

Freedman, J. and Combs, G. (1996) *Narrative Therapy: The Social Construction of Preferred Realities.* New York: Norton.

Gergen, K. (1991) *The Saturated Self.* New York: Basic Books.

Gergen, K. (1994) *Toward Transformation in Social Knowledge,* 2nd edn. London: Sage.

Janesick, V. (2000) 'The choreography of qualitative research design.' In N. Denzin and Y. Lincoln (eds) *Handbook of Qualitative Research.* Thousand Oaks, CA: Sage.

McLeod, J. (1997) *Narrative and Psychotherapy.* London: Sage.

McLeod, J. (1999)'Counselling as a social process.' *Counselling 10,* 217–227.

Monk, G., Winslade, J. Crocket, K. and Epston, D. (eds) (1997) *Narrative Therapy in Practice: The Archaeology of Hope.* San Fransisco: Jossey-Bass.

Nouwen, H. (1994) *The Wounded Healer.* New York: Image Books.

Oliver, M. (1990) *The Politics of Disablement.* Basingstoke: Macmillan.

Oliver, M. (1993) 'Re-defining disability.' In J. Swain, V. Finkelstein, S. French and M. Oliver (eds) *Disabling Barriers – Enabling Environments.* London: Sage.

Oliver, M. (1996) *Understanding Disability: From Theory to Practice.* London: Macmillan.

Payne, M. (2000) *Narrative Therapy: An Introduction for Counsellors.* London: Sage.

Reissman, C. K. (1993) *Narrative Analysis.* London: Sage.

Richardson, L. (1994) 'Writing: A method of inquiry.' In N.K. Denzin and Y.S. Lincoln (eds) *Handbook of Qualitative Research.* Thousand Oaks, CA: Sage.

Speedy, J. (2000) 'The storied helper: narrative ideas and practices in counselling and psychotherapy.' *European Journal of Psychotherapy, Counselling and Health 3,* 3, 361–374.

Swain, J., Finkelstein, V., French, S. and Oliver, M. (eds) (1993) *Disabling Barriers – Enabling Environments.* London: Sage.

White, M. and Epston, D. (1990) *Narrative Means to Therapeutic Ends.* New York: Norton.

Woolley, M. (1993) 'Acquired hearing loss: Acquired oppression.' In J. Swain, V. Finkelstein, S. French and M. Oliver (eds) *Disabling Barriers – Enabling Environments.* London: Sage.

Contributors

Diane Aronson works as a counsellor in the Bath Head Injury Unit, and also at the University of Bath Medical Centre. She has a diploma and MSc in Counselling from the University of Bristol, and used her research about her work in the Head Injury Unit towards her MSc. She previously worked for many years as an Occupational Therapist in Mental Health, and values and uses the therapeutic approaches she developed in that field within her counselling practice.

Cindi Bedor holds a Diploma and an MSc in Counselling from the University of Bristol. She has worked with drug users for the past ten years and within different settings, including voluntary organisations, a day programme and residential rehabilitation. She trains other professionals to understand and work with drug users. She has recently moved from Kent to the West Country.

Kevin Brenton is a Registered Psychiatric Nurse, and has an MSc in Rehabilitation Counselling from Brunel University. He has worked in area of Mental Health Rehabilitation since 1988 and is currently a clinical practitioner and the manager of the Assertive Outreach Team within Sussex Weald and Downs NHS Trust in Chichester. He has particular interest in the use of psychosocial and psychoeducational interventions with people suffering from severe and enduring mental illness and their families. He also teaches on supervision and reflective practice on courses accredited by the University of Portsmouth.

Richard Bryant-Jefferies trained in person-centred counselling with the Institute for Person-Centred Learning in the UK. Since 1995 he has specialised in working with people with alcohol problems. He offers and co-ordinates a National Health Service alcohol counselling service in GP surgeries and has run community support groups in Surrey, UK as part of the Acorn Community Drug and Alcohol Service. He also has a small private counselling and supervision practice. He has had a number of papers and articles published on themes such as: alcohol and the older person; person-centred counselling in Primary Health Care; training in alcohol awareness. Richard's book entitled 'Counselling the Person Beyond the Alcohol Problem' was published in June 2001. He regards the therapeutic relationship as the primary factor in enabling a process of rehabilitation.

Kim Etherington is a BAC Accredited Counsellor and Supervisor in private practice. She is a lecturer at the University of Bristol where she teaches on the MSc in Counselling. Having started out in the early 60s as an Occupational Therapist,

Kim worked in NHS general and psychiatric hospitals, and charitable organisations including a child guidance clinic and a community for autistic people, and in the 80s as a community OT for Social Services. She then trained as a counsellor at the University of Bristol. Her previous books 'Adult Male Survivors of Childhood Sexual Abuse' (1995) and 'Narrative Approaches to Working with Adult Male survivors of Child Sexual Abuse' (2000) follow from the research she undertook for her PhD. She and her husband have an ever-increasing family of three adult sons, three daughters-in-law and three grandsons and one (very new) granddaughter.

Pamela Griffiths is a BACP accredited counsellor and UKCP registered psychotherapist. Since 1990 she has developed and run the post-graduate Diploma/ MSc in Rehabilitation Counselling at Brunel University and has a private practice in counselling and psychotherapy in London. She has worked as a physiotherapist in Southern Africa, the USA and the UK. Her research interests include counselling asylum seekers and refugees, and remembrance of trauma; her publications cover these and other aspects of rehabilitation counselling. Currently she is completing a clinical Phd in child and family psychology at Birbeck College, University of London and the Tavistock Clinic, London.

Sally Lockwood CQSW Dip Couns. MSc is a qualified social worker and counsellor who has worked in Northamptonshire, Bedfordshire and Bristol in the statutory, voluntary and commercial sectors. She is currently manager/senior co-ordinator of the Bristol Area Stroke Foundation which offers individual and group support services to people affected by stroke.

Ruth Morgan-Jones trained as a social group worker at the University of Chicago in 1966-68. After migrating with her British husband to England in 1970, she followed the birth of her two children by working with RELATE for ten years as she has always been extremely interested in the dynamics of couples. Eventually in mid-life, she acknowledged that her mild sensorineural hearing loss had become profound. Her PhD at the London School of Economics on 'The Impact of Hearing Impairment on Family Life' was Ruth's attempt to continue with her career in a way which made use of her developing disability. Her research suggested the need for a counselling service, HearSay, for people with acquired hearing loss which she founded in 1990. This service now includes people with many other problems, physical and emotional. Ruth's book, 'Hearing Differently', has just been published by Whurr Publishers Ltd, and developed from her thesis.

Julia Segal MA is a BACP accredited counsellor who works within the North West London Hospitals NHS Trust counselling people with multiple sclerosis and members of their families. She also works privately training professionals who work with people who have various disabilities. She is particularly interested in using the insights of Melanie Klein and her colleagues to increase understanding in relationships, particularly those including mental or physical disabilities. She has written extensively on counselling people with disabilities, (including Helping Children with Ill or Disabled Parents, Jessica Kingsley 1992) and on the work of Melanie Klein.

Diana Sheppard was a Legal Secretary for five years before joining the Police as an Administrator in 1990. After suffering a Stroke in 1997 she now carries out some voluntary work for the Bristol Area Stroke Foundation.

Frances Taylor[1] has been a counsellor in the field of addiction for nine years. She has worked in various agencies in Bristol and is currently working with clients recovering from substance dependency. She lives peacefully and enjoys close relationships with her children and grandchild.

Gillian Thomas was the first counsellor to work within the NHS exclusively with people with Inflammatory Bowel disease. She trained as a counsellor at the University of Reading where she also completed a PhD on the place of counselling in the care of people affected by Inflammatory Bowel disease. The resulting findings assisted the National Association for Colitis and Crohn's disease in securing a Department of Health grant to train other counsellors in this field. Gillian has written a number of articles and chapters about her work and experience, given numerous talks to both lay and professional audiences and is currently completing a book on the subject. She has recently become involved in the NHS patient participation initiative.

1   Frances Taylor would like to add this comment on her contribution (Chapter 11):

'Since writing my story I have uncovered incidents of sexual abuse by my father's brother. It happened when I was four or five years old. Now I know this happened I am better equipped to make sense of my life. A vital piece of the jigsaw is now found. I believe that my parents knew what my uncle did to me.

My father banished him and we never saw or spoke about him again. My mother's reaction had a profound effect on me. She attempted to bury the incident and her feelings along with the impact it had on me. She projected her shame of the abuse on to me, hence I always felt there was something wrong with me. No wonder she couldn't approve of me: I was no longer unconditionally loveable. I needed her comfort and reassurance to heal the violation: instead she gave me food. Food became a substitute for love. My promiscuity and attraction to dangerous and abusive men is now more understandable. I was unconsciously re-enacting the abuse in an attempt to find a satisfactory resolution. My body had been violated as a little girl. No-one said that it was wrong so how could I have known that my body was precious?

I grew up confused and unhappy. I held myself in poor esteem. No wonder I was vulnerable to the kind of comfort narcotics provide!'

Author Index

Subject Index